SOME LONGER ELIZABETHAN POEMS

AN ENGLISH GARNER

SOME LONGER
ELIZABETHAN POEMS

WITH AN INTRODUCTION BY

A. H. BULLEN

NEW YORK

COOPER SQUARE PUBLISHERS, INC.

1964

PUBLISHERS' NOTE

THE texts contained in the present volume are re-printed with very slight alterations from the *English Garner* issued in eight volumes (1877-1890, London, 8vo) by Professor Arber, whose name is sufficient guarantee for the accurate collation of the texts with the rare originals, the old spelling being in most cases carefully modernised. The contents of the original *Garner* have been rearranged and now for the first time classified, under the general editorial supervision of Mr. Thomas Seccombe. Certain lacunae have been filled by the interpolation of fresh matter. The Introductions are wholly new and have been written specially for this issue.

Published by
Cooper Square Publishers, Inc.
59 Fourth Avenue, New York, N. Y. 10003
Library of Congress Catalog Card No. 64-16741
Printed in the United States of America

PAGE

elegies by Spenser and other hands printed as an
Appendix to Spenser's Colin Clouts come home again,
1595, ... 271

J. C.—Alcilia : Philoparthen's Loving Folly, 1595, . . 319

Antony Scoloker—Daiphantus, or The Passions of Love, by
An. Sc. Whereunto is added The Passionate Man's
Pilgrimage, 1604, ... 363

CONTENTS

PAGE

———————

* The items indicated by an asterisk are new additions to *An English Garner.*

INTRODUCTION

As there is no need to adopt a strictly chronological order for the poems included in the present volume, I have begun with the *Orchestra* and *Nosce Teipsum* of Sir John Davies (1569-1626), who was undoubtedly one of the most brilliant figures of the Elizabethan Age. Well-born and gently bred, educated at Winchester and at New College, Oxford, Davies was exceptionally fortunate in escaping the pecuniary cares that harassed so many Elizabethan men of letters. From the Middle Temple he was called to the bar in 1595 (at the age of twenty-six). In the previous year *Orchestra* had been entered in the Stationers' Register, but the poem was first published in 1596. From the dedicatory sonnet to Richard Martin we learn that it was written in fifteen days. There are, however, no signs of haste in the writing, and it may fairly be claimed that this poem in praise of dancing is a graceful monument of ingenious fancy. Lucian composed a valuable and entertaining treatise on dancing, and I suspect that Περὶ Ὀρχήσεως gave Davies the idea of writing *Orchestra*.

In the opening stanzas[1] we are presented with a picturesque description of

> ' The sovereign castle of the rockly isle
> Wherein Penelope the Princess lay,'

---

[1] Ben Jonson (*Conversations with William Drummond of Hawthornden*) took exception to the opening lines :—

> ' He scorned such verses as could be transponed—
> Where is the man that never yett did hear
> Of faire Penelope, Ulisses Queene?
> Of faire Penelope Ulisses Queene,
> Wher is the man that never yett did hear?'

lit with a thousand lamps on a festal night when the
suitors had assembled, at the queen's invitation, to hear
the minstrel Phœmius sing the praises of the heroes who
had fought at Troy. With such beauty shone Penelope
that the suitors were abashed at their temerity in having
dared to woo her. But one 'fresh and jolly knight,'
Antinous, so far from being dismayed,

> 'boldly gan advance
> And with fair manners wooed the Queen to dance.'

She blushingly declined, and mildly chided him for trying
to persuade her to new-fangled follies. Forthwith he
launched into a rapturous disquisition on the antiquity of
dancing, which began when Love persuaded the jarring
elements—fire, air, earth, and water—to cease from con-
flict and observe true measure. The sun and moon, the
fixed and wandering stars, the girdling sea and running
streams, all 'yield perfect forms of dancing.' With exu-
berant fancy, fetching his illustrations from near and far,
he pursues his theme through many richly-coloured stanzas.
It may be worth while to remark (as his editors have been
silent on the subject) that Davies does not scruple to
borrow freely from Lucian. Take, for instance, stanza
80 :—

> ' Wherefore was Proteus said himself to change
> Into a stream, a lion, and a tree,
> And many other forms fantastic strange
> As in his fickle thought he wished to be?
> But that he danced with such facility,
>   As, like a lion, he could prance with pride,
>   Ply like a plant and like a river glide.'

Now hear Lucian :—

δοκεῖ γάρ μοι ὁ παλαιὸς μῦθος καὶ Πρωτέα τὸν Αἰγύπτιον οὐκ ἄλλο τι

ἢ ὀρχηστήν τινα γενέσθαι λέγειν, μιμητικὸν ἄνθρωπον καὶ πρὸς πάντα
σχηματίζεσθαι καὶ μεταβάλλεσθαι δυνάμενον, ὡς καὶ ὕδατος ὑγρότητα
μιμεῖσθαι καὶ πυρὸς ὀξύτητα ἐν τῇ τῆς κινήσεως σφοδρότητι καὶ λέοντος
ἀγριότητα καὶ παρδάλεως θυμὸν καὶ δένδρου δόνημα, καὶ ὅλως ὅ τι καὶ
θελήσειεν.[1]

Here is another example (Stanza 17):—

> ' Dancing, bright Lady, then began to be
>   When the first seeds whereof the world did spring,
>   The Fire, Air, Earth, and Water did agree
>   By Love's persuasion (Nature's mighty King)
>   To leave their first disordered combating,
>   And in a dance such measures to observe
>   As all the world their motion should preserve.'

With this compare Lucian (as Englished by Jasper Mayne):
'First, then, you plainly seem to me not to know that
dancing is no new invention or of yesterday's or the other
day's growth, or born among our forefathers or their
ancestors. But they who most truly derive dancing, say
it sprung with the first beginning of the universe, and had
a birth equally as ancient as love.' It would be easy to
multiply instances. Of course Davies' borrowings from
Lucian do not for a moment detract from his poem's merit :
indeed they give an added zest.

In the 1596 edition *Orchestra* ends with a compliment to
Queen Elizabeth, and stanzas in praise of Spenser, Daniel,
and others. Davies had evidently intended to write
a sequel ; for, when *Orchestra* was republished in the

----

[1] The passage is thus rendered by Jasper Mayne (*Part of Lucian, made
English . . . in the year* 1638):—'Nor were it amiss, having passed through
India and Aethiopia, to draw our discourse down to their neighbouring Aegypt.
Where the ancient fiction which goes of Proteus, methinks, signifies him only to
be a certain dancer and mimic ; who could transform and change himself into all
shapes, sometimes acting the fluidness of water, sometimes the sharpness of fire,
occasioned by the quickness of its aspiring motion, sometimes the fierceness of a
lion, and fury of a libbard, and waving of an oak, and whatever he liked.'

collective edition of his poems (1622), it was described on the title-page as 'not finished,' some new stanzas were added, and it ended abruptly in the middle of a simile. The poem is quite long enough as we have it in the 1596 edition, and we need not lament that Davies failed to carry out his intention of continuing it : μηδὲν ἄγαν.

To his youthful days belong the *Epigrams*, which were bound up with Marlowe's translation of Ovid's *Amores* (with a Middleburgh imprint): occasionally indecorous, they are seldom wanting in wit and pleasantry.

In February 1597-8, Davies was disbarred for a breach of discipline. He quarrelled with Richard Martin (afterwards Recorder of London)—to whom he had dedicated *Orchestra*—and assaulted him at dinner in the Middle Temple Hall, breaking a cudgel over his head. Retiring to Oxford, he engaged in the more peaceful occupation of composing *Nosce Teipsum*, a poem on the immortality of the soul, which was published in 1599. It was an ambitious task that this young disbarred bencher took in hand, but he acquitted himself ably. Some of his modern admirers have exceeded all reasonable bounds in their praise of the poem. Rejecting these extravagant eulogies, we may claim that Davies, while he was leading the life of an inns-of-court man of fashion, had remained a steadfast lover of learning and letters; that he had stored his mind richly; and that his well-turned quatrains have had an inspiring influence on later poets. Young, in *Night Thoughts*, was under special obligation to Davies. Matthew Arnold had no enthusiasm for Elizabethan writers; but, unless I am greatly mistaken, he had glanced at *Nosce Teipsum*. In 'A Southern Night' Arnold wrote—

> . . . 'And see all things from pole to pole,[1]
> And glance, and nod, and bustle by,
> And never once possess our soul
> Before we die,'

—a stanza that bears a very suspicious resemblance to Davies' quatrain—

> 'We that acquaint ourselves with every zone,
> And pass both tropics, and behold both poles;
> When we come home, are to ourselves unknown
> And unacquainted still with our own souls.'

All the arguments for and against the immortality of the soul were threshed out ages ago, and there is little or nothing new to say on the subject. A poet's skill lies in graciously attiring the old commonplaces; in searching out the right persuasive words and uttering them so melodiously that dull 'approved verities'—sparkling with sudden lustre —are transmuted into something rich and strange. It is idle to talk about Davies' 'deep and original thinking.' Many stanzas can be brushed aside as tiresome and uncouth; but something will be left. In his handling of the ten-syllabled quatrain (with alternate rhymes) Davies showed considerable deftness. The metre has weight and dignity, but is apt to become stiff and monotonous. Davies certainly succeeded in securing more freedom and variety than might have been anticipated. Inspired by his example, Davenant chose this metre for *Gondibert*; and Davenant was followed by Dryden, who in the preface to *Annus Mirabilis* says all that can be said in favour of the quatrain (which was seen to best advantage in Gray's *Elegy*).

---

[1] Cf. also Arnold's 'Obermann once more':—

> '"Poor World," she cried, "so deep accurst,
> That runn'st from pole to pole
> To seek a draught to quench thy thirst,
> Go seek it in thy soul."'

Though few may be at the pains to read through *Nosce Teipsum* at a blow, it is a poem that lends itself admirably to quotation. Towards the end there is a cluster of fine stanzas ('O ignorant poor man,' etc.) that have found their way into many volumes of selected poetry; and even the arid tracts are dotted with green oases. Tennyson, with somewhat wearisome iteration, pleaded through stanza after stanza of *In Memoriam* that the longing which most men unquestionably have for immortality must needs be based on a sure foundation :—

> 'We think we were not made to die,
> And Thou hast made us, Thou art just.'

Davies sums up pithily in a single line :—

> 'If Death do quench us quite, we have great wrong.'

A poet greater than Davies, greater than Tennyson, the august Lucretius, in the noble verses that he pondered through the still nights (seeking to do justice to the doctrine of his Master Epicurus), scathingly checks our vaulting aspirations. If we have enjoyed the banquet of life, why should we not rise content and pass to our dreamless sleep? If our life has been wastefully squandered and is become a weariness to us, why should we hesitate to make an end of it? 'Aufer abhinc lacrimas, balatro, et compesce querellas!'

Astræa, a series of acrostic verses on Queen Elizabeth, is merely a *tour de force* of courtly ingenuity. Much more interesting is Davies' group of graceful little poems, *Twelve Wonders of the World*, published in the second edition (1608) of Davison's *Poetical Rhapsody*.

In 1603 Davies was appointed Solicitor-General for Ireland, and in 1606 Attorney-General. His letters to Cecil give a valuable and vivid account of the state of Ireland;

and his *Discovery of the True Cause why Ireland was never entirely subdued*, 1612, is a treatise of the first importance. Davies' political writings wait the attention of a competent editor, who would undoubtedly find absorbing interest in his task.

It was the poet's misfortune to marry a crazy rhapsodical woman (Eleanor Touchet, sister of the notorious Baron Audley), who annoyed him by putting herself into mourning and bidding him 'within three years to expect the mortal blow.' Three days before his death she 'gave him pass to take his long sleep.' He resented these admonitions, and testily exclaimed, 'I pray you weep not while I am alive, and I will give you leave to laugh when I am dead.' On 7th December 1626 he dined with Lord Keeper Coventry, and on the following morning was found dead of apoplexy. It was perhaps fortunate that his life had not been prolonged, for his views of kingly prerogative were high. He had supported the king's demand for a forced loan, and (when 'the mortal blow' really came) was about to succeed Lord Chief Justice Crew, who had been removed from office for refusing to affirm the legality of such loans.

Not much need be said about *Six Idillia*, 1588, the anonymous translations (pp. 123-146) from Theocritus. It is a performance worthy of George Turberville or 'that painful furtherer of learning' Barnabe Googe. On the verso of the title page is the Horatian inscription :—

'E. D.

Libenter hic et omnis exantlabitur
Labor, in tuæ spem gratiæ.'

Collier, misreading this dedication, claimed the *Idillia* for Sir Edward Dyer, and his mistake has been followed by some later bibliographers. But in the first place there is nothing to show that 'E. D.' was Sir Edward Dyer; and in the second it is perfectly plain that the translations were dedicated to 'E. D.,' not written by him. The rhymed fourteen-syllable lines are somewhat uncouth and do scant justice to the liquid melody of Theocritus' hexameters; but though these *Idillia* have no great literary value, the hardy pioneer is entitled to some credit for breaking new ground. Only one copy (preserved in the Bodleian Library) of the original edition is known. Some years ago a small edition, for private circulation, was issued from the press of Rev. H. C. Daniel.

Richard Barnfield (1574-1627) had genuine poetical gifts, but seldom displayed them to advantage. Born in 1574 at Norbury, near Newport, Shropshire, he was educated at Brasenose College, Oxford, and is conjectured to have been a member of Gray's Inn. He seems to have spent most of his time in the country, leading the life of a country gentleman. In 1594 he published *The Affectionate Shepheard* (with a dedication to Lady Penelope Rich), and in 1595 *Cynthia*. His last work, *The Encomion of Lady Pecunia*, followed in 1598, a second edition (with changes and additions) appearing in 1605. He died in March 1626-7, leaving a son and a grand-daughter. In his will he is described as of 'Dorlestone, in the Countie of Stafford, Esquire.' [1]

The Affectionate Shepheard was inspired by Virgil's Second Eclogue. Though the choice of subject was not happy, it must be allowed that in describing country contentment and the pastimes of silly shepherds Barnfield shows un-

---

[1] The poems of Barnfield were not in the original *Garner* and are now incorporated for the first time.

laboured fluency and grace, with playful touches of quaint
extravagance. The passage beginning 'And when th'art
wearie of thy keeping Sheepe' (pp. 159, 160) and ending
'Like Lillyes in a bed of roses shed' is a pleasant piece of
poetical embroidery. Barnfield doubtless adopted the six-
line stanza in imitation of *Venus and Adonis*, 1593 (which
had in turn been modelled on Lodge's *Glaucus and Scylla*,
1589). It has been recently pointed out—by Mr. Charles
Crawford in *Notes and Queries*—that some passages in *The
Affectionate Shepheard* were closely imitated from Marlowe
and Nashe's *Dido* (published in 1594), and that one line has
been taken straight out of Marlowe's *Edward II*. Appended
to *The Affectionate Shepheard* are *The Complainte of Chastitie*,
in imitation of Michael Drayton, and *Hellens Rape*—a copy
of 'English Hexameters' so atrociously bad that one
wonders whether it was written to bring contempt on the
metre which Gabriel Harvey and others were vainly striving
to popularise.

To *Cynthia* is prefixed a copy of high-flying commenda-
tory verses, from which very little sense can be extracted,
by 'T. T.,' possibly Thomas Thorpe, the publisher of
Shakespeare's Sonnets. In the address to 'The Curteous
Gentlemen Readers' Barnfield claims indulgence for *Cynthia*
on the ground that it was the first 'imitation of the verse of
that excellent Poet, Maister *Spencer*, in his *Fayrie Queene*.'
The poem is a compliment to Queen Elizabeth, who is
adjudged by Jove to have merited the golden apple wrongly
given by Paris to Venus. When Barnfield mentioned that he
borrowed the metre of *Cynthia* from Spenser, he forgot to
add that the matter was drawn from Peele's *Arraignment of
Paris*. To *Cynthia* succeed twenty sonnets extolling, after the

fashion of the age, the beauty and virtues of an imaginary
youth, Ganymede. In the last sonnet Barnfield introduces
compliments to Spenser (Colin) and Drayton (Rowland):—

> 'Ah had great *Colin*, chiefe of sheepheards all,
>   Or gentle *Rowland*, my professed friend,
>   Had they thy beautie, or my pennance pend,
>   Greater had beene thy fame, and lesse my fall:
>   But since that euerie one cannot be wittie,
>   Pardon I craue of them, and of thee pitty.'

The 'Ode' that follows the sonnets runs trippingly away in
easy trochaics; but *Cassandra* is laboured and languid.

The Encomion of Lady Pecunia has an 'Address to the
Gentlemen Readers,' in which Barnfield states that he had
been at much pains to find an unhackneyed subject for his
pen. After long consideration he had determined to write
the praises of money, a theme both new (for none had
ventured upon it before) and pleasing (for money is always
in esteem). It was in pursuit of money that Hawkins and
Drake had lost their lives. Barnfield wrote a fine epitaph
on Hawkins:—

> 'The[1] Waters were his Winding sheete, the Sea was made his Toome;
>   Yet for his fame the Ocean Sea was not sufficient roome.'

His lines on Drake are not quite so happy:—

> 'England[2] his hart; his Corps the Waters have;
>   And that which raysed his fame, became his grave.'

---

[1] Prince in his *Worthies of Devon* (1701) quotes this couplet as an epitaph, by
an anonymous writer, on Drake.

[2] There is a better epitaph on Drake in *Wit's Recreations* (1640):—

> 'Sir Drake, whom well the world's end knew,
>   Which thou didst compasse round,
> And whom both Poles of Heaven once saw,
>   Which North and South do bound:
> The Stars above would make thee known
>   If men here silent were:
> The Sun himselfe cannot forget
>   His fellow-passenger.'

The *Encomion* is smoothly written, and is not without humour. A country gentleman in easy circumstances, Barnfield could dally playfully with a subject that had for him no terrors. His example probably led 'T. A.' (Thomas Acheley?) to write *The Massacre of Money*, 1602. *The Complaint of Poetrie for the Death of Liberalitie* seems to be an imitation of Spenser's *Teares of the Muses*. More interesting are the *Poems ; in divers humors* at the end of the booklet, for among them are the sonnet 'If Musique and sweet Poetrie agree,' and the 'Ode' beginning 'As it fell upon a day,' which were long ascribed erroneously to Shakespeare. In the poem entitled 'A Remembrance of some English Poets' Barnfield praises Spenser, Daniel, Drayton, and Shakespeare. For Sir Philip Sidney he had a deep admiration, but his 'Epitaph' was a poor tribute. The verse with which the tract ends, 'A Comparison of the Life of Man,' is distinctly impressive :—

> 'Mans life is well compared to a feast,
> Furnisht with choice of all Varietie :
> To it comes Tyme ; and as a bidden guest
> Hee sets him downe, in Pompe and Maiestie ;
> The three-folde Age of Man the Waiters bee :
> Then with an earthen voyder (made of clay)
> Comes Death, and takes the table clean away.'

We now reach a group of elegies (pp. 271-318) by various hands on Sir Philip Sidney, printed as an Appendix to Spenser's *Colin Clouts Come Home Againe*, 1595, with a dedication to Sidney's widow, who by her second marriage had become Countess of Essex. There was no man more generally beloved than Sidney, and none whose loss was more sincerely deplored. Numberless were the tributes paid in verse and prose to his memory. The present collection embraces 'Astrophel,' by Spenser; the 'Dolefull Lay of Clorinda,' by Sidney's sister, the Countess of Pembroke; 'The Mourning Muse of Thestylis' and 'A Pastorall Æglogue,' both by Lodowick Bryskett; 'An Elegie, or Friends Passion, for his Astrophel,' by Matthew Roydon; 'An Epitaph,' probably by Sir Walter Ralegh; and 'Another of the same' (*i.e.* on the same subject), which Malone was inclined to attribute to Sir Edward Dyer, while Charles Lamb ascribed it on internal evidence to Fulke Greville. Although *Colin Clouts Come Home Againe* was first published in 1595, the dedicatory epistle to Sir Walter Ralegh is dated from Kilcolman, 27th December 1591. All the elegies were doubtless written soon after Sidney's death. Lodowick Bryskett's two poems had been entered in the Stationers' Register on 22nd August 1587, but are not known to have been separately published. Matthew Roydon's elegy had appeared in the *Phœnix Nest*, 1593, where also are found the 'Epitaph' and 'Another of the Same. Excellently written by a most woorthy gentleman.'

In *The Ruines of Time* (1591) there are some fine stanzas to Sidney's memory; but if the literary public expected an elaborate elegy from Spenser, 'Astrophel' must have disappointed their hopes. When we recall Moschus' lament over Bion, or Ovid's tribute to Tibullus, or *Lycidas*, or *Adonais*, Spenser's elegy on Sidney seems thin and colourless. Scores of poets who had not a tithe of Spenser's genius have left elegies that far transcend 'Astrophel.' Lady Pembroke's sisterly tribute of affection will be read with respect; but however much we may commend the pious intentions of the naturalised Italian

Ludowick Bryskett, it is impossible to find a word of praise
for such 'rude rhymes' as

> 'Come forth, ye Nymphes, come forth, forsake your watry boures !
>   Forsake your mossy caves and help me to lament ;
>   Help me to tune my dolefull notes to gurgling sound
>   Of Liffies tumbling streames ; come, let salt teares of ours
>   Mix with his waters fresh,' etc.

Matthew Roydon's elegy is too diffuse, but has some most
happy and memorable stanzas.   As we gaze at Isaac
Oliver's beautiful miniature of Sidney, in the Windsor
Palace collection, those oft-quoted lines of Roydon inevit-
ably leap to the lips :—

> 'A sweet attractive kind of grace,
>   A full assurance given by lookes,
>   Continuall comfort in a face,
>   The lineaments of Gospell bookes :
>   I trowe that countenance cannot lie
>   Whose thoughts are legible in the eie.'

The 'Epitaph' beginning, 'To praise thy life, or waile thy
worthie death,' appears to have been written by Sir Walter
Ralegh.   Sir John Harington, in the notes appended to the
sixteenth book of his translation of *Orlando Furioso* (1591),
refers to 'our English Petrarke, Sir Philip Sidney, or (as
Sir Walter Rawleigh in his Epitaph worthily calleth him)
the Scipio and the Petrarke of our time' (see the last stanza
of the poem).   Harington had evidently seen the 'Epitaph'
in MS. ; and there is not the slightest reason for questioning
the accuracy of his ascription, for he was well acquainted
with the poets of the time, and curious information may be
gathered from his Notes.   I find Ralegh's elegy somewhat
obscure; pregnant, but harshly worded.   Nor can I profess
any great admiration for 'Another of the same,' where the
vehemence of the writer's grief choked his utterance.

Of the first edition of *Alcilia : Philoparthen's Loving Folly*, 1595 (pp. 319-362), only one copy is known, preserved in the public library at Hamburgh. On the last page are subscribed the author's initials 'J. C.', which have been altered in ink to 'J. G.' in the Hamburgh copy. The poem was reprinted in London in 1613, 1619, and 1628, being accompanied by Marston's *Pygmalion's Image* and Samuel Page's *Amos and Laura*. Who 'J. C.' may have been is unknown ; for the wild conjecture that he was John Chalkhill, author of *Thealma and Clearchus* and friend of Izaak Walton, is chronologically untenable. For the space of two years the unknown poet had pressed his attentions upon the lady whom he called Alcilia. She finally rejected his addresses, and young 'J. C.' was not sorry to escape from bondage. Hardly a trace of genuine passion can be found in *Alcilia*, which is merely (as the author freely admits) a collection of odds and ends written 'at divers times and upon divers occasions.' It is somewhat surprising that there was a demand for new editions. 'J. C.' wrote with elegance and facility, but the note of originality is wanting. Had the poem appeared a few years earlier, it would have been entitled to more consideration ; but the achievements of Greene, Lodge, and others had made it possible in the closing years of the sixteenth century for any young writer of respectable talents to compose such verse as we find in *Alcilia*.

Daiphantus, or The Passions of Love, 1604 (pp. 363-404), is described on the title-page as 'By An. Sc. Gentleman,' assumed to stand for Antony Scoloker. In the days of Henry VIII. there was an Antony Scoloker, a printer and translator, with whom 'An. Sc.' was doubtless connected.

In the humorous prose address there is an interesting
reference to Shakespeare :—' It should be like the never-too-
well-read *Arcadia* where the Prose and Verse, Matter and
Words, are like his Mistress eyes, one still excelling
another and without corrival ; or to come home to the
Vulgar's element, like friendly Shake-speare's *Tragedies*,
where the Comedian rides when the Tragedian stands on
tiptoe. Faith it should please all like Prince HAMLET.
But, in sadness, then it were to be feared he would run
mad. In sooth I will not be moonsick to please, nor out of
my wits though I displease all. What? Poet, are you in
passion or out of Love? This is as strange as true.' In
the poem itself there is another reference to 'mad Hamlet,'
though Scoloker there seems to be glancing at the older
play on the subject of Hamlet. For the reader's guidance
an 'Argument' is obligingly prefixed, but it is to be feared
that even with the help of this Argument he will not find
the poem very intelligible or of engrossing interest. *Daiphantus*, of which only one copy (in the Douce Collection)
is known, was perhaps intended merely for circulation
among the author's friends, who may have been able to
read between the lines. Appended is the fine poem, 'The
Passionate Man's Pilgrimage,' beginning :—

> ' Give me my Scalop Shell of quiet,
> My Staff of faith to walk upon,
> My Scrip of joy, immortal diet,
> My Bottle of salvation,
> My Gown of glory, hope's true gage,
> And thus I'll take my Pilgrimage,' etc.

Possibly the publisher tacked on these verses without
Scoloker's knowledge. It is quite certain that they were
not written by the author of *Daiphantus*, and there are

good reasons for assigning them to Sir Walter Ralegh (*see* Hannah's edition of Ralegh's *Poems*, 1885).

The 'Odes' of Michael Drayton (pp. 405-441), drawn from *Poems Lyrick and Pastorall* (1606?), and the later collection of 1619, contain some of his best writing.   There is no need to praise the glorious 'Ballad of Agincourt,' but it may be noted that Drayton spent considerable pains over the revision of this poem.   It was fine in its original form, but every change found in the later version was a clear improvement.   No signs of the file are visible, and we should certainly judge—unless we had evidence to the contrary—that this imperishable 'ballad' had been thrown off at a white heat.   Only inferior to 'Agincourt' is the stirring ode 'To the Virginian Voyage.'   Professor Arber, a high authority, is of opinion that it was composed some time before 12th August 1606, on which day the Plymouth Company despatched Captain Henry Challons' ship to North Virginia.   In this valedictory address Drayton writes:—

> 'Your course securely steer,
> West-and-by-South forth keep !
>   Rocks,[1] Lee-shores, nor Shoals,
>   When Æolus scowls,
> You need not fear :
> So absolute the deep.'

Captain Challons sailed to Madeira, St. Lucia, Porto Rico,

[1] On March 31, 1605, Captain George Weymouth started from the Downs with a crew of twenty-nine to discover a North-West Passage to the East Indies. On May 14 he 'descries land in 41° 30′ N. in the midst of dangerous rocks and shoals. Upon which he puts to sea, the wind blowing south-south-west and west-south-west many days' (Prince's *New England Chronology ap.* Garner, ii. 356). Drayton advises the Virginian voyagers to keep the west-by-south course and so avoid misadventures. He had not reckoned on the Spanish fleet.

and thence towards North Virginia.   His little ship of
fifty-five tons, with a crew of twenty-nine Englishmen (and
two native Virginians), had the ill-luck on 10th November
to fall in with the Spanish fleet of eight ships returning
from Havanna.   It was captured by the Spaniards and the
crew were taken prisoners to Spain.

In a lighter vein, the ode beginning 'Maidens, why spare
ye,' was worthy to have been set to music by Robert Jones.
The seventh ode was written from the Peak in winter—

> 'Amongst the mountains bleak,
> Exposed to sleet and rain'—

where Charles Cotton afterwards resided.   Drayton's state-
ment in the ninth ode—

> 'My resolution such
> How well and not how much
> To write'—

will draw a smile from any reader who has ever seriously
attempted to grapple with his multitudinous works.   But
in these odes, and in the other 'lyric poesies' added in the
1619 edition, he was careful to curb his tendency to diffuse-
ness.   He employed a variety of metres, and his experiments
were not always happy.   Ode 5, 'An Amouret Anacreontic,'
cannot be unreservedly commended, and Ode 9, 'A
Skeltoniad,' could be spared.   One of the most attractive
poems is the address 'To his Rival,' a capital piece of
good-natured raillery.   In his early work Drayton frequently
taxes the reader's patience by his disregard for grammatical
proprieties, and some of these maturer Odes are so ineptly
harsh that one has to grope for the writer's meaning (while
one bans the punctuation of old printers and modern
editors alike).   Hence it is particularly pleasant to meet

such a poem as 'To his Rival,' which never swerves awry, but runs on blithely without an encountering obstacle. The 'Hymn to his Lady's Birthplace' is a polished compliment, and very charming is the canzonet 'To his Coy Love.' I end with expressing a hope that the extracts here given from Michael Drayton may induce the reader to make further acquaintance [1] with the writings of one of the most lovable of our elder poets.

A. H. BULLEN.

---

[1] Several of Drayton's works have been reprinted by the Spenser Society, and an excellent Introduction to them has been written by Professor Oliver Elton (1895).

ORCHESTRA,

or,

A Poem of Dancing.

Judicially proving the true observation of Time and Measure, in the authentical and laudable use of Dancing.

Ovid, *Art. Aman.* lib. 1.

Si vox est, canta : si mollia brachia, salta :
Et quacunque potes dote placere, place.

At London,
Printed by J. Robarts for N. Ling.
1596.

[The following entries at Stationers' Hall prove that this Poem, composed in fifteen days, was written not later than June, 1594; though it did not come to the press till November, 1596.

25 Junij [1594].

Master HARRISON.
Senior.

Entred for his copie in Court holden this day/ a booke entituled, *Orchestra, or a poeme of Daunsing.*

vjd.

Transcript &c. ii. 655. *Ed.* 1875.

xxj° Die Nouembris [1596].

NICHOLAS LYNG/

Entered for his copie under th[e h]andes of Master JACKSON and master Warden DAWSON, a booke called *Orchestra, or a poeme of Dauncinge.* vjd.

Transcript &c. iii. 74. *Ed.* 1876.]

To his very friend,
Master RICHARD MARTIN.

T O WHOM, shall I, this Dancing Poem send;
This sudden, rash, half-capreol of my wit?
To you, first mover and sole cause of it,
Mine own-self's better half, my dearest friend!
  Oh would you, yet, my Muse some honey lend
  From your mellifluous tongue (whereon doth sit
  Suada in majesty) that I may fit
  These harsh beginnings with a sweeter end!
You know the modest sun, full fifteen times,
Blushing did rise, and blushing did descend,
While I, in making of these ill made rhymes,
My golden hours unthriftily did spend:
  Yet if, in friendship, you these Numbers praise,
  I will mispend another fifteen days.

[The following Dedication was substituted in the edition of 1622.

To the Prince.

[*i.e.,* CHARLES, *Prince of* WALES.]

IR, whatsoever You are pleased to do,
It is your special praise, that you are bent,
And sadly set your Princely mind thereto :
Which makes You in each thing so excellent.

Hence is it, that You came so soon to be
A Man-at-arms in every point aright,
The fairest flower of noble Chivalry,
And of Saint GEORGE his Band the bravest Knight.

And hence it is, that all your youthful train
In activeness and grace You do excel,
When You do Courtly dancings entertain :
Then Dancing's praise may be presented well

To You, whose action adds more praise thereto
Than all the Muses, with their pens can do.]

ORCHESTRA,

or,

A Poem of Dancing.

1.

HERE lives the man, that never yet did hear
Of chaste PENELOPE, ULYSSES's Queen?
Who kept her faith unspotted twenty year;
Till he returned, that far away had been,
And many men and many towns had seen:
  Ten year at Siege of Troy, he ling'ring lay;
  And ten year in the midland sea did stray.

2.

HOMER, to whom the Muses did carouse
A great deep cup, with heavenly nectar filled;
The greatest deepest cup in JOVE's great house
(For JOVE himself had so expressly willed):
He drank of all, ne let one drop be spilled;
  Since when, his brain, that had before been dry,
  Became the Wellspring of all Poetry.

3.

Homer doth tell, in his abundant verse,
The long laborious travails of the Man ;
And of his Lady too, he doth rehearse,
How she illudes, with all the art she can,
Th'ungrateful love which other Lords began ;
    For of her Lord, false Fame, long since, had sworn
    That NEPTUNE'S monsters had his carcass torn.

4.

All this he tells, but one thing he forgot,
One thing most worthy his eternal Song,
But he was old, and blind, and saw it not :
Or else he thought he should ULYSSES wrong,
To mingle it his tragic acts among :
    Yet was there not, in all the world of things,
    A sweeter burden for his Muse's wings :

5.

The Courtly love ANTINOUS did make,
ANTINOUS, that fresh and jolly Knight,
Which of the Gallants that did undertake
To win the Widow, had most Wealth and Might,
Wit to persuade, and Beauty to delight :
    The Courtly love he made unto the Queen,
    HOMER forgot, as if it had not been.

6.

Sing then, TERPSICHORE, my light MUSE, sing
His gentle art and cunning courtesy !
You, Lady, can remember everything,
For you are daughter of Queen MEMORY :
But sing a plain and easy melody,
    For the soft mean that warbleth but the ground,
    To my rude ear doth yield the sweetest sound.

7.

Only one night's Discourse I can report :
When the great Torchbearer of heaven was gone
Down, in a masque, unto the Ocean's Court,
To revel it with TETHYS, all alone ;
ANTINOUS disguised, and unknown,
　　Like to the Spring in gaudy ornament,
　　Unto the Castle of the Princess went.

8.

The sovereign Castle of the rocky isle,
Wherein PENELOPE the Princess lay,
Shone with a thousand lamps, which did exile
The dim dark shades, and turned the night to day.
Not JOVE's blue tent, what time the sunny ray
　　Behind the bulwark of the earth retires,
　　Is seen to sparkle with more twinkling fires.

9.

That night, the Queen came forth from far within,
And in the presence of her Court was seen.
For the sweet singer PHŒMIUS did begin
To praise the Worthies that at Troy had been :
Somewhat of her ULYSSES she did ween,
　　In his grave Hymn, the heavenly man would sing,
　　Or of his wars, or of his wandering.

10.

PALLAS, that hour, with her sweet breath divine,
Inspired immortal beauty in her eyes,
That with celestial glory she did shine
Brighter than VENUS, when she doth arise
Out of the waters to adorn the skies.
　　The Wooers, all amazèd, do admire
　　And check their own presumptuous desire.

11.

Only ANTINOUS, when at first he viewed
Her star-bright eyes, that with new honour shined,
Was not dismayed ; but therewithal renewed
The *noblesse* and the splendour of his mind :
And, as he did fit circumstances find,
  Unto the throne, he boldly 'gan advance,
  And, with fair manners, wooed the Queen to dance.

12.

Goddess of women ! sith your heavenliness
Hath now vouchsafed itself to represent
To our dim eyes ; which though they see the less,
Yet are they blest in their astonishment :
Imitate heaven, whose beauties excellent
  Are in continual motion day and night,
  And move thereby more wonder and delight.

13.

Let me the mover be, to turn about
Those glorious ornaments that Youth and Love
Have fixed in you, every part throughout :
Which if you will in timely measure move ;
Not all those precious gems in heaven above
  Shall yield a sight more pleasing to behold
  With all their turns and tracings manifold.

14.

With this, the modest Princess blushed and smiled
Like to a clear and rosy eventide,
And softly did return this answer mild :
Fair Sir !   You needs must fairly be denied,
Where your demand cannot be satisfied.
  My feet, which only Nature taught to go,
  Did never yet the Art of Footing know.

15.

But why persuade you me to this new rage?
For all Disorder and Misrule is new :
For such misgovernment in former Age
Our old divine forefathers never knew ;
Who if they lived, and did the follies view,
    Which their fond nephews make their chief affairs,
    Would hate themselves, that had begot such heirs.

16.

Sole Heir of Virtue, and of Beauty both!
Whence cometh it, ANTINOUS replies,
That your imperious Virtue is so loath
To grant your Beauty her chief exercise?
Or from what spring doth your opinion rise
    That Dancing is a Frenzy and a Rage,
    First known and used in this new-fangled Age?

17.

Dancing, bright Lady! then, began to be,
When the first seeds whereof the world did spring;
The Fire, Air, Earth, and Water did agree
By LOVE's persuasion (Nature's mighty King)
To leave their first disordered combating;
    And, in a dance, such Measure to observe,
    As all the world their motion should preserve.

18.

Since when, they still are carried in a round;
And changing come one in another's place :
Yet do they neither mingle nor confound,
But every one doth keep the bounded space,
Wherein the Dance doth bid it turn or trace:
    This wondrous miracle did LOVE devise,
    For Dancing is LOVE's proper exercise.

19.

Like this, he framed the gods' eternal bower,
And of a shapeless and confusèd mass,
By his through-piercing and digesting power,
The turning Vault of Heaven formèd was;
Whose starry wheels he hath so made to pass
  As that their movings do a Music frame,
  And they themselves still dance unto the same.

20.

Or if " this All, which round about we see,"
As idle MORPHEUS *some sick brains hath taught,*
" Of undivided motes compactèd be,"
How was this goodly architecture wrought?
Or by what means were they together brought?
  They err, that say, " they did concur by Chance!"
  LOVE *made them meet in a well ordered Dance!*

21.

As when AMPHION *with his charming Lyre*
Begot so sweet a Siren of the air,
That, with her rhetoric, made the stones conspire,
The ruins of a city to repair
(A work of Wit and Reason's wise affair):
  So LOVE's *smooth tongue the motes such measnre taught,*
  That they joined hands; and so the world was wrought!

22.

How justly then is Dancing termèd new,
Which, with the world, in point of time began?
Yea Time itself (whose birth JOVE *never knew,*
And which is far more ancient than the sun)
Had not one moment of his age outrun,
  When out leaped Dancing from the heap of things
  And lightly rode upon his nimble wings.

23.

Reason hath both their pictures in her Treasure;
Where Time the Measure of all moving is,
And Dancing is a moving all in measure.
Now, if you do resemble that to this,
And think both One, I think you think amiss:
But if you judge them Twins, together got,
And Time first born, your judgement erreth not.

24.

Thus doth it equal age with Age enjoy,
And yet in lusty youth for ever flowers;
Like LOVE, his Sire, whom painters make a boy,
Yet is he Eldest of the Heavenly Powers;
Or like his brother Time, whose wingèd hours,
Going and coming, will not let him die,
But still preserve him in his infancy.

25.

This said, the Queen, with her sweet lips divine,
Gently began to move the subtle air,
Which gladly yielding, did itself incline
To take a shape between those rubies fair;
And being formed, softly did repair,
With twenty doublings in the empty way,
Unto ANTINOUS' ears, and thus did say.

26.

What eye doth see the heaven, but doth admire
When it the movings of the heavens doth see?
Myself, if I, to heaven may once aspire,
If that be Dancing, will a dancer be;
But as for this, your frantic jollity,
How it began, or whence you did it learn,
I never could, with Reason's eye discern?

27.

ANTINOUS answered, *Jewel of the earth !*
Worthy you are, that heavenly Dance to lead;
But for you think our Dancing base of birth,
And newly born but of a brain-sick head,
I will forthwith his antique gentry read,
  And (for I love him) will his herald be,
  And blaze his arms, and draw his pedigree.

28.

When LOVE *had shaped this world, this great fair wight,*
(That all wights else in this wide womb contains),
And had instructed it to dance aright
A thousand measures, with a thousand strains,
Which it should practise with delightful pains,
  Until that fatal instant should revolve,
  When all to nothing should again resolve :

29.

The comely Order and Proportion fair
On every side did please his wand'ring eye;
Till, glancing through the thin transparent air,
A rude disordered rout he did espy
Of men and women, that most spitefully
  Did one another throng and crowd so sore
  That his kind eye, in pity, wept therefore.

30.

And swifter than the lightning down he came,
Another shapeless chaos to digest.
He will begin another world to frame
(For LOVE, *till all be well, will never rest).*
Then with such words as cannot be expresst,
  He cuts the troops, that all asunder fling,
  And ere they wist, he casts them in a ring.

31.

Then did he rarify the Element,
And in the centre of the ring appear ;
The beams that from his forehead shining went
Begot a horror and religious fear
In all the souls that round about him were,
    Which in their ears attentiveness procures,
    While he, with such like sounds, their minds allures.

32.

" How doth Confusions's Mother, headlong Chance,
Put Reason's noble squadron to the rout ?
Or how should you, that have the governance
Of Nature's children, heaven and earth throughout,
Prescribe them rules, and live yourselves without ?
    Why should your fellowship a trouble be,
    Since Man's chief pleasure is Society ?

33.

" If Sense hath not yet taught you, learn of me
A comely moderation and discreet ;
That your assemblies may well ordered be,
When my uniting power shall make you meet,
With heavenly tunes it shall be tempered sweet ;
    And be the model of the world's great frame,
    And you, Earth's children, Dancing shall it name.

34.

" Behold the world, how it is whirlèd round !
And for it is so whirled, is namèd so :
In whose large volume, many rules are found
Of this new Art, which it doth fairly show.
For your quick eyes in wandering to and fro,
    From East to West, on no one thing can glance ;
    But (if you mark it well) it seems to dance.

35.

"*First, you see fixed, in this huge mirror blue,*
Of trembling lights a number numberless;
Fixed, they are named but with a name untrue;
For they are moved and in a dance express
The great long Year that doth contain no less
    Than threescore hundreds of those years in all,
    Which the Sun makes with his course natural.

36.

"*What if to you these sparks disordered seem,*
As if by chance they had been scattered there?
The gods a solemn measure do it deem
And see a just proportion everywhere,
And know the points whence first their movings were
    To which first points, when all return again,
    The Axletree of Heaven shall break in twain.

37.

"*Under that spangled sky, five wandering Flames,*
Besides the King of Day and Queen of Night,
Are wheeled around, all in their sundry frames,
And all in sundry measures do delight;
Yet altogether keep no measure right;
    For by itself each doth itself advance,
    And by itself each doth a Galliard dance.

38

"VENUS (*the mother of that bastard* LOVE,
Which doth usurp the world's Great Marshal's name),
Just with the sun, her dainty feet doth move;
And unto him doth all her gestures frame
Now after, now afore, the flattering Dame,
    With divers cunning passages doth err,
    Still him respecting, that respects not her.

39.

" For that brave SUN, the Father of the Day,
Doth love this EARTH, the Mother of the Night,
And like a reveller, in rich array,
Doth dance his Galliard in his leman's sight;
Both back, and forth, and sideways passing light.
  His gallant grace doth so the gods amaze,
  That all stand still, and at his beauty gaze.

40.

" But see the EARTH, when she approacheth near,
How she for joy doth spring and sweetly smile;
But see again, her sad and heavy cheer
When, changing places, he retires a while;
But those black clouds he shortly will exile,
  And make them all before his presence fly,
  As mists consumed before his cheerful eye.

41.

" Who doth not see the Measures of the MOON?
Which thirteen times she danceth every year,
And ends her Pavin thirteen times as soon
As doth her brother, of whose golden hair
She borroweth part, and proudly doth it wear.
  Then doth she coyly turn her face aside
  That half her cheek is scarce sometimes descried.

42.

" Next her, the pure, subtle, and cleansing fire
Is swiftly carried in a circle even :
Though VULCAN be pronounced by many, a liar,
The only halting god that dwells in heaven.
But that foul name may be more fitly given
  To your false fire, that far from heaven is fall,
  And doth consume, waste, spoil, disorder all.

43.

" *And now, behold your tender nurse, the Air,*
And common neighbour that aye runs around ;
How many pictures and impressions fair,
Within her empty regions are there found,
Which to your senses, Dancing do propound ?
　　For what are breath, speech, echoes, music, winds
　　But Dancings of the Air, in sundry kinds ?

44.

" *For when you Breathe, the air in order moves ;*
Now in, now out, in time and measure true
And when you Speak, so well the Dancing loves
That doubling oft, and oft redoubling new,
With thousand forms she doth herself endue.
　　For all the words that from your lips repair,
　　Are nought but tricks and turnings of the Air.

45.

" *Hence is her prattling daughter, ECHO, born,*
That dances to all voices she can hear.
There is no sound so harsh that she doth scorn ;
Nor any time, wherein she will forbear
The airy pavement with her feet to wear ;
　　And yet her hearing sense is nothing quick,
　　For after time she endeth every trick."

46.

" *And thou, sweet Music, Dancing's only life,*
The ear's sole happiness, the Air's best speech,
Loadstone of fellowship, Charming rod of strife,
The soft mind's Paradise, the sick mind's Leech,
With thine own tongue, thou trees and stones canst teach,
　　That when the Air doth dance her finest measure,
　　Then art thou born, the gods' and men's sweet pleasure."

47.

" *Lastly, where keep the Winds their revelry,*
Their violent turnings, and wild whirling Hayes ;
But in the Air's tralucent gallery ?
Where she herself is turned a hundred ways,
While with those Maskers, wantonly she plays.
         Yet in this misrule, they such rule embrace
         As two, at once, encumber not the place.

48.

" *If then Fire, Air, Wandering and Fixed Lights,*
In every province of th'imperial sky,
Yield perfect forms of Dancing to your sights ;
In vain I teach the ear, that which the eye,
With certain view, already doth descry ;
         But for your eyes perceive not all they see,
         In this, I will your senses' master be

49.

" *For lo, the Sea that fleets about the land,*
And like a girdle clips her solid waist,
Music and Measure both doth understand
For his great Crystal Eye is always cast
Up to the Moon, and on her fixèd fast ;
         And as she danceth, in her pallid sphere,
         So danceth he about the centre here

50.

" *Sometimes his proud green waves, in order set,*
One after other, flow unto the shore ;
Which when they have with many kisses wet,
They ebb away in order, as before :
And to make known his Courtly Love the more,
         He oft doth lay aside his three-forked mace,
         And with his arms the timorous Earth embrace.

51.

" *Only the Earth doth stand for ever still :*
Her rocks remove not, nor her mountains meet
(Although some wits enriched with learning's skill,
Say ' Heaven stands firm, and that the Earth doth fleet,
And swiftly turneth underneath their feet') ;
    Yet, though the Earth is ever steadfast seen,
    On her broad breast hath Dancing ever been.

52.

" *For those blue veins, that through her body spread ;*
Those sapphire streams which from great hills do spring,
(The Earth's great dugs ! for every wight is fed
With sweet fresh moisture from them issuing)
Observe a Dance in their wild wandering ;
    And still their Dance begets a murmur sweet,
    And still the Murmur with the Dance doth meet.

53.

" *Of all their ways, I love Mæander's path ;*
Which, to the tunes of dying swans, doth dance
Such winding slights.   Such turns and tricks he hath,
Such creeks, such wrenches, aad such daliance
That (whether it be hap or heedless chance)
    In his indented course and wringing play,
    IIe seems to dance a perfect cunning Hay.

54.

" *But wherefore do these streams for ever run ?*
To keep themselves for ever sweet and clear ;
For let their everlasting course be done,
They straight corrupt and foul with mud appear.
O ye sweet Nymphs, that beauty's loss do fear,
    Contemn the drugs that physic doth devise ;
    And learn of LOVE, this dainty exercise.

55.

" See how those flowers, that have sweet beauty too,
The only jewels that the EARTH doth wear
When the young SUN in bravery her doth woo)
As oft as they the whistling wind do hear,
Do wave their tender bodies here and there :
    And though their dance no perfect measure is ;
    Yet oftentimes their music makes them kiss.

56.

" What makes the Vine about the Elm to dance
With turnings, windings, and embracements round ?
What makes the loadstone to the North advance
His subtle point, as if from thence he found
His chief attractive virtue to redound ?
    Kind Nature, first, doth cause all things to love ;
    Love makes them dance, and in just order move.

57.

" Hark how the birds do sing ! and mark then how,
Jump with the modulation of their lays,
They lightly leap, and skip from bough to bough ;
Yet do the cranes deserve a greater praise,
Which keep such measure in their airy ways:
    As when they all in order rankèd are,
    They make a perfect form triangular.

58.

" In the chief angle, flies the watchful guide ;
And all the followers their heads do lay
On their foregoers' backs, on either side :
But, for the Captain hath no rest to stay
His head forwearied with the windy way,
    He back retires ; and then the next behind,
    As his Lieutenant, leads them through the wind.

59.

"By why relate I every singular?
Since all the world's great fortunes and affairs
Forward and backward rapt and whirlèd are,
According to the music of the spheres;
And Chance herself her nimble feet upbears
    On a round slippery wheel, that rolleth aye,
      And turns all states with her impetuous sway.

60.

"Learn then to dance you, that are princes born
And lawful Lords of earthly creatures all;
Imitate them, and thereof take no scorn,
For this new Art to them is natural.
And imitate the stars celestial;
    For when pale Death your vital twist shall sever,
      Your better parts must dance with them for ever."

61.

Thus LOVE persuades, and all the crowd of men
That stands around, doth make a murmuring,
As when the wind, loosed from his hollow den,
Among the trees a gentle bass doth sing;
Or as a brook, through pebbles wandering:
    But in their looks, they uttered this plain speech,
      "That they would learn to dance, if LOVE would teach.

62.

Then, first of all, he doth demonstrate plain,·
The motions seven that are in Nature found;
Upward and downward, forth and back again,
To this side, and to that, and turning round:
Whereof a thousand Brawls he doth compound,
    Which he doth teach unto the multitude:
      And ever, with a turn they must conclude.

63.

As when a *Nymph* arising from the land,
Leadeth a dance, with her long watery train,
Down to the sea, she wries to every hand,
And every way doth cross the fertile plain ;
But when, at last, she falls into the Main,
    Then all her traverses concluded are,
    And with the sea *her course is circular*

64.

Thus, when, at first, LOVE had them marshallèd,
(As erst he did the shapeless mass of things)
He taught them Rounds and winding Heyes to tread,
And about trees to cast themselves in rings :
As the two Bears, whom the First Mover flings
    With a short turn about Heaven's Axle-tree,
    In a round dance for ever wheeling be.

65.

But after these, as men more civil grew,
He did more grave and solemn Measures frame ;
With such fair order and proportion true,
And correspondence every way the same,
That no fault-finding eye did ever blame :
    For every eye was movèd at the sight
    With sober wondering, and with sweet delight.

66.

Not those old students of the heavenly book,
ATLAS the great, PROMETHEUS the wise ;
Which on the stars did all their lifetime look,
Could ever find such measures in the skies,
So full of change and rare varieties :
    Yet all the feet whereon these measures go
    Are only Spondees, solemn, grave, and slow.

67.

But for more divers and more pleasing show,
A swift and wandering dance She did invent;
With passages uncertain, to and fro,
Yet with a certain Answer and Consent
To the quick music of the instrument.
    Five was the number of the Music's feet;
    Which still the Dance did with five paces meet.

68.

A gallant Dance! that lively doth bewray
A spirit and a virtue masculine;
Impatient that her house on earth should stay,
Since she herself is fiery and divine.
Oft doth she make her body upward flyne
    With lofty turns and caprioles in the air,
    Which with the lusty tunes accordeth fair.

69.

What shall I name those current travases,
That on a triple Dactyl foot, do run
Close by the ground, with sliding passages?
Wherein that dancer greatest praise hath won,
Which with best order can all orders shun;
    For everywhere he wantonly must range,
    And turn, and wind, with unexpected change.

70.

Yet is there one, the most delightful kind,
A lofty jumping, or a leaping round,
When, arm in arm, two dancers are entwined,
And whirl themselves, with strict embracements bound,
And still their feet an Anapest do sound;
    An Anapest is all their music's song,
    Whose first two feet are short, and third is long.

71.

As the victorious twins of *LÆDA* and *JOVE*,
(*That taught the Spartans dancing on the sands
Of swift Eurotas*) *dance in heaven above,
Knit and united with eternal bands ;
Among the stars their double image stands,
    Where both are carried with an equal pace,
    Together jumping in their turning race.*

72.

*This is the net wherein the sun's bright eye
VENUS and MARS entangled did behold ;
For in this dance their arms they so imply,
As each doth seem the other to enfold.
What if lewd wits another tale have told,
    Of jealous VULCAN, and of iron chains ?
    Yet this true sense that forged lie contains.*

73.

*These various forms of dancing LOVE did frame,
And besides these, a hundred millions moe ;
And as he did invent, he taught the same :
With goodly gesture, and with comely show,
Now keeping state, now humbly honouring low.
    And ever for the persons and the place,
    He taught most fit, and best according grace.*

74.

*For LOVE, within his fertile working brain,
Did then conceive those gracious Virgins three,
Whose civil moderation did maintain
All decent order and conveniency,
And fair respect, and seemly modesty :
    And then he thought it fit they should be born,
    That their sweet presence Dancing might adorn.*

75.

Hence is it, that these Graces painted are
With hand in hand, dancing an endless round ;
And with regarding eyes, that still beware
That there be no disgrace amongst them found :
With equal foot they beat the flowery ground,
  Laughing, or singing, as their Passions will ;
  Yet nothing that they do, becomes them ill.

76.

Thus LOVE taught men ! and men thus learned of LOVE
Sweet Music's sound with feet to counterfeit :
Which was long time before high-thundering JOVE
Was lifted up to Heaven's imperial seat.
For though by birth he were the Prince of Crete,
  Nor Crete nor Heaven should that young Prince have
  If dancers with their timbrels had not been. [seen,

77.

Since when all ceremonious mysteries,
All sacred orgies and religious rites,
All pomps, and triumphs, and solemnities,
All funerals, nuptials, and like public sights,
All parliaments of peace, and warlike fights,
  All learned arts, and every great affair,
  A lively shape of Dancing seems to bear.

78.

For what did he, who, with his ten-tongued Lute,
Gave beasts and blocks an understanding ear ;
Or rather into bestial minds and brutes
Shed and infused the beams of Reason clear ?
Doubtless, for men that rude and savage were,
  A civil form of Dancing he devised,
  Wherewith unto their gods they sacrificed.

79.

So did MUSÆUS, so AMPHION did,
And LINUS with his sweet enchanting Song,
And he whose hand the earth of monsters rid,
And had men's ears fast chainèd to his tongue,
And THESEUS to his wood-born slaves among,
     Used Dancing, as the finest policy
     To plant Religion and Society.

80.

And therefore, now, the Thracian ORPHEUS' lyre
And HERCULES himself are stellified,
And in high heaven, amidst the starry quire
Dancing their parts, continually do slide.
So, on the Zodiac, GANYMEDE doth ride,
     And so is HEBE with the Muses nine,
     For pleasing JOVE with dancing, made divine.

81.

Wherefore was PROTEUS said himself to change
Into a stream, a lion, and a tree,
And many other forms fantastic strange,
As, in his fickle thought, he wished to be?
But that he danced with such facility,
     As, like a lion, he could pace with pride,
     Ply like a plant, and like a river slide.

82.

And how was CŒNEUS made, at first, a man,
And then a woman, then a man again,
But in a Dance? which when he first began
He the man's part in measure did sustain:
But when he changed into a second strain,
     He danced the woman's part another space;
     And then returned unto his former place.

83.

Hence sprang the fable of TIRESIAS,
That he the pleasure of both sexes tried ;
For, in a dance, he man and woman was,
By often change of place, from side to side,
But, for the woman easily did slide,
    And smoothly swim with cunning hidden Art,
    He took more pleasure in a woman's part.

84.

So to a fish VENUS herself did change,
And swimming through the soft and yielding wave,
With gentle motions did so smoothly range,
As none might see where she the water drave ;
But this plain truth that falsèd fable gave,
    That she did dance with sliding easiness,
    Pliant and quick in wandering passages.

85.

And merry BACCHUS practised dancing too,
And to the Lydian numbers Rounds did make.
The like he did in th' Eastern India do,
And taught them all, when PHŒBUS did awake,
And when at night he did his coach forsake,
    To honour heaven, and heaven's great rolling eye,
    With turning dances and with melody.

86.

Thus they who first did found a Common weal,
And they who first Religion did ordain,
By dancing first the people's hearts did steal :
Of whom we now a thousand tales do feign.
Yet do we now their perfect rules retain,
    And use them still in such devices new ;
    As in the world, long since, their withering grew.

87.

For after Towns and Kingdoms founded were,
Between great states arose well-ordered war,
Wherein most perfect Measure doth appear :
Whether their well set Ranks respected are,
In quadrant forms or semicircular ;
  Or else the March, when all the troops advance,
  Unto the drum in gallant order dance.

88.

And after wars, when white-winged Victory
Is with a glorious Triumph beautified ;
And every one doth Iô ! Iô ! cry,
While all in gold the Conqueror doth ride ;
The solemn pomp, that fills the city wide,
  Observes such Rank and Measure everywhere,
  As if they altogether dancing were.

89.

The like just order Mourners do observe,
But with unlike affection and attire,
When some great man, that nobly did deserve,
And whom his friends impatiently desire,
Is brought with honour to his latest fire.
  The dead corpse, too, in that sad dance is moved
  As if both dead and living dancing loved.

90.

A diverse cause, but like solemnity,
Unto the Temple leads the bashful bride,
Which blusheth like the Indian ivory
Which is with dip of Tyrian purple dyed :
A golden troop doth pass on every side,
  Of flourishing young men and virgins gay,
  Which keep fair Measure all the flowery way.

91.

And not alone the general multitude
But those choice NESTORS, which in counsel grave
Of cities and of kingdoms do conclude,
Most comely order in their sessions have ;
Wherefore the wise Thessalians ever gave
  The name of Leader of their Country's Dance
  To him that had their country's governance.

92.

And those great Masters of the liberal arts,
In all their several Schools, do Dancing teach ;
For humble Grammar first doth set the parts
Of congruent and well according Speech,
Which Rhetoric, whose state the clouds doth reach,
  And heavenly Poetry do forward lead,
  And divers Measures diversely do tread.

93.

For Rhetoric clothing Speech in rich array,
The looser numbers teacheth her to range
With twenty tropes, and turnings every way,
And various figures and licentious change :
But Poetry, with rule and order strange,
  So curiously doth move each single pace
  As all is marred if she one foot misplace.

94.

These Arts of Speech the Guides and Marshals are,
But Logic leadeth Reason in a dance
(Reason, the Cynosure and bright Loadstar
In this world's sea, t'avoid the rocks of Chance),
For with close following, and continuance,
  One reason doth another so ensue
  As, in conclusion, still the Dance is true.

95.

So Music to her own sweet tunes doth trip,
With tricks of 3, 5, 8, 15, and more ;
So doth the Art of Numbering seem to skip
From Even to Odd, in her proportioned score ;
So do those skills, whose quick eyes do explore
  The just dimension both of earth and heaven,
  In all their rules observe a measure even.

96.

Lo, this is Dancing's true nobility ;
Dancing, the Child of Music and of Love ;
Dancing itself, both Love and Harmony ;
Where all agree, and all in order move ;
Dancing, the art that all Arts doth approve ;
  The sure Character of the world's consent,
  The heaven's true figure, and th'earth's ornament.

97.

The Queen, whose dainty ears had borne too long
The tedious praise of that she did despise,
Adding once more the music of the tongue
To the sweet speech of her alluring eyes ;
Began to answer in such winning wise
  As that forthwith ANTINOUS' tongue was tied,
  His eyes fast fixed, his ears were open wide.

98.

Forsooth, quoth she, *great glory you have won*
To your trim minion, Dancing, all this while,
By blazing him LOVE'*s first begotten son,*
Of every ill the hateful father vile,
That doth the world with sorceries beguile,
  Cunningly mad, religiously profane,
  Wit's monster, Reason's canker, Sense's bane.

99.

Love taught the mother that unkind desire
To wash her hands in her own infant's blood;
Love taught the daughter to betray her sire
Into most base unworthy servitude;
Love taught the brother to prepare such food
  To feast his brothers that the all-seeing sun,
  Wrapt in a cloud, the wicked sight did shun.

100.

And even this self-same Love hath Dancing taught,
An Art that shewed th'Idea of his mind
With vainness, frenzy, and misorder fraught;
Sometimes with blood and cruelties unkind,
For in a dance Tereus' mad wife did find
  Fit time and place, by murdering her son,
  T'avenge the wrong his traitorous sire had done.

101.

What mean the Mermaids, when they dance and sing,
But certain death unto the mariner?
What tidings do the dancing Dolphins bring,
But that some dangerous storm approacheth near?
Then since both Love and Dancing liveries bear
  Of such ill hap unhappy may they prove
  That, sitting free, will either dance or love!

102.

Yet, once again, Antinous did reply,
Great Queen! condemn not Love the innocent,
For this mischievous Lust, which traitorously
Usurps his Name, and steals his Ornament;
For that True Love, which Dancing did invent,
  Is he that tuned the world's whole harmony,
  And linked all men in sweet society

103.

He first extracted from th'earth-mingled mind
That heavenly fire, or quintessence divine,
Which doth such sympathy in Beauty find
As is between the Elm and fruitful Vine,
And so to Beauty ever doth incline;
    Life's life it is, and cordial to the heart,
    And of our better part the better part.

104.

This is True Love, by that true CUPID got;
Which danceth Galliards in your amorous eyes,
But to your frozen heart approacheth not;
Only your heart he dares not enterprise,
And yet through every other part he flies,
    And everywhere he nimbly danceth now,
    Though in yourself yourself perceive not how.

105.

For your sweet beauty daintily transfused
With due proportion, throughout every part;
What is it but a dance where LOVE hath used
His finer cunning, and more curious Art?
Where all the Elements themselves impart,
    And turn, and wind, and mingle with such measure
    That th' eye that sees it surfeits with the pleasure.

106.

LOVE in the twinkling of your eyelids danceth,
LOVE dances in your pulses and your veins,
LOVE, when you sew, your needle's point advanceth,
And makes it dance a thousand curious strains
Of winding rounds; whereof the form remains
    To shew that your fair hands can dance the Hey,
    Which your fine feet would learn as well as they.

107.

And when your ivory fingers touch the strings
Of any silver-sounding instrument,
LOVE makes them dance to those sweet murmurings,
With busy skill and cunning excellent!
O that your feet, those tunes would represent
With artificial motions to and fro,
That LOVE this Art in every part might shew!

108.

Yet your fair soul, which came from heaven above
To rule this house (another heaven below)
With divers powers in harmony doth move;
And all the virtues that from her do flow
In a round measure, hand in hand do go:
Could I now see, as I conceive this dance,
Wonder and Love would cast me in a trance.

109.

The richest jewel in all the heavenly treasure,
That ever yet unto the earth was shown,
Is Perfect Concord th' only perfect pleasure,
That wretched earthborn men have ever known:
For many hearts it doth compound in one,
That what so one doth will, or speak, or do,
With one consent they all agree thereto.

110.

Concord's true picture shineth in this Art
Where divers men and women rankèd be,
And every one doth dance a several part,
Yet all as one in measure do agree,
Observing perfect uniformity:
All turn together, all together trace,
And all together honour and embrace.

III.

If they whom sacred Love hath linked in one,
Do, as they dance, in all their course of life;
Never shall burning grief nor bitter moan,
Nor factious difference, nor unkind strife,
Arise between the husband and the wife;
  For whether forth, or back, or round he go,
  As doth the man, so must the woman do.

112.

What, if by often interchange of place,
Sometimes the woman gets the upper hand?
That is but done for more delightful grace,
For on that part, she doth not ever stand;
But, as the Measures' law doth her command,
  She wheels about, and, ere the dance doth end,
  Into her former place she doth transcend.

113.

But not alone this correspondence meet
And uniform consent doth Dancing praise;
For Comeliness, the child of Order sweet,
Enamels it with her eye-pleasing rays:
Fair Comeliness, ten hundred thousand ways,
  Through Dancing sheds itself, and makes it shine
  With glorious beauty, and with grace divine.

114.

For Comeliness is a disposing fair
Of things and actions in fit time and place;
Which doth in Dancing shew itself most clear
When troops confused, which here and there do trace,
Without distinguishment or bounded space,
  By dancing rule, into such ranks are brought,
  As glads the eye, and ravisheth the thought.

115.

Then why should Reason judge that reasonless
Which is Wit's Offspring, and the work of *Art*,
Image of Concord, and of Comeliness ?
Who sees a clock moving in every part,
A sailing pinnace, or a wheeling cart,
  But thinks that Reason, ere it came to pass,
  The first impulsive cause and mover was ?

116.

Who sees an army all in rank advance,
But deems a wise Commander is in place,
Which leadeth on that brave victorious dance ?
Much more in Dancing's Art, in Dancing's grace,
Blindness itself may Reason's footsteps trace ;
  For of Love's Maze it is the curious plot,
  And of Man's Fellowship the true-love knot.

117.

But if these eyes of yours (Loadstars of Love !
Shewing the world's great Dance to your mind's eye)
Cannot, with all their demonstrations, move
Kind apprehension in your Phantasy
Of Dancing's virtue and nobility ;
  How can my barbarous tongue win you thereto,
  Which heaven's and earth's fair speech could never do ?

118.

O LOVE ! my King ! If all my Wit and power
Have done you all the service that they can ;
O be you present, in this present hour,
And help your servant and your true liegeman !
End that persuasion, which I erst began !
  For who in praise of Dancing can persuade
  With such sweet force, as LOVE, which Dancing made ?

119.

LOVE heard his prayer; and swifter than the wind,
(Like to a page in habit, face, and speech),
He came; and stood ANTINOUS behind,
And many secrets of his thoughts did teach.
At last a crystal Mirror he did reach
    Unto his hands, that he with one rash view
    All forms therein by LOVE'S revealing knew.

120.

And humbly honouring, gave it to the Queen,
With this fair speech, *See, fairest Queen!* quoth he,
The fairest sight that ever shall be seen,
And th'only wonder of posterity!
The richest work in Nature's treasury!
    Which she disdains to shew on this world's stage,
    And thinks it far too good for our rude age.

121.

But in another world, divided far,
In the great fortunate triangled Isle,
Thrice twelve degrees removed from the North Star,
She will this glorious Workmanship compile,
Which she hath been conceiving all this while
    Since the world's birth; and will bring forth at last,
    When six and twenty hundred years are past.

122.

PENELOPE the Queen, when she had viewed
The strange eye-dazzling admirable sight,
Fain would have praised the State and Pulchritude;
But she was stricken dumb with wonder quite,
Yet her sweet mind retained her thinking might.
    Her ravished mind in heavenly thoughts did dwell;
    But what she thought, no mortal tongue can tell.

123.

You, Lady Muse, whom JOVE the Counsellor
Begot of MEMORY, Wisdom's Treasuress,
To your divining tongue is given a power
Of uttering secrets, large and limitless;
You can PENELOPE'S strange thoughts express;
    Which she conceived, and then would fain have told,
    When she the wondrous Crystal did behold.

124.

Her wingèd thoughts bore up her mind so high
As that she weened she saw the glorious throne,
Where the bright Moon doth sit in Majesty:
A thousand sparkling stars about her shone,
But she herself did sparkle more, alone,
    Than all those thousand beauties would have done,
    If they had been confounded all in one.

125.

And yet she thought those stars moved in such measure,
To do their Sovereign honour and delight,
As soothed her mind with sweet enchanting pleasure,
Although the various Change amazed her sight,
And her weak judgement did entangle quite:
    Besides, their moving made them shine more clear;
    As diamonds moved more sparkling do appear.

126.

This was the Picture of her wondrous thought!
But who can wonder that her thought was so,
Sith VULCAN, King of Fire, that Mirror wrought
(Which things to come, present, and past doth know),
And there did represent in lively show
    Our glorious English Court's divine Image,
    As it should be in this our Golden Age?

[*See duplicate ending from this point on the next pages.*]

127.

Away, TERPSICHORE, light Muse, away!
And come, URANIA, Prophetess divine!
Come, Muse of Heaven, my burning thirst allay!
Even now, for want of sacred drink, I pine:
In heavenly moisture dip this pen of mine,
  And let my mouth with nectar overflow,
  For I must more than mortal glory show!

128.

O that I had HOMER's abundant vein,
I would hereof another Ilias make!
Or else the Man of Mantua's charmèd brain,
In whose large throat great JOVE the thunder spake!
O that I could old GEOFFREY's Muse awake,
  Or borrow COLIN's fair heroic style,
  Or smooth my rhymes with *DELIA's* servant's file!

129.

O could I, sweet Companion, sing like you
Which of a *Shadow*, under a shadow sing!
Or like fair SALVES' sad lover true!
Or like the Bay, the marigold's darling,
Whose sudden verse, Love covers with his wing!
  O that your brains were mingled all with mine,
  T'enlarge my Wit for this great work divine!

130.

Yet ASTROPHEL might one for all suffice,
Whose supple Muse camelion-like doth change
Into all forms of excellent device:
So might the Swallow, whose swift Muse doth range
Through rare *Idæas* and inventions strange,
  And ever doth enjoy her joyful Spring,
  And Sweeter than the Nightingale doth sing.

131.

O that I might that singing Swallow hear,
To whom I owe my service and my love !
His sugared tunes would so enchant mine ear,
And in my mind such sacred fury move,
As I should knock at heaven's great gate above,
    With my proud rhymes ; while, of this heavenly state,
    I do aspire the Shadow to relate.

FINIS.

[*In later editions a different ending of the poem was substituted for the above, from after Stanza 126, thus :*

     ❋   ❋   ❋   ❋

Here are wanting some stanzas describing Queen ELIZABETH.

Then follow these :

127.

Her brighter dazzling beams of Majesty
Were laid aside : for she vouchsafed awhile
With gracious, cheerful, and familiar eye,
Upon the Revels of her Court to smile,
For so Time's journey she doth oft beguile :
    Like sight no mortal eye might elsewhere see
    So full of State, Art, and variety.

128.

For of her Barons brave, and Ladies fair
(Who had they been elsewhere, most fair had been),
Many an incomparable lovely pair
With hand-in-hand were interlinkèd seen,
Making fair honour to their sovereign Queen:
    Forward they paced, and did their pace apply
    To a most sweet and solemn melody.

129.

So subtle and curious was the measure
With such unlooked-for change in every strain,
As that PENELOPE rapt with sweet pleasure
Weened she beheld the true proportion plain
Of her own web, weaved and unweaved again:
    But that her Art was somewhat less, she thought
    And on a mere ignoble subject wrought.

130.

For here, like to the silkworm's industry,
Beauty itself out of itself did weave
So rare a work, and of such subtlety,
As did all eyes entangle and deceive;
And in all minds a strange impression leave.
    In this sweet labyrinth did CUPID stray,
    And never had the power to pass away.

131.

As when the Indians, neighbours of the Morning,
In honour of the cheerful rising Sun,
With pearl and painted plumes themselves adorning,
A solemn stately measure have begun;
The god well pleased with that fair honour done,
    Sheds forth his beams, and doth their faces kiss
    With that immortal glorious face of his:

132.

So　　＊　　＊　　＊　　＊]

Nosce teipsum!

This Oracle expounded in two Elegies.

1. Of Human Knowledge.
2. Of the Soul of Man, and the Immortality thereof.

LONDON:
Printed by RICHARD FIELD, for JOHN STANDISH.
1599.

[This work was thus registered for publication at Stationers' Hall :
10 Aprilis [1599].

JOHN STANDYSHE. Entred for his copie A booke called *Nosce Teipsum
The oracle expounded in two Elegies.* j. *of human
kno*[w]*ledge.* 2. *of the soule of Man and th*[e] *immortality thereof.*

Master PONSONBYES   This is aucthorised vnder the hand of the I.[ord]
[*the junior Warden*   Bysshop of LONDON PROVYED that yt must not be
at the time] hand is   printed without his L[ordships] hand to yt again.
to yt.   *Transcript &c.* iii. 142. *Ed.* 1876.

To my most gracious dread Sovereign.

O THAT clear Majesty which in the North
  Doth like another sun in glory rise;
  Which standeth fixt, yet spreads her heavenly worth
  Loadstone to hearts, and loadstar to all eyes:

Like heaven in all; like th' earth in this alone,
  That though great States by her support do stand,
  Yet she herself supported is of none,
  But by the finger of th' Almighty's hand:

To the divinest and the richest Mind,
  Both by Art's purchase and by Nature's dower,
  That ever was from heaven to earth confined,
  To shew the utmost of a creature's power:

To that great Spirit which doth great kingdoms move,
  The sacred spring, whence Right and Honour streams,
  Distilling Virtue, shedding Peace and Love
  In every place, as CYNTHIA sheds her beams:

I offer up some sparkles of that fire,
  Whereby we Reason, Live, and Move, and Be.
  These sparks, by nature, evermore aspire;
  Which makes them to so high a Highness flee.

Fair Soul, since to the fairest body knit,
 You give such lively life, such quick'ning power,
 Such sweet celestial influence to it
 As keeps it still in youth's immortal flower;

(As where the sun is present all the year,
 And never doth retire his golden ray,
 Needs must the Spring be everlasting there,
 And every season, like the month of May)

O many, many years, may you remain
 A happy Angel to this happy land!
 Long, long may you on earth our Empress reign!
 Ere you in heaven, a glorious angel stand.

  Stay long, sweet Spirit, ere thou to heaven depart,
  Which mak'st each place a heaven, wherein thou art.

  Her Majesty's least and unworthiest subject,

    John Davies.

Of Human Knowledge.

Hy did my parents send me to the Schools,
    That I with knowledge might enrich my
       mind ?
Since the Desire to Know first made men
       fools,
And did corrupt the root of all mankind.

For when GOD's hand had written in the
       hearts
Of the First Parents, all the rules of good ;
So that their skill infused, did pass all Arts
That ever were, before, or since the Flood ;

And when their Reason's eye was sharp and clear,
    And, as an eagle can behold the sun,
Could have approached the Eternal Light as near
    As th'intellectual angels could have done :

Even then, to them the Spirit of Lies suggests
    That they were blind, because they saw not Ill ;
And breathes into their incorrupted breasts,
    A curious Wish, which did corrupt their Will.

For that same Ill they straight desired to know,
    Which Ill (being nought but a defect of Good);
In all GOD's works, the Devil could not show,
    While Man, their Lord, in his perfection stood.

So that themselves were first to *do* the Ill
    Ere they thereof the *knowledge* could attain ;
    Like him, that knew not poison's power to kill,
    Until, by tasting it, himself was slain.

Even so, by tasting of that fruit forbid,
    Where they sought Knowledge, they did Error find ;
    Ill they desired to know, and Ill, they did ;
    And to give Passion eyes, made Reason blind.

For then their minds did first in Passion see,
    Those wretched Shapes of Misery and Woe,
    Of Nakedness, of Shame, of Poverty,
    Which then their own experience made them know.

But then grew Reason dark, that she no more
    Could the fair forms of Good and Truth discern :
    Bats they became, that eagles were before ;
    And this they got by their Desire to Learn.

But we, their wretched offspring, what do we ?
    Do not we still taste of the fruit forbid ?
    Whiles, with fond fruitless curiosity,
    In books profane we seek for knowledge hid ?

What is this Knowledge but the sky-stol'n fire
    For which the Thief still chained in ice doth sit,
    And which the poor rude Satyr did admire,
    And needs would kiss, but burnt his lips with it ?

What is it, but the cloud of empty rain,
    Which when JOVE'S guest embraced, he monsters got ?
    Or the false pails, which oft being filled with pain,
    Received the water, but retained it not ?

Shortly, what is it but the fiery Coach
    Which the Youth sought, and sought his death withal ?
    Or the Boy's wings, which when he did approach
    The sun's hot beams, did melt, and let him fall ?

And yet, alas, when all our lamps are burned,
 Our bodies wasted, and our spirits spent ;
 When we have all the learned volumes turned,
 Which yield men's wits, both help and ornament :

What can we know? or what can we discern?
 When Error chokes the windows of the Mind ;
 The divers Forms of things how can we learn,
 That have been, ever from our birthday, blind?

When Reason's lamp (which, like the sun in sky,
 Throughout man's little world her beams did spread)
 Is now become a Sparkle, which doth lie
 Under the ashes, half extinct, and dead ;

How can we hope, that through the Eye and Ear,
 This dying Sparkle, in this cloudy place,
 Can re-collect these beams of knowledge clear,
 Which were infused in the first minds, by grace?

So might the heir, whose father hath in play
 Wasted a thousand pounds of ancient rent,
 By painful earning of one groat a day,
 Hope to restore the patrimony spent.

The wits that dived most deep, and soared most high,
 Seeking man's powers, have found his weakness such ;
 "Skill comes so slow, and life so fast doth fly ;
 "We learn so little, and forget so much."

For this, the wisest of all moral men
 Said, *He knew nought, but that he nought did know !*
 And the great mocking Master, mocked not then,
 When he said, *Truth was buried deep below !*

For how may we, to other's things attain,
 When none of us, his own Soul understands?
 For which, the Devil mocks our curious brain,
 When, *Know thyself !* his oracle commands.

For why should we the busy Soul believe,
 When boldly she concludes of that and this?
 When of herself, she can no judgement give,
 Nor How, nor Whence, nor Where, nor What she is?

All things without, which round about we see,
 We seek to know, and have therewith to do;
 But that, whereby we Reason, Live, and Be,
 Within ourselves, we strangers are thereto.

We seek to know the moving of each sphere,
 And the strange cause of th'ebbs and floods of Nile;
 But of that Clock, which in our breasts we bear,
 The subtle motions we forget the while!

We that acquaint ourselves with every zone,
 And pass both tropics, and behold both poles;
 When we come home, are to ourselves unknown
 And unacquainted still with our own souls!

We study Speech, but others we persuade;
 We Leechcraft learn, but others cure with it;
 We interpret Laws which other men have made,
 But read not those which in our hearts are writ.

Is it because the Mind is like the Eye,
 (Through which it gathers knowledge by degrees)
 Whose rays reflect not but spread outwardly,
 Not seeing itself, when other things it sees?

No, doubtless, for the Mind can backward cast
 Upon herself, her understanding light;
 But she is so corrupt, and so defac't,
 As her own image doth herself affright.

As in the fable of that Lady fair,
 Which, for her lust, was turned into a cow;
 When thirsty to a stream she did repair,
 And saw herself transformed (she wist not how;)

At first, she startles! then, she stands amazed!
 At last, with terror, she from thence doth fly,
 And loathes the wat'ry glass wherein she gazed,
 And shuns it still, though she for thirst do die.

Even so, Man's Soul, which did God's Image bear,
 And was, at first, fair, good, and spotless pure;
 Since with her sins, her beauties blotted were,
 Doth, of all sights, her own sight least endure.

For even, at first reflection, she espies
 Such strange CHIMERAS and such monsters there!
 Such toys! such antics! and such vanities!
 As she retires, and shrinks for shame and fear.

And as the man loves least at home to be,
 That hath a sluttish house, haunted with sprites;
 So she, impatient her own faults to see,
 Turns from herself, and in strange things delights.

For this, few *know themselves!* for merchants broke,
 View their estate with discontent and pain;
 And seas are troubled, when they do revoke
 Their flowing waves into themselves again.

And while the face of outward things we find,
 Pleasing and fair, agreeable and sweet;
 These things transport and carry out the mind,
 That with herself, herself can never meet.

Yet if Affliction once her wars begin,
 And threat the feeble Sense with sword and fire;
 The Mind contracts herself, and shrinketh in,
 And to herself she gladly doth retire,

As spiders touched, seek their web's inmost part;
 As bees in storms, unto their hives return;
 As blood in danger, gathers to the heart;
 And men seek towns, when foes the country burn.

If ought can teach us ought, Affliction's looks
(Making us look into ourselves so near)
Teach us to *know ourselves*, beyond all books,
Or all the learned Schools that ever were !

This Mistress, lately, plucked me by the ear,
And many a golden lesson hath me taught,
Hath made my Senses quick, and Reason clear,
Reformed my Will, and rectified my Thought.

So do the winds and thunders cleanse the air ;
So working lees settle and purge the wine ;
So lopt and pruned trees do flourish fair ;
So doth the fire the drossy gold refine.

Neither MINERVA, nor the learned Muse,
Nor Rules of Art, nor Precepts of the Wise,
Could in my brain, those beams of skill infuse,
As but the glance of this Dame's angry eyes.

She, within lists, my ranging mind hath brought,
That now beyond myself I list not go ;
Myself am Centre of my circling thought,
Only Myself, I study, learn, and know.

I *know* my Body's of so frail a kind,
As force without, fevers within, can kill ;
I *know* the heavenly nature of my Mind ;
But 'tis corrupted, both in Wit and Will.

I *know* my Soul hath power to know all things,
Yet is she blind and ignorant in all ;
I *know* I am one of Nature's little kings,
Yet to the least and vilest things am thrall !

I *know* my Life's a pain, and but a span ;
I *know* my Sense is mocked with every thing :
And to conclude, I *know* myself a Man ;
Which is a proud, and yet a wretched thing !

Of the Soul of Man;

and the Immortality thereof.

THE Lights of Heaven, which are the world's
  fair eyes,
  Look down into the world, the world to
   see ;
  And as they turn, or wander in the skies,
  Survey all things, that on this Centre be.

  And yet the Lights which in my Tower do
   shine,
Mine Eyes ! (which view all objects, nigh and far)
Look not into this little world of mine,
Nor see my face, wherein they fixèd are.

Since Nature fails us in no needful thing ;
  Why want I means, mine inward self to see ?
  Which sight, the Knowledge of Myself might bring ;
  Which, to true wisdom, is the first degree.

That Power (which gave me eyes, the world to view)
  To view myself, infused an Inward Light,
  Whereby my Soul, as by a Mirror true,
  Of her own form, may take a perfect sight.

But as the sharpest Eye discerneth nought,
  Except the sunbeams in the air do shine ;
  So the best Soul, with her reflecting thought,
  Sees not herself, without some light Divine.

O LIGHT! (which makest the Light, which makest the Day;
    Which settest the Eye without, and Mind within)
    Lighten my spirit, with one clear heavenly ray!
    Which now to view itself, doth first begin.

For her true form, how can my Spark discern?
    Which dim by Nature, Art did never clear;
    When the great wits, of whom all skill we learn,
    Are ignorant, both What She is! and Where!

One thinks the Soul is Air, another Fire,
    Another, Blood diffused about the heart;
    Another saith, the Elements conspire,
    And to her Essence, each doth give a part.

Musicians think our Souls are Harmonies;
    Physicians hold that they Complexions be;
    Epicures make them Swarms of Atomies,
    Which do, by change, into our bodies flee!

Some think one General Soul fills every brain,
    As the bright sun sheds light in every star;
    And others think the name of Soul is vain,
    And that We, only Well-mixed Bodies are.

In judgement of her Substance, thus they vary;
    And thus they vary in judgement of her Seat;
    For some, her chair up to the Brain do carry,
    Some thrust it down into the Stomach's heat!

Some place it in the root of life, the Heart;
    Some, in the Liver, fountain of the veins;
    Some say, "She is all in all, and all in part!"
    Some say, "She is not contained, but all contains!"

Thus these great Clerks their little wisdom show,
    While with their doctrines, they at hazard play;
    Tossing their light opinions to and fro,
    To mock the lewd; as learned in this, as they!

For no crazed brain could ever yet propound,
    Touching the Soul, so vain and fond a thought ;
    But some among these Masters, have been found,
    Which in their Schools, the selfsame thing have taught.

GOD, only-Wise ! to punish Pride of Wit,
    Among men's wits hath this confusion wrought !
    As the proud Tower, whose points the clouds did hit,
    By Tongues' Confusion, was to ruin brought.

But, Thou ! which didst Man's Soul, of nothing make !
    And when to nothing, it was fallen again ;
    To make it new, the Form of Man didst take,
    And, GOD with GOD, becam'st a Man with men !

Thou ! that hast fashioned twice, this Soul of ours,
    So that She is, by double title, Thine ;
    Thou, only, knowest her nature and her powers,
    Her subtle form, Thou, only, canst define !

To judge herself, She must herself transcend,
    As greater circles comprehend the less :
    But She wants power, her own powers to extend,
    As fettered men cannot their strength express.

But Thou, bright morning Star ! Thou, rising Sun !
    Which, in these later times, has brought to light
    Those mysteries, that, since the world began,
    Lay hid in darkness and eternal night !

Thou, like the sun, doth with indifferent ray,
    Into the palace and the cottage shine !
    And showest the Soul, both to the Clerk and Lay,
    By the clear Lamp of thy Oracle Divine !

This Lamp, through all the regions of my brain,
    Where my Soul sits, doth spread such beams of grace,
    As now, methinks ! I do distinguish plain
    Each subtle line of her immortal face.

The Soul, a Substance and a Spirit is,
What the Soul is? Which GOD Himself doth in the body make,
Which makes the Man ; for every man, from this,
The Nature of a man and Name doth take.

And though the Spirit be to the Body knit,
As an apt meane her powers to exercise ;
Which are Life, Motion, Sense, and Will, and Wit :
Yet she survives, although the Body dies.

That the Soul is a thing subsisting by itself, without the Body. She is a Substance, and a real thing,
1. Which hath, itself, an actual working Might,
2. Which neither from the Sense's power doth spring,
3. Nor from the Body's humours tempered right.

She is a Vine, which doth no propping need,
To make her spread herself, or spring upright ;
She is a Star, whose beams do not proceed
From any sun, but from a native light.

I. That the Soul hath a proper operation, without the Body. For when She sorts things present with the past,
And thereby things to come doth oft foresee ;
When She doth doubt at first, and choose at
last :
These acts her own, without the Body, be.

When of the dew, which the Eye and Ear do take,
From flowers abroad, and bring into the brain ;
She doth, within, both wax and honey make :
This work is hers, this is her proper pain !

When She from sundry acts, one Skill doth draw ;
Gathering from divers fights, one Art of War ;
From many Cases like, one Rule of Law :
These, her collections, not the Sense's, are.

When in th'Effects, She doth the Causes know;
    And seeing the stream, thinks where the spring doth
        rise ;
    And seeing the branch, conceives the root below :
    These things She views, without the Body's eyes.

When She, without a Pegasus, doth fly
    Swifter than lightning's fire, from East to West ;
    About the Centre, and above the Sky :
    She travels then, although the Body rest.

When all her works She formeth first within ;
    Proportions them, and sees their perfect end,
    Ere She in act, doth any part begin :
    What instruments doth then, the Body lend ?

When without hands, She thus doth castles build ;
    Sees without eyes, and without feet doth run ;
    When She digests the world, yet is not filled :
    By her own power, these miracles are done.

When She defines, argues, divides, compounds ;
    Considers Virtue, Vice, and General Things ;
    And marrying diverse principles and grounds,
    Out of their match, a true conclusion brings :

These actions, in her closet, all alone,
    (Retired within herself) She doth fulfil ;
    Use of her Body's organs, She hath none,
    When She doth use the powers of Wit and Will.

Yet in the Body's prison, so She lies,
    As through the Body's windows She must look,
    Her divers powers of Sense to exercise,
    By gathering notes out of the world's great book.

Nor can herself discourse, or judge of ought,
    But what the Sense collects, and home doth bring,
    And yet the Power of her discoursing Thought,
    From these Collections, is a diverse thing.

For though our eyes can nought but colours see,
    Yet colours give them not their Power of Sight;
    So, though these fruits of Sense, her objects be,
    Yet She discerns them by her proper light.

The workman on his stuff, his skill doth shew,
    And yet the stuff gives not the man his skill;
    Kings, their affairs, do, by their servants know,
    But order them by their own royal will.

So though this cunning Mistress, and this Queen
    Doth, as her instruments, the Senses use,
    To know all things that are Felt, Heard, or Seen;
    Yet She herself doth only Judge and Choose:

Even as our great wise Empress (that now reigns
    By sovereign title over sundry lands)
    Borrows, in mean affairs, her subjects' pains,
    Sees by their eyes, and writeth by their hands:

But things of weight and consequence indeed,
    Herself doth in her chamber them debate;
    Where, all her Councillors she doth exceed
    As far in judgement, as she doth in State.

Or as the man, whom she doth now advance,
    Upon her gracious Mercy Seat to sit,
    Doth common things, of course and circumstance,
    To the Reports of common men commit:

But when the Cause itself must be decreed,
    Himself in person, in his proper Court,
    To grave and solemn hearing doth proceed,
    Of every proof, and every by-report.

Then, like God's angel, he pronounceth right,
    And milk and honey from his tongue do flow:
    Happy are they, that still are in his sight,
    To reap the wisdom, which his lips do sow.

Right so, the Soul, which is a Lady free,
    And doth the justice of her State maintain ;
    Because the Senses, ready servants be,
    Attending nigh about her Court, the Brain ;

By them, the forms of outward things She learns,
    For they return unto the Fantasy,
    Whatever each of them abroad discerns ;
    And there enrol it for the Mind to see.

But when She sits to judge the good and ill,
    And to discern betwixt the false and true ;
    She is not guided by the Senses' skill,
    But doth each thing in her own mirror view.

Then She the Senses checks ! which oft do err,
    And even against their false reports, decrees ;
    And oft She doth condemn, what they prefer,
    For with a power above the Sense, She sees :

Therefore, no Sense, the precious joys conceives,
    Which in her private contemplations be ;
    For then, the ravished Spirit, the Senses leaves,
    Hath her own powers, and proper actions free.

Her harmonies are sweet and full of skill,
    When on the Body's instrument She plays :
    But the proportions of the Wit and Will,
    Those sweet accords are even the angels' lays.

These tunes of Reason are Amphion's lyre,
    Wherewith he did the Theban city found ;
    These are the notes, wherewith the heavenly Quire,
    The praise of Him, which spreads the heaven, doth sound.

Then her self-being nature shines in this,
    That She performs her noblest works alone !
    " The work, the touchstone of the nature is ! "
    And " by their operations, things are known ! "

2.
That the
Soul is
more than
a perfec-
tion or re-
flection of
the Sense.

Are they not senseless then! that think the Soul
　　Nought but a fine perfection of the Sense,
　　Or of the forms which Fancy doth enrol,
　　A quick Resulting, and a Consequence?

What is it, then, that doth the Sense accuse,
　　Both of false judgements, and fond appetites?
　　Which makes us do, what Sense doth most refuse?
　　Which oft, in torment of the Sense delights?

Sense thinks the planets' spheres not much asunder;
　　What tells us, then, their distance is so far?
　　Sense thinks the lightning born before the thunder,
　　What tells us, then, they both together are?

When men seem crows, far off upon a tower;
　　Sense saith, "They are crows!" What makes us think
　　　　them men?
　　When we, in agues, think all sweet things sour;
　　What makes us know our tongue's false judgements then?

What power was that, whereby MEDEA saw,
　　And well approved and praised the better course,
　　When her rebellious Sense did so withdraw
　　Her feeble powers, as she pursued the worst?

Did Sense persuade ULYSSES not to hear
　　The Mermaid's songs? which so his men did please,
　　As they were all persuaded through the ear,
　　To quit the ship, and leap into the seas.

Could any power of Sense the Roman move,
　　To burn his own right hand, with courage stout?
　　Could Sense make MARIUS sit unbound, and prove
　　The cruel lancing of the knotty gout?

Doubtless in Man, there is a Nature found
　　Beside the senses, and above them far;
　　Though "most men being in sensual pleasures drowned,
　　It seems their souls but in their senses are."

If we had nought but sense, then only they
    Should have sound minds, which have their senses sound ;
    But Wisdom grows, when senses do decay,
    And Folly most, in quickest sense is found.

If we had nought but Sense, each living wight,
    Which we call brute, would be more sharp than we ;
    As having Sense's apprehensive might
    In a more clear and excellent degree.

But they do want that quick discoursing Power,
    Which doth, in us, the erring Sense correct :
    Therefore the bee did suck the painted flower,
    And birds, of grapes the cunning shadow peckt.

Sense, outsides knows ! the Soul, through all things sees,
    Sense, circumstance ! She doth, the substance view;
    Sense sees the bark ! but She, the life of trees ;
    Sense hears the sounds ! but She, the concords true.

But why do I the Soul and Sense divide ?
    When Sense is but a power, which She extends,
    Which being in divers parts diversified,
    The divers Forms of objects apprehends ?

This power spreads outward ; but the root doth grow
    In th'inward Soul, which only doth perceive;
    For the Eyes and Ears, no more their objects know,
    Than glasses know what faces they receive.

For if we chance to fix our thoughts elsewhere ;
    Although our eyes be ope, we do not see,
    And if one Power did not both see and hear,
    Our sights and sounds would always double be.

Then is the Soul a Nature which contains
    The power of Sense within a greater power ;
    Which doth employ and use the senses' pains,
    But sits and rules within her private bower.

3.

That the
Soul is
more than
the Tem-
perature
of the
Humoursof
the Body.
If She doth then the subtle Sense excel,
How gross are they, that drown her in the blood !
Or in the Body's humours tempered well,
As if in them, such high perfection stood.

As if most skill in that musician were,
Which had the best and best-tuned instrument;
As if the pencil neat, and colours clear
Had power to make the painter excellent

Why doth not Beauty then refine the Wit ?
And good Complexion rectify the Will ?
Why doth not Health bring Wisdom still with it ?
Why doth not Sickness make men brutish still ?

Who can in Memory, or Wit, or Will ;
Or Air ! or Fire ! or Earth ! or Water find !
What alchemist can draw, with all his skill,
The Quintessence of these, out of the Mind ?

If th'Elements (which have, nor Life, nor Sense)
Can breed in us so great a power as this !
Why give they not themselves, like excellence,
Or other things wherein their mixture is ?

If She were but the Body's quality
Then would She be, with it, sick ! maimed ! and blind !
But we perceive, when these privations be,
A healthy, perfect, and sharp-sighted Mind.

If She, the Body's nature did partake,
Her strength would, with the Body's strength decay ;
But when the Body's strongest sinews slake,
Then is the Soul most active ! quick ! and gay !

If She were but the Body's accident,
And her sole Being did in it subsist
As white in snow ; She might herself absent !
And in the Body's substance not the mist.

But it on Her, not She on it depends,
    For She the Body doth sustain and cherish.
    Such secret powers of life to it, She lends ;
    That when they fail, then doth the Body perish.

Since, then, the Soul works by herself alone,
    Springs not from Sense, nor Humours well agreeing ;
    Her nature is peculiar, and her own.
    She is a Substance ! and a Perfect Being.

But though this Substance be the root of Sense,
That the Sense knows her not ! (which doth but bodies know)
Soul is a She is a Spirit, and a heavenly influence ;
Spirit.   Which from the fountain of GOD's Spirit doth flow.

She is a Spirit ; yet not like air, or wind,
    Nor like the spirits about the heart or brain,
    Nor like those spirits which alchemists do find,
    When they, in everything, seek gold, *in vain*.

For She, all natures under heaven doth pass;
    Being like those spirits, which GOD's bright face do see,
    Or like Himself ! whose Image once She was,
    Though now, alas, She scarce his Shadow be.

Yet of the forms, She holds the first degree,
    That are to gross material bodies knit ;
    Yet She herself is bodiless and free,
    And, though confined, is almost infinite.

Were She a Body, how could She remain
That it   Within this body, which is less than She ?
cannot be Or how could She, the world's great shape contain ;
a Body.   And in our narrow breasts containèd be ?

All bodies are confined within some place ;
    But She all place within herself confines;
    All bodies have their measure and their space;
    But who can draw the Soul's dimensive lines ?

No Body can, at once, two forms admit,
    Except the one, the other do deface;
    But in the Soul, ten thousand forms do sit,
    And none intrudes into her neighbour's place.

All bodies are, with other bodies filled,
    But She receives both heaven and earth together,
    Nor are their Forms, by rash encounter, spilled,
    For there they stand, and neither toucheth either.

Nor can her wide embracements fillèd be;
    For they that most and greatest things embrace,
    Enlarge thereby their mind's capacity,
    As streams enlarged, enlarge the channel's space.

All things received, do such proportion take,
    As those things have, wherein they are received:
    So little glasses, little faces make;
    And narrow webs, on narrow frames be weaved:

Then, what vast body must we make the Mind?
    Wherein are men, beasts, trees, towns, seas, and lands,
    And yet each thing a proper place doth find,
    And each thing in the true proportion stands.

Doubtless, this could not be, but that She turns
    Bodies to Spirits, by sublimation strange;
    As fire converts to fire, the things it burns;
    As we, our meats into our nature change.

From their gross Matter, she abstracts the Forms,
    And draws a kind of Quintessence from things,
    Which to her proper nature, She transforms,
    To bear them light on her celestial wings.

This doth She, when from things particular,
    She doth abstract the universal kinds,
    Which bodiless and immaterial are,
    And can be lodged but only in our minds.

And thus, from divers accidents and acts,
　　Which do within her observation fall ;
　　She, goddesses and Powers Divine abstracts,
　　As Nature, Fortune, and the Virtues all.

Again, how can She, several bodies know,
　　If in herself a body's form She bears ?
　　How can a mirror sundry faces show,
　　If from all shapes and forms it be not clear ?

Nor could we by our eyes, all colours learn,
　　Except our eyes were, of all colours void,
　　Nor sundry tastes can any tongue discern,
　　Which is with gross and bitter humours cloyed.

Nor may a man, of Passions judge aright,
　　Except his mind be from all Passions free ;
　　Nor can a Judge, his office well acquite,
　　If he possest of either party be !

If, lastly, this quick power a Body were,
　　Were it as swift, as is the wind or fire,
　　(Whose atomies do, th' one down sideways bear,
　　And make the other, in pyramids aspire) ;

Her nimble body, yet in *time* must move,
　　And not in instants through all places slide :
　　But She is nigh ! and far ! beneath ! above !
　　In point of time which thought can not divide.

She's sent as soon to China, as to Spain,
　　And thence returns, as soon as She is sent,
　　She measures with one time and with one pain,
　　An ell of silk, and heaven's wide-spreading tent.

As then, the Soul a Substance hath alone
　　Besides the Body, in which She is confined ;
　　So hath She *not* a body of her own,
　　But is a Spirit and immaterial Mind.

Since Body and Soul have such diversities;

That the Soul is created immediately by God.— *Zach.* xii. 1.

Well, might we muse, how first their match began,
But that we learn, that He, that spread the skies
And fixed the earth, first formed the Soul in Man.

This true PROMETHEUS, first, made man of earth,
    And shed in him a beam of heavenly fire:
    Now, in their mother's womb, before their birth,
    Doth in all sons of men, their souls inspire.

And as MINERVA is, in fables, said,
    From JOVE, without a mother, to proceed ;
    So our true JOVE, without a mother's aid,
    Doth, daily, millions of MINERVAS breed.

Then neither, from Eternity before,

Erroneous opinions of the creation of souls.

Nor from the time, when time's first point began;
Made He all souls ! which now He keeps in store,
Some in the moon, and others in the sun :

Nor in the secret cloister doth He keep,
    These virgin spirits until their marriage day,
    Nor locks them up in chambers, where they sleep,
    Till they awake within these beds of clay.

Nor did He first a certain number make,
    Infusing part in beasts, and part in men,
    And as unwilling farther pains to take,
    Would make no more, than those He framèd then.

So that the widow Soul, her Body dying,
    Unto the next born Body married was ;
    And so by often changing and supplying,
    Men's souls to beasts, and beasts' to men did pass.

(These thoughts are fond ! for since the bodies born
    Be more in number far than those that die;
    Thousands must be abortive, and forlorn,
    Ere others' deaths, to them their souls supply.)

But as GOD's handmaid, Nature, doth create
　　Bodies, in time distinct and order due ;
　　So GOD gives souls the like successive date,
　　Which Himself makes in bodies formèd new.

Which Himself makes, of no material things,
　　For unto angels, He no power hath given,
　　Either to form the shape, or stuff to bring,
　　From air, or Fire, or substance of the heaven.

Nor He, in this, doth Nature's service use,
That the　For though from bodies she can bodies bring ;
Soul is not
traduced　Yet could she never, souls from souls traduce,
from the　As fire from fire, or light from light doth spring.
parents.

Alas ! that some that were great lights of old,
　　And in their hands the Lamp of GOD did bear,
　　Some reverend Fathers did this error hold,
　　Having their eyes dimmed with religious fear.

" For when," say they, " by rule of faith we find,
　　That every soul unto her body knit,
　　Brings from the mother's womb, the Sin of Kind,
　　The root of all the ill She doth commit."

" How can we say, that GOD, the Soul doth make,
　　But we must make Him author of her sin ;
　　Then from man's soul, She doth beginning take,
　　Since in man's soul, corruption did begin."

" For if GOD make her, first he makes her ill,
　　(Which GOD forbid ! our thoughts should yield unto)
　　Or makes the body, her fair form to spill ;
　　Which, of itself, it hath no power to do."

" Not Adam's Body, but his Soul did sin,
　　And so herself unto corruption brought :
　　But our poor Soul corrupted is within,
　　Ere She hath sinned, either in act or thought " ;

E　　　　　　　　　　　　　　10

" And yet we see in her such powers divine,
  As we could gladly think, from GOD she came;
  Fain would we make Him author of the wine,
  If for the dregs, we could some other blame."

 Thus these good men, with holy zeal were blind,
The Answer   When on the other part the truth did shine,
to the
Objection.   Whereof we do clear demonstrations find,
  By light of Nature, and by light Divine.

None are so gross, as to contend for this,
  That Souls from Bodies may traducèd be;
  Between whose natures no proportion is,
  When root and branch in nature still agree.

But many subtle wits have justified
  That Souls from Souls, spiritually may spring;
  Which (if the nature of the Soul be tried)
  Will even, in Nature, prove as gross a thing.

 For all things made, are either made of nought,
Reasons   Or made of stuff that ready made doth stand:
derived
from   Of nought, no creature ever formed ought,
Nature.   For that is proper to th'Almighty's hand.

If then the Soul, another soul do make;
  Because her power is kept within a bound,
  She must some former stuff or matter take;
  But in the Soul, there is no matter found.

Then if her heavenly Form do not agree,
  With any matter which the world contains;
  Then She of nothing must created be,
  And to Create, to GOD alone, pertains!

Again, if Souls do other Souls beget,
  'Tis by themselves, or by the Body's power!
  If by themselves! what doth their working let,
  But they might Souls engender every hour?

If by the Body! how can Wit and Will,
    Join with the body, only in this act?
    Since when they do their other works fulfil,
    They from the Body, do themselves abstract!

Again, if Souls, of Souls begotten were,
    Into each other they should change and move;
    And Change and Motion still corruption bear;
    How shall we then, the Soul immortal prove?

If, lastly, Souls did generation use,
    Then should they spread incorruptible seed:
    What then becomes of that which they to lose,
    When the acts of generation do not speed?

And though the Soul *could* cast spiritual seed,
    Yet *would* She not, because She never dies;
    For mortal things desire, their like to breed;
    That so they may their kind immortalise.

Therefore the angels, Sons of God are named,
    And marry not, nor are in marriage given;
    Their spirits and ours are of one Substance framed,
    And have one Father, even the Lord of heaven:

Who would at first, that in each other thing,
    The earth and water, living souls should breed;
    But that Man's Soul (whom He would make their king)
    Should from Himself immediately proceed.

And when He took the woman from man's side,
    Doubtless Himself inspired her soul alone;
    For 'tis not said, he did, Man's *soul* divide,
    But took *flesh of his flesh, bone of his bone.*

Lastly, GOD, being made Man, for man's own sake,
    And being like man in all, except in sin:
    His Body, from the Virgin's womb did take;
    But all agree, *GOD formed His soul within.*

Then is the Soul from God? So Pagans say,
 Which saw by Nature's light, her heavenly kind,
 Naming her " Kin to God!" and "GOD's bright ray,"
 " A citizen of heaven, to earth confined!"

But now I feel they pluck me by the ear,
 (Whom my young Muse so boldly termèd blind)
 And crave more heavenly light; that cloud to clear,
 Which makes them think GOD doth not make the
  Mind!

GOD doubtless makes her! and doth make her good!
 And grafts her in a Body, there to spring;
 Which though it be corrupted, flesh and blood,
 Can no way to the Soul, corruption bring.

Reasons drawn from Divinity.

And yet this Soul (made good by GOD at first,
 And not corrupted by the Body's ill)
 Even in the womb, is sinful and accurst,
 Ere she can judge by Wit, or choose by Will.

Yet is not GOD, the author of her Sin;
 Though author of her Being, and being there;
 And if we dare to judge our Judge therein;
 He can condemn us, and Himself can clear.

First, GOD, from infinite eternity
 Decreed what hath been, is, or shall be done;
 And was resolved that every man should Be,
 And, in his turn, his race of life should run.

And so did purpose all the souls to make,
 That ever have been made, or ever shall;
 And that their Being, they should only take
 In human bodies, or not Be at all.

Was it then fit, that such a weak event
 (Weakness, itself! the sin and fall of Man)
 His counsel's execution should prevent?
 Decreed and fixed before the world began.

Or that one penal law, by ADAM broke,
    Should make GOD break His own eternal law;
    The settled order of the world revoke,
    And change all forms of things, which He foresaw.

Could EVE's weak hand, extended to the tree,
    In sunder rent that Adamantine Chain,
    Whose golden links, Effects and Causes be ;
    And which to GOD's own chair, doth fixt remain ?

O could we see ! how Cause from Cause doth spring !
    How mutually they linked and folded are!
    And hear how oft one disagreeing string,
    The harmony doth rather make, than mar!

And view at once, how Death by sin is brought !
    And how from Death a better Life doth rise;
    How this, GOD's Justice and his Mercy taught;
    We, this decree, would praise, as right and wise !

But we (that measure times, by First and Last)
    The sight of things successively do take;
    When GOD, on all at once, His view doth cast ;
    And of all times, doth but one instant make.

All in Himself, as in a glass, He sees,
    And from Him, by Him, through Him, all things be ;
    His sight is not discursive, by degrees ;
    But seeing the whole, each single part doth see.

He looks on ADAM, as a root, or well,
    And on his heirs, as branches, and as streams;
    He sees all men as one man ! though they dwell
    In sundry cities, and in sundry realms.

And as the root and branch are but one tree,
    And well and stream do but one river make;
    So, if the root and well corrupted be ;
    The stream and branch the same corruption take.

So when the root and fountain of Mankind ;
    Did draw corruption, and GOD's curse by sin :
    This was a charge that all his heirs did bind ;
    And all his offspring grew corrupt therein !

And as when th' hand doth strike, the man offends,
    (For part from whole, Law severs not in this !)
    So ADAM's sin to the whole Kind extends,
    For all their natures are but part of his.

Therefore, this sin, of Kind, not personal ;
    But real, and hereditary was :
    The guilt whereof, and punishment to all,
    By Course of Nature, and of Law doth pass.

For as that easy law was given to all !
    To ancestor and heir ! to first and last !
    So was the first transgression general ;
    And All did pluck the fruit ! and All did taste !

Of this, we find some footsteps in our Law,
    Which doth her root from GOD and Nature take.
    Ten thousand men she doth together draw,
    And of them all, one Corporation make !

Yet these and their successors are but One ;
    And if they gain or lose their liberties ;
    They harm or profit not themselves alone,
    But such, as in succeeding time, shall rise !

And so the ancestor and all his heirs,
    (Though they in number pass the stars of heaven)
    Are still but One ! His forfeitures are theirs !
    And unto them, are his advancements given !

His civil acts to bind and bar them all !
    And as from ADAM, all corruption take ;
    So if the father's crime be capital ;
    In all the blood, Law doth *corruption* make !

Is it, then, just with us, to disinherit
 The unborn nephews, for the father's fault?
 And to advance again, for one man's merit,
 A thousand heirs that have deserved nought?

And is not GOD's decree as just as ours,
 If He, for ADAM's sins, his sons deprive
 Of all those native virtues, and those powers;
 Which He to him, and to his race did give?

For what is this contagious Sin of Kind,
 But a privation of that grace within,
 And of that great rich dowry of the mind;
 Which all had had, but for the first man's sin?

If then a man, on light conditions, gain
 A great estate, to him and his, for ever;
 If wilfully, he forfeit it again:
 Who doth bemoan his heir? or blame the giver?

So, though GOD make the Soul good, rich, and fair;
 Yet when her form is to the Body knit,
 Which makes the Man: which Man is ADAM's heir
 Justly, forthwith, he takes his grace from it.

And then the Soul, being first from nothing brought,
 When GOD's grace fails her, doth to nothing fall;
 And this *declining Proneness unto nought,*
 Is even that Sin, that we are born withal.

Yet not, alone, the first good qualities,
 Which in the first Soul were, deprivèd are;
 But in their place the contrary do rise,
 And real spots of sin, her beauty mar.

Nor is it strange that ADAM's ill desert,
 Should be transferred unto his guilty race;
 When CHRIST, His grace and justice doth impart
 To men unjust! and such as have no grace!

Lastly, the Soul were better so to be
    Born slave to sin, than not to Be at all !
    Since, if She do believe, One sets her free,
    That makes her mount the higher, from her fall.

Yet this, the curious Wits will not content !
    They yet will know (since GOD foresaw this Ill)
    Why His high providence did not prevent
    The declination of the first Man's will.

If by His word, He had the current stayed,
    Of Adam's will, which was by nature free ;
    It had been one as if His word had said,
    " I will, henceforth, that man, no Man shall be ! "

For what is Man, without a moving Mind ;
    Which hath a judging Wit, and choosing Will ?
    Now, if GOD's power should her election bind ;
    Her motions then would cease, and stand all still.

And why did GOD in Man this Soul infuse ;
    But that he should his Maker know and love ?
    Now if love be compelled, and cannot choose ;
    How can it grateful, or thankworthy prove ?

Love must free hearted be, and voluntary,
    And not enchanted, or by Fate constrained :
    Not like that love, which did ULYSSES carry
    To CIRCE's isle, with mighty charms enchained

Besides ! Were we unchangeable in Will,
    And of a Wit, that nothing could misdeem ;
    Equal to GOD (whose wisdom shineth still,
    And never errs) we might ourselves esteem.

So that if Man would be unvariable ;
    He must be GOD ! or like a rock, or tree !
    For even the perfect angels were not stable ;
    But had a fall, more desperate than we.

Then let us praise that Power, which makes us be
 Men, as we are ! and rest contented so !
 And knowing man's fall was Curiosity,
 Admire GOD's counsels ! which we cannot know.

And let us know that GOD, the Maker is
 Of all the Souls, in all the men that be :
 Yet their corruption is no fault of His ;
 But the first man's, that broke GOD's first decree

This Substance, and this Spirit, of God's own making,
 Is in the Body placed, and planted there :
 That both of GOD, and of the world partaking ;
 Of all that is, Man might the Image bear !

Why the Soul is united to the Body.

GOD, first, made Angels ! bodiless pure minds !
 Then, other things, which mindless bodies be.
 Last, He made Man, the Horizon 'twixt both kinds,
 In whom, we do the World's Abridgement see.

Besides ! This world below did need one wight,
 Which might thereof, distinguish every part ;
 Make use thereof, and take therein delight ;
 And order things with industry and Art.

Which, also, GOD, might (in His works) admire,
 And here, beneath, yield Him both prayer and praise ;
 As there, above, the holy Angels' Quire
 Doth spread His glory, with spiritual lays.

Lastly, the brute unreasonable wights,
 Did want a Visible King, on them to reign ;
 And GOD Himself, thus to the world unites,
 That so the world might endless bliss obtain.

But how shall we this Union well express ?
 Nought ties the Soul, her subtility is such :
 She moves the body, which She doth possess ;
 Yet no part toucheth, but by virtue's touch !

In what manner, the Soul is united to the Body.

Then dwells She *not* therein, as in a tent,
    Nor as a pilot, in his ship doth sit,
    Nor as a spider, in her web is pent,
    Nor as the wax retains the print in it:

Nor as a vessel, water doth contain,
    Nor as one liquor, in another shed,
    Nor as the heat doth in the fire remain,
    Nor as a voice, throughout the air is spread.

But as the fair and cheerful Morning Light
    Doth, here and there, her silver beams impart:
    And, in an instant, doth herself unite
    To the transparent air, in all and part.

Still resting whole, when blows, the air divide,
    Abiding pure, when th'air is most corrupted;
    Throughout the air, her beams dispersing wide;
    And, when the air is tost, not interrupted!

So doth the piercing Soul, the Body fill,
    Being all in all, and all in part diffused:
    Indivisible! incorruptible still!
    Not forced! encountered! troubled! or confused!

And as the Sun above, the light doth bring,
    Though we behold it in the air below;
    So from th' Eternal Light, the Soul doth spring,
    Though in the body, She her powers do show.

But as this world's sun doth effects beget,

How the Soul doth exercise her powers in the Body.

    Diverse in divers places, every day,
    Here, Autumn's temperature! there, Summer's heat!
    Here, flowery Spring-tide! and there, Winter grey!

Here, Even! there, Morn! here, Noon! there, Day! there,
        Night!
    Melts wax! dries clay! makes flowers some quick, some
        dead!
    Makes the Moor black! and th'European, white!
    Th'American tawny! and th'East Indian red!

So in our little world, this Soul of ours,
    Being only One, and to one Body tied,
    Doth use on divers objects, diverse powers.
    And so are her effects diversified.

Her Quick'ning Power in every living part,
    Doth as a Nurse, or as a Mother serve;
    And doth employ her economic art,
    And busy care, her household to preserve.

The Vegetative or Quick-ening Power.

Here, She attracts ! and there, She doth retain,
    There, She decocts, and doth the food prepare,
    There, She distributes it to every vein,
    There, She expels, what She may fitly spare.

This power to MARTHA, may comparèd be,
    Which busy was, the household things to do ;
    Or to a Dryas living in a tree,
    For even to trees, this power is proper too.

And though the Soul may not this power extend
    Out of the body, but still use it there ;
    She hath a Power, which she abroad doth send,
    Which views and searcheth all things everywhere.

This Power is Sense, which from abroad doth bring,
    The Colour, Taste, and Touch, and Scent, and Sound,
    The Quantity, and Shape of everything
    Within th'earth's centre or heaven's circle found.

The power of Sense.

This Power, in parts made fit, fit objects takes,
    Yet not the Things, but Forms of Things receives:
    As when a seal in wax impression makes,
    The print therein, but not itself, it leaves:

And though things sensible be numberless,
    But only five the Sense's organs be;
    And in those five, All Things their Forms express,
    Which we can Touch, Taste, Feel, or Hear, or See.

These are the Windows, through the which She views
  The Light of Knowledge, which is Life's Load-star;
  And yet whiles She, these spectacles doth use,
  Oft, worldly things seem greater than they are.

First, the two Eyes, which have the Seeing Power,
  Stand as one Watchman, Spy, or Sentinel,
Sight. Being placed aloft within the head's high Tower
  And though both see, yet both but one thing tell.

These Mirrors take into their little space,
  The Forms of moon, and sun, and every star ;
  Of every body, and of every place,
  Which, with the world's wide arms, embracèd are.

Yet their best object, and their noblest use,
  Hereafter in another world will be ;
  When GOD in them, shall heavenly light infuse,
  That face to face, they may their Maker see.

Here are they guides, which do the Body lead,
  Which else would stumble in eternal night :
  Here in this world, they do much knowledge *read*,
  And are the Casements, which admit most light.

They are her farthest-reaching instrument ;
  Yet they no beams unto their objects send :
  But all the rays are from their objects sent ;
  And in the Eyes, with pointed angles end.

If th'objects be far off, the rays do meet
  In a sharp point, and so things seem but small ;
  If they be near, their rays do spread and fleet,
  And make broad points, that things seem great withal.

Lastly. Nine things to Sight requirèd are.
  The Power to see ! the Light ! the Visible thing !
  Being not too small ! too thin ! too nigh ! too far !
  Clear space ! and Time, the Form distinct to bring.

Thus see we, how the Soul doth use the Eyes,
 As instruments of her quick power of sight ;
 Hence do th'Arts Optic, and fair Painting rise.
 Painting, which doth all gentle minds delight !

Now let us hear, how She the Ears employs:
 Their office is the troubled air to take,
Hearing. Which in their mazes, forms a sound or noise ;
 Whereof herself doth true distinction make.

These Wickets of the Soul are placed on high,
 Because all sounds do lightly mount aloft ;
 And that they may not pierce too violently ;
 They are delayed with turns and windings oft.

For should the voice directly strike the brain,
 It would astonish and confuse it much ;
 Therefore these plaits and folds the sound restrain,
 That it, the Organ may more gently touch !

As streams, which, with their winding banks, do play,
 Stopt by their creeks, run softly through the plain ;
 So in the Ear's labyrinth, the voice doth stray,
 And doth, with easy motion, touch the brain !

It is the slowest, yet the daintiest Sense !
 For even the ears of such as have no skill,
 Perceive a discord, and conceive offence,
 And knowing not what's good, yet find the ill !

And though this Sense, first, gentle Music found ;
 Her proper object is the Speech of Man !
 But that speech chiefly which GOD's heralds sound,
 When their tongues utter, what his Spirit did pen.

Our Eyes have lids, our Ears still ope we see !
 Quickly to hear, how every tale is proved ;
 Our Eyes still move, our Ears unmoved be !
 That though we hear quick, we be not quickly moved.

Thus by the organs of the Eye and Ear,
 The Soul with knowledge doth herself endue !
Thus She her prison, may with pleasure bear ;
 Having such prospects, all the world to view !

These Conduit Pipes of Knowledge feed the Mind :
 But th'other three attend the Body still ;
For by their services the Soul doth find
 What things are to the Body, good or ill.

The Body's life, with meats and air is fed,
 Therefore the Soul doth use the Tasting power !
Taste. In veins, which through the tongue and palate spread,
 Distinguish every relish, sweet and sour.

This is the Body's Nurse ! But since Man's wit
 Found th'art of cookery to delight his Sense :
More bodies are consumed and killed with it !
 Than with the sword, famine, or pestilence.

Next, in the nostrils, She doth use the Smell,
 As GOD the breath of life in them did give ;
Smell. So makes He, now, His power in them to dwell ;
 To judge all airs, whereby we breath and live.

This Sense is also mistress of an Art,
 Which to soft people, sweet perfumes doth sell ;
Though this dear Art doth little good impart,
 Since " they smell best ; that do of nothing smell ! "

And yet good scents do purify the Brain,
 Awake the Fancy, and the Wits refine.
Hence Old Devotion, incense did ordain,
 To make men's spirits more apt for thoughts divine

Lastly, the Feeling power, which is Life's Root,
 Through every living part itself doth shed ;
Feeling. By sinews, which extend from head to foot,
 And like a net, all o'er the Body spread.

Much like a subtle spider, which doth sit
    In middle of her web, which spreadeth wide ;
    If ought do touch the utmost thread of it ;
    She feels it, instantly, on every side !

By touch; the first pure qualities we learn,
    Which quicken all things, Hot, Cold, Moist, and Dry !
    By touch; Hard, Soft, Rough, Smooth, we do discern !
    By touch ; sweet Pleasure, and sharp Pain we try !

These are the outward instruments of Sense !
    These are the Guards, which every thing must pass ;
    Ere it approach the Mind's intelligence !
    Or touch the Phantasy " Wits Looking Glass ! "

And yet these Porters which all things admit,
The   Themselves perceive not, nor discern the things;
Imagina- One Common Power doth in the forehead sit,
tion, or
Common Which all their proper forms together brings.
Sense.

For all those Nerves, which spirits of Sense do bear,
    And to those outward organs spreading go,
    United are as in a centre there !
    And, there, this power, those sundry forms doth know !

Those outward Organs present things receive ;
    This inward Sense doth absent things retain !
    Yet, straight, transmits all Forms she doth perceive,
    Unto a higher region of the brain ;

Where Phantasy (near handmaid to the Mind!)
    Sits and beholds, and doth discern them all ;
The   Compounds in one, things diverse in their kind,
Phantasy. Compares the black and white, the great and small.

Besides those single forms, She doth esteem,
    And in her balance doth their values try ;
    Where some things good, and some things ill do seem,
    And neutral some in her Phantastic eye.

This busy power is working day and night,
　　For when the outward senses rest do take;
　　A thousand dreams, phantastical and light,
　　With fluttering wings, do keep her still awake!

Yet, always, all may not afore her be;
The　　　Successively, she this, and that intends:
sensative　Therefore such forms as she doth cease to see,
Memory.　To Memory's large volume she commends!

The Ledger Book lies in the brain behind,
　　Like JANUS' eye, which in his poll was set;
　　The Layman's Tables! Storehouse of the Mind!
　　Which doth remember much, and much forget.

Here, Sense's Apprehensions end doth take;
　　As, when a stone is into water cast,
　　One circle doth another circle make,
　　Till the last circle touch the bank at last!

But though the Apprehensive Power do pause,
The　　　The Motive Virtue then begins to move!
Passions　Which in the heart below, doth Passions cause,
of Sense.　Joy, Grief, and Fear, and Hope, and Hate, and Love

These Passions have a free commanding might,
　　And divers actions in our life do breed;
　　For all acts done without true Reason's light,
　　Do from the Passion of the Sense proceed.

But sith the Brain doth lodge these powers of Sense,
　　How makes it, in the Heart those passions spring?
　　The mutual love, the kind intelligence
　　'Twixt heart and brain, this Sympathy doth bring.

From the kind heat, which in the heart doth reign,
　　The spirits of Life do their beginning take!
　　These spirits of Life ascending to the brain,
　　When they come there, the spirits of Sense do make.

These spirits of Sense in Phantasy's high court,
    Judge of the Forms of Objects, ill or well !
    And so, they send a good or ill report
    Down to the heart, where all Affections dwell.

If the report be good; it causeth love !
    And longing hope ! and well assured joy !
    If it be ill ; then doth it hatred move !
    And trembling fear ! and vexing grief's annoy !

Yet were these natural affections good
    (For they which want them, blocks or devils be !) ;
    If Reason in her first perfection stood,
    That she might Nature's Passions rectify.

Besides, another Motive Power doth rise
    Out of the heart : from whose pure blood do spring
The motion   The Vital Spirits, which born in arteries,
of Life.   Continual motion to all parts do bring.

This makes the pulses beat, and lungs respire,
    This holds the sinews, like a bridle's reins;
The local   And makes the body to advance, retire,
motion.   To turn or stop, as she them slacks or strains !

Thus the Soul tunes the Body's instrument ;
    These harmonies She makes with Life and Sense :
    The organs fit, are by the Body lent ;
    But th'actions flow from the Soul's influence.

But now I have a Will, yet want a Wit,
The In-   To express the workings of the Wit and Will ;
tellectual Which, though their root be to the body knit,
Powers of
the Soul.   Use not the Body, when they use their skill.

These powers the nature of the Soul declare,
    For to Man's Soul, these only proper be !
    For on the earth, no other wights there are,
    Which have these heavenly powers, but only

The Wit (the pupil of the Soul's clear eye!

The Wit or Uner-standing. And in Man's world, th'only shining star!)
Looks in the Mirror of the Phantasy,
Where all the gatherings of the senses are

From thence this Power, the Shapes of things abstracts,
  And them within her *Passive* part receives;
  Which are enlightened by that part which *Acts*,
  And so the Forms of single things perceives.

But after, by discoursing to and fro,
  Anticipating, and comparing things;
  She doth all universal natures know,
  And all Effects into their Causes brings.

When She rates things, and moves from ground to ground,
Reason. The name of Reason, She obtains by this!
Under-standing. But when, by reasons, She the truth hath found,
  And standeth fixt, She, Understanding is!

When her assent, She lightly doth incline
Opinion. To either part, She is Opinion light!
  But when She doth by principles define
Judgment. A certain truth, She hath true Judgement's sight.

And as from senses, Reason's work doth spring;
  So many reasons, Understanding gain :
  And many understandings, Knowledge bring,
  And by much knowledge, Wisdom we obtain.

So, many stairs we must ascend upright,
  Ere we attain to Wisdom's high degree:
  So doth this earth eclipse our Reason's light,
  Which else (in instants) would like angels see.

Yet hath the Soul a dowry natural,
  And Sparks of Light some common things to see;
  Not being a blank, where nought is writ at all,
  But what the writer will, may written be.

For Nature, in man's heart her laws doth pen,
    Prescribing Truth to Wit! and Good to Will!
    Which do accuse, or else excuse all men,
    For every thought or practice, good or ill!

And yet these sparks grow almost infinite,
    Making the world and all therein, their food;
    As fire so spreads, as no place holdeth it,
    Being nourished still with new supplies of wood.

And though these sparks were almost quenched with sin,
    Yet they, whom that Just One hath justified,
    Have them increased, with Heavenly Light within!
    And, like the Widow's oil, still multiplied!

And as this Wit should goodness truly know,
      We have a Wit which that true good should choose!
The power   Though Will do oft (when Wit, false Forms doth show)
of Will.   Take Ill, for Good; and Good, for Ill refuse.

Will puts in practice what the Wit deviseth;
The   Will ever acts, and Wit contemplates still:
relations   And as from Wit the power of Wisdom riseth;
betwixt   All other virtues, daughters are of Will!
Wit and
Will.

Will is the Prince! and Wit, the Councillor!
    Which doth for common good in council sit;
    And when Wit is resolved; Will lends her power
    To execute what is advised by Wit.

Wit is the Mind's Chief Judge! which doth control,
    Of Fancy's Court, the judgements false and vain!
    Will holds the royal sceptre in the Soul;
    And on the Passions of the Heart doth reign!

Will is as free as any Emperor,
    Nought can restrain her gentle liberty;
    No tyrant, nor no torment hath the power
    To make us will; when we unwilling be!

To these high powers, a Storehouse doth pertain;
The Where they, all Arts and general reasons lay!
intellectual Which in the Soul (even after death!) remain,
Memory. And no Lethean flood can wash away!

This is the Soul! and those, her virtues be!
Which, though they have their sundry proper ends,
And one exceeds another in degree;
Yet each on other mutually depends.

Our Wit is given, Almighty GOD to know!
Our Will is given to love Him, being known!
But GOD could not be *known* to us below,
But by His works, which through the Sense are shown.

And as the Wit doth reap the fruits of Sense;
So doth the Quick'ning Power, the Senses feed!
Thus while they do their sundry gifts dispense,
The best, the service of the least doth need!

Even so, the King, his magistrates do serve;
Yet Commons feed both magistrate and King!
The Commons' peace, the magistrates preserve
By borrowed power, which from the Prince doth spring.

The Quickening Power would *be*, and so would rest!
The Sense would not *be* only, be *be well*!
But Wit's ambition longeth to *be best*!
For it desires in endless bliss, to dwell.

And these three Powers, three sorts of men do make.
For some, like plants, their veins do only fill;
And some, like beasts, their senses' pleasure take,
And some, like angels, do contemplate still.

Therefore the fables turned some men to flowers,
And others, did with brutish forms invest;
And did of others, make celestial powers
Like angels! which still travail, yet still rest!

Yet these three Powers are not three Souls but one,
　　As one and two are both contained in three;
　　Three being one number by itself alone.
　　A shadow of the blessed Trinity !

O what is Man ! (Great Maker of mankind !)
　　That Thou to him so great respect dost bear !
An accla-　　That Thou adorn'st him with so bright a Mind !
mation.　　Mak'st him a king ! and even an angel's peer !

O what a lively life ! what heavenly power !
　　What spreading virtue ! what a sparkling fire !
　　How great ! how plentiful ! how rich a dower !
　　Dost Thou, within this dying flesh inspire !

Thou leav'st Thy Print in other works of Thine !
　　But Thy whole Image, Thou, in Man hast writ !
　　There cannot be a creature more divine;
　　Except, (like Thee !) it should be infinite.

But it exceeds Man's thought, to think how high
　　GOD hath raised Man, since GOD, a man became :
　　The angels do admire this mystery,
　　And are astonished when they view the same !

NOR hath He given these blessings for a day,
　　Nor made them on the Body's life
　　　　depend, That the
　　The Soul, though made in Time, survives Soul is im-
　　　　for Aye ; mortal, and
　　　　 cannot die.
　　And though it hath beginning, sees no end !

Her only end, in never-ending bliss ;
　　Which is, th' eternal face of GOD to see :
　　Who Last of Ends and First of Causes is,
　　And to do this, She must Eternal be !

How senseless then, and dead a Soul hath he,
    Which thinks his soul doth with his body die :
    Or thinks not so, but so would have it be,
    That he might sin with more security !

For though these light and vicious persons say,
    " Our Soul is but a smoke ! or airy blast !
    Which, during life, doth in our nostrils play ;
    And when we die, doth turn to wind at last ! "

Although they say, " Come, let us eat, and drink !
    Our life is but a spark, which quickly dies ! "
    Though thus they *say*, they know not what to *think*,
    But in their minds, ten thousand doubts arise.

Therefore no heretics desire to spread
    Their light opinions, like these Epicures ;
    For so their staggering thoughts are comforted,
    And other men's assent, their doubt assures.

Yet though these men against their conscience strive,
    There are some sparkles in their flinty breasts,
    Which cannot be extinct, but still revive,
    That (though they would) they cannot, quite be beasts !

But whoso makes a Mirror of his Mind ;
    And doth, with patience, view himself therein ;
    His Soul's *eternity* shall clearly find,
    Though th'other beauties be defaced with sin.

First, In man's mind, we find an appetite
    1 Reason.   To Learn and Know the Truth of everything:
    Drawn from the   Which is connatural, and born with it ;
    Desire of Knowledge.   And from the essence of the Soul doth spring.

With this Desire, She hath a native Might,
    To find out every truth, if She had time
    Th' innumerable effects to sort aright ;
    And, by degrees, from cause to cause to climb !

But since our life so fast away doth slide !
    (As doth a hungry eagle through the wind,
    Or as a ship transported with the tide ;
    Which in their passage, leave no print behind.)

Of which swift little time, so much we spend,
    While some few things, we, through the Sense, do strain;
    That our short race of life is at an end,
    Ere we, the Principles of Skill attain :

Or GOD (which to vain ends, hath nothing done)
    In vain, this Appetite and Power hath given ;
    Or else our knowledge, which is here begun,
    Hereafter must be perfected in heaven.

GOD never gave a Power to one whole Kind ;
    But most of that Kind did use the same !
    Most eyes have perfect sight ! though some be blind ;
    Most legs can nimbly run ! though some be lame.

But in this life, *no* Soul, the Truth can know
    So perfectly, as it hath power to do !
    If then perfection be not found below,
    A higher place must make her mount thereto.

Again, how can She but immortal be ?
2 *Reason.*   When with the motions of both Will and Wit,
Drawn   She still aspireth to Eternity,
from the
motion of   And never rests, till she attain to it.
the Soul.

Water in conduit pipes can rise no higher
    Than the well head, from whence it first doth spring !
    Then since to eternal GOD, She doth aspire ;
    She cannot be but an eternal thing.

" All moving things to other things do move
    Of the same kind," which shows their natures such ;
    So earth falls down, and fire doth mount above,
    Till both their proper Elements do touch.

And as the moisture which the thirsty earth

The Soul
compared
to a river.

    Sucks from the sea, to fill her empty veins;
    From out her womb at last doth take a birth,
    And runs, a Nymph! along the grassy plains:

Long doth she stay, as loath to leave the land,
    From whose soft side, she first did issue make:
    She tastes all places! turns to every hand!
    Her flow'ry banks unwilling to forsake:

Yet Nature, so her streams doth lead and carry,
    As that her course doth make no final stay
    Till she, herself unto the Ocean marry;
    Within whose watry bosom first she lay.

Even so the Soul, which in this earthy mould,
    The Spirit of GOD doth secretly infuse;
    Because, at first, She doth the earth behold,
    And only this material world She views!

At first, our Mother Earth, She holdeth dear!
    And doth embrace the World, and worldly things!
    She flies close by the ground, and hovers here!
    And mounts not up with her celestial wings!

Yet, under heaven, She cannot light on ought,
    That with her heavenly nature doth agree:
    She cannot rest! She cannot fix her thought!
    She cannot in this world contented be!

For who did ever yet in Honour, Wealth,
    Or Pleasure of the Sense, contentment find?
    Who ever ceased to *wish*, when he had Health?
    Or having Wisdom, was not *vext in mind*?

Then as a bee, which among weeds doth fall,
    Which seem sweet flowers, with lustre fresh and gay;
    She lights on that! and this! and tasteth all;
    But pleased with none, doth rise and soar away!

So, when the Soul finds here no true content,
 And, like NOAH's dove, can no sure footing take;
 She doth return from whence She first was sent,
 And flies to Him, that first her wings did make!

Wit seeking Truth, from Cause to Cause ascends;
 And never rests, till it the First attain;
 Will seeking Good, finds many middle Ends,
 But never stays, till it the Last do gain.

Now, GOD, the Truth! and First of Causes is!
 GOD is the Last Good End! which lasteth still:
 Being *Alpha* and *Omega* named for this,
 Alpha to Wit! *Omega* to the Will!

Since then, her heavenly kind She doth bewray,
 In that to GOD, She doth directly move:
 And on no mortal thing can make her stay;
 She cannot be from hence, but from *above*.

And yet this First True Cause and Last Good End,
 She cannot hear so *well*, and *truly* see;
 For this perfection, She must yet attend,
 Till to her Maker, She espousèd be.

As a King's daughter, being in person sought
 Of divers Princes, which do neighbour near;
 On none of them can fix a constant thought,
 Though she to all do lend a gentle ear.

Yet can she love a foreign Emperor!
 Whom, of great worth and power, she hears to be;
 If she be wooed but by Ambassador;
 Or but his letters, or his picture see.

For well she knows, that when she shall be brought
 Into the kingdom, where her Spouse doth reign;
 Her eyes shall see what she conceived in thought,
 Himself! his State! his glory! and his train!

So while the virgin Soul on earth doth stay
 She wooed and tempted is, ten thousand ways,
 By these great Powers, which on the earth bear sway;
 The WISDOM OF THE WORLD, WEALTH, PLEASURE, PRAISE.

With these, sometime, She doth her time beguile,
 These do, by fits, her Phantasy possess,
 But She distastes them all, within a while;
 And in the sweetest, finds a tediousness:

But if, upon the world's Almighty King,
 She once do fix her humble loving thought;
 Which, by his Picture drawn in everything,
 And sacred Messages, her love hath sought,

Of Him, She thinks She cannot think too much,
 This honey tasted, still is ever sweet;
 The pleasure of her ravished thought is such,
 As almost here, She, with her bliss doth meet.

But when in heaven, She shall His Essence see,
 This is her Sovereign Good! and Perfect Bliss!
 Her longings, wishings, hopes, all finished be!
 Her joys are full! her motions rest in this!

There, is She crowned with Garlands of Content,
 There, doth She manna eat, and nectar drink,
 That Presence doth such high delights present,
 As never tongue could speak, nor heart could think!

3 *Reason.* For this! the better Souls do oft despise
From con- The body's death, and do it oft desire;
tempt of For when on ground, the burdened balance lies;
death in
the better The empty part is lifted up the higher!
sort of
spirits.

But if the body's death, the Soul should kill?
 Then death must needs *against her nature* be;
 And were it so, all Souls would fly it still,
 " For Nature hates, and shuns her contrary."

For all things else, which Nature makes to be ;
    Their Being to preserve, are chiefly taught !
    For though some things desire a change to see,
    " Yet never thing did long to turn to *nought* ! "

If then, by death, the Soul were quenchèd quite,
    She could not thus against her nature run !
    Since every senseless thing, by Nature's light,
    Doth *preservation* seek ! *destruction* shun !

Nor could the world's best spirits so much err,
    (If Death took all !) that they should *all* agree,
    Before this life, their Honour to prefer !
    For what is praise, to things that nothing be ?

Again, if by the body's prop, She stand ?
    If on the body's life, her life depend ?
    As MELEAGER's on the fatal brand !
    The body's good, She only would intend !

We should not find her half so brave and bold,
    To lead it to the wars, and to the seas !
    To make it suffer watchings ! hunger ! cold !
    When it might feed with plenty ! rest with ease !

Doubtless, *all* Souls have a surviving thought ;
    Therefore of Death, we think with quiet mind ;
    But if we think of being *turned to nought*,
    A trembling horror in our Souls we find !

And as the better spirit, when She doth bear
4. Reason.   A scorn of death, doth shew She cannot die ;
From the   So when the wicked Soul, Death's face doth fear,
fear of
death in   Even then, She proves her own eternity !
the wicked
souls.

For, when Death's form appears, She feareth not
    An utter quenching or extinguishment !
    She would be glad to meet with such a lot !
    That so She might all future ill prevent.

But She doth doubt what after may befall,
    For Nature's law accuseth her within,
    And saith, " 'Tis true, that is affirmed by all,
    That after death, there is a pain for sin ! "

Then She, which hath been hoodwinked from her birth,
    Doth first herself within Death's Mirror see ;
    And when her body doth return to earth,
    She first takes care, how She alone shall be.

Whoever sees these irreligious men,
    With burden of a sickness, weak and faint ;
    But hears them talking of religion then,
    And vowing of their souls to every saint ?

When was there ever cursed atheist brought
    Unto the gibbet, but he did adore
    That blessed Power ! which he had set at nought,
    Scorned, and blasphemed, all his life before ?

These light vain persons, still are drunk and mad,
    With surfeitings and pleasures of their youth ;
    But, at their deaths, they are fresh ! sober ! sad !
    Then, they discern ! and then, they speak the truth !

If then, all souls, both good and bad, do teach
    With general voice, that souls can never die ;
    'Tis not Man's flattering Gloss, but Nature's Speech,
    Which, like GOD's Oracle, can never lie.

Hence, springs that *universal* strong desire,
    Which all men have, of Immortality :
    Not some few spirits unto this thought aspire,
    But all men's minds in this, united be.

5. Reason. From the general desire of Immortality.

Then this desire of Nature is not vain !
    " She covets not impossibilities ! "
    " Fond thoughts may fall into some idle brain ;
    But one Assent of All, is ever true ! "

From hence, that general care and study springs,
    That *launching* and *progression* of the Mind,
    Which all men have, so much of Future things,
    As they no joy, do in the Present find.

From this desire, that main Desire proceeds,
    Which all men have, surviving Fame to gain;
    By tombs, by books, by memorable deeds;
    For She that this desires, doth still remain.

Hence, lastly, springs Care of Posterities!
    For things, their kind would everlasting make!
    Hence is it, that old men do plant young trees,
    The fruit whereof, another age shall take!

If we these rules unto ourselves apply,
    And view them by reflection of the mind;
    All these True Notes of Immortality,
    In our hearts' tables, we shall written find!

And though some impious wits do questions move,
    And doubt "if souls immortal be or no?"
    That *doubt*, their immortality doth prove!
    Because they seem immortal things to know.

6. Reason. From the very doubt and disputation of Immortality.

For he which reasons, on both parts doth bring,
    Doth some things mortal, some immortal call;
    Now if himself were but a mortal thing;
    He could not judge immortal things, *at all*!

For when we judge, our Minds we Mirrors make,
    And as those glasses, which material be,
    Forms of material things do only take
    (For Thoughts or Minds in them, we cannot see);

So when we GOD and Angels do conceive,
    And think of Truth (which is eternal too),
    Then do our Minds, immortal Forms receive,
    Which if they mortal were, they could not do.

And as if beasts conceived what Reason were,
    And that conception should distinctly shew;
    They should the name of *reasonable* bear
    (For without Reason, none could reason know).

So when the Soul mounts with so high a wing,
    As of eternal things, She *doubts* can move,
    She, proofs of her eternity doth bring;
    Even when She strives the contrary to prove.

For even the *thought* of Immortality,
    Being an act done without the body's aid,
    Shews, that herself alone could move, and be,
    Although the body in the grave were laid.

And if herself She can so lively move,
    And never need a foreign help to take,
    Then must her motion everlasting prove,
    "Because her self She never can forsake."

" But though Corruption cannot touch the Mind,

That the Soul cannot be destroyed.
    By any cause, that from itself may spring;
    Some Outward Cause, Fate hath perhaps designed,
    Which to the Soul, may utter quenching bring ? "

"Perhaps her Cause may cease, and She may die !"

Her Cause ceaseth not.
    GOD is her Cause ! His WORD, her Maker was !
    Which shall stand fixed for all eternity !
    When heaven and earth shall like a shadow pass.

" Perhaps something repugnant to her kind,

She hath no contrary.
    By strong antipathy, the Soul may kill ! "
    But what can be contrary to the Mind,
    Which holds all contraries in concord still ?

She lodgeth heat, and cold ! and moist, and dry !
    And life, and death ! and peace, and war together :
    Ten thousand fighting things in her do lie,
    Yet neither troubleth or disturbeth either.

" Perhaps, for want of food, the Soul may pine ! "

She cannot
die for
want of
food.   But that were strange ! since all things bad and good,
Since all GOD's creatures, mortal and divine ;
Since GOD Himself is her eternal food.

Bodies are fed with things of mortal kind,
  And so are subject to mortality ;
  But Truth, which is eternal, feeds the Mind,
  The Tree of Life, which will not let her die.

" Yet violence perhaps the Soul destroys,

Violence
cannot de-
stroy her.   As lightning or the sunbeams dim the sight ;
Or as a thunder-clap or cannon's noise,
The power of hearing doth astonish quite ? "

But high perfection to the Soul it brings,
  T'encounter things most excellent and high ;
  For when She views the best and greatest things,
  They do not hurt, but rather clear the eye.

Besides as HOMER's gods 'gainst armies stand ;
  Her subtle form can through all dangers slide ;
  Bodies are captive, Minds endure no band,
  " And Will is free, and can no force abide ! "

" But lastly, Time perhaps, at last, hath power,

Time can-
not destroy
her.   To spend her lively powers, and quench her light ? "
But old god SATURN, which doth all devour,
Doth cherish her, and still augment her might.

Heaven waxeth old ; and all the spheres above
  Shall, one day, faint, and their swift motion stay ;
  And Time itself, in time, shall cease to move,
  Only the Soul survives, and lives for aye.

Our bodies, every footstep that they make,
  March towards death, until at last they die :
  Whether we work, or play, or sleep, or wake,
  Our life doth pass, and with Time's wings doth fly

But to the Soul, time doth perfection give,
    And adds fresh lustre to her beauty still,
    And makes her in eternal youth to live,
    Like her which nectar to the gods doth fill.

The more She lives, the more She feeds on Truth;
    The more She feeds, her Strength doth more increase :
    And what is Strength, but an effect of Youth !
    Which if Time nurse, how can it ever cease ?

But now these Epicures begin to smile,
Objections against the Immortality of the Soul.   And say, " My doctrine is more safe, than true ! "
    And that " I fondly do myself beguile,
    While these received opinions I ensue."

" For what ! " they say, " doth not the Soul wax old ?
Objection.   How comes it, then, that aged men do dote,
    And that their brains grow sottish, dull, and cold ;
    Which were in youth, the only spirits of note ? "

" What ! are not Souls within themselves corrupted ?
    How can there idiots then by Nature be ?
    How is it that some wits are interrupted,
    That now they dazzled are, now clearly see ? "

These questions make a subtle argument
Answer.   To such as think both Sense and Reason one :
    To whom, nor Agent, from the Instrument ;
    Nor Power of Working, from the Work is known.

But they that know that Wit can show no skill,
    But when she things in Sense's glass doth view ;
    Do know, if accident this glass do spill,
    It *nothing* sees ! or sees the *false* for *true*.

For if that region of the tender brain,
    Wherein th'inward sense of Phantasy should sit,
    And th'outward senses' gatherings should retain,
    By Nature, or by chance become unfit,

Either at first uncapable it is ;
    And so few things or none at all receives ;
    Or marred by accident which haps amiss,
    And so amiss it everything perceives ;

Then as a cunning Prince that useth spies ;
    If they return no news, doth nothing know;
    But if they make advertisement of lies,
    The Prince's Council all awry do go.

Even so, the Soul, to such a Body knit,
    Whose inward senses undisposèd be,
    And to receive the Forms of things unfit ;
    Where nothing is brought in, can nothing see.

This makes the Idiot, which hath yet a mind,
    Able to know the Truth, and choose the Good ;
    If she such figures in the brain did find,
    As might be found, if it in temper stood.

But if a frenzy do possess the brain ;
    It so disturbs and blots the forms of things,
    As Phantasy proves altogether vain,
    And to the Wit, no true relation brings.

Then doth the Wit, admitting all for true,
    Build fond conclusions on those idle grounds ;
    Then doth it fly the Good, and Ill pursue,
    Believing all that this false spy propounds.

But purge the humours, and the rage appease ;
    Which this distemper in the Fancy wrought :
    Then will the Wit, which never had disease,
    Discourse and judge discreetly, as it ought.

So though the clouds eclipse the Sun's fair light,
    Yet from his face they do not take one beam :
    So have our eyes their perfect power of sight,
    Even when they look into a troubled stream.

Then these defects in Sense's organs be,
    Not in the Soul, or in her working might;
    She cannot lose her perfect Power to See,
    Though mists and clouds do choke her window light.

These imperfections then we must impute,
    Not to the Agent, but the Instrument ;
    We must not blame APOLLO, but his Lute,
    If false accords from her false strings be sent.

The Soul, in all, hath one intelligence,
    Though too much moisture in an infant's brain,
    And too much dryness in an old man's sense
    Cannot the prints of outward things retain.

Then doth the Soul want work, and idle sit :
    And this we Childishness and Dotage call :
    Yet hath She then a quick and active Wit,
    If She had stuff and tools to work withal.

For, give her organs fit, and objects fair,
    Give but the aged man, the young man's sense :
    Let but MEDEA, ÆSON's youth repair,
    And straight She shews her wonted excellence.

As a good harper, stricken far in years,
    Into whose cunning hands, the gout is fall :
    All his old crotchets, in his brain he bears,
    But on his harp, plays ill, or not at all.

But if APOLLO take his gout away,
    That he, his nimble fingers may apply;
    APOLLO's self will envy at his play,
    And all the world applaud his minstrelsy !

Then Dotage is no weakness of the Mind,
    But of the Sense ; for if the Mind did waste ;
    In *all* old men, we should this wasting find,
    When they some certain term of years had past.

But most of them, even to their dying hour,
  Retain a Mind more lively, quick, and strong,
  And better use their Understanding Power,
  Than when their brains were warm, and limbs were
    young.

For though the body wasted be and weak,
  And though the leaden form of earth it bears;
  Yet when we hear that half-dead body speak,
  We oft are ravished to the heavenly spheres.

Yet say these men, " If all her organs die,
2. Objection. Then hath the Soul no power, her Powers to use !
  So in a sort her Powers extinct do lie,
  When into Act She cannot them reduce."

" And if her Powers be dead, then what is She ?
  For since from everything, some Powers do spring,
  And from those Powers some Acts proceeding be :
  Then kill both Power and Act, and kill the Thing."

Doubtless the Body's death, when once it dies,
Answer.   The Instruments of Sense and Life doth kill;
  So that She cannot use those faculties,
  Although their root rest in her substance still.

But as, the Body living, Wit and Will
  Can judge and choose without the Body's aid,
  Though on such objects, they are working still,
  As through the Body's organs are conveyed :

So, when the Body serves her turn no more,
  And all her Senses are extinct and gone,
  She can discourse of what She learned before,
  In heavenly contemplations all alone.

So if one man well on the lute doth play,
  And have good horsemanship, and learning's skill :
  Though both his lute and horse we take away;
  Doth he not keep his former learning still ?

He keeps it doubtless! and can use it too!
 And doth both th'other skills, in power retain!
 And can of both the proper actions do,
 If with his Lute, or Horse he meet again.

So, though the instruments by which we live
 And view the world, the Body's death doth kill:
 Yet with the Body, they shall all revive;
 And all their wonted offices fulfil.

"But *how*, till then, shall She herself employ?
3. Objection. Her spies are dead; which brought home news before:
 What she hath got and keeps, she may enjoy;
 But She hath means to understand no more."

"Then what do those poor Souls which nothing get?
 Or what do those which get and nothing keep,
 Like buckets bottomless, which all out let?
 Those Souls, for want of exercise, must sleep"

See *how* Man's Soul, against itself doth strive:
Answer. Why should we not have other means to know?
 As children, while within the womb they live,
 Feed by the navel; Here, they feed not so.

These children (if they had some use of Sense,
 And should by chance their mothers talking, hear;
 That, in short time, they shall come forth from thence)
 Would fear their birth, more than our death we fear.

They would cry out, "If we, this place shall leave,
 Then shall we break our tender navel strings:
 How shall we then our nourishment receive,
 Since our sweet food, no other conduit brings?"

And if a man should, to these babes reply,
 That "Into this fair world they shall be brought,
 Where they shall see the earth, the sea, the sky,
 The glorious sun, and all that GOD hath wrought:

That there ten thousand dainties they shall meet,
    Which by their mouths they shall with pleasure take :
    Which shall be cordial too, as well as sweet,
    And of their little limbs, tall bodies make ! "

This, would they think a fable ! even as we
    Do think the story of the Golden Age;
    Or as some sensual spirits amongst us be,
    Which hold the World to Come, " a feigned Stage. "

Yet shall these infants, after, find all true ;
    Though, then, thereof, they nothing could conceive.
    As soon as they are born, the world they view,
    And with their mouths, the nurse's milk receive.

So when the Soul is born (for Death is nought
    But the Soul's Birth, and so we should it call!)
    Ten thousand things She sees, beyond her thought ;
    And, in an unknown manner, knows them all.

Then doth She see by spectacles no more,
    She hears not by report of double spies,
    Herself, in instants, doth all things explore,
    For each thing present, and before her lies.

But still this Crew, with questions me pursues ;
4. Objection. " If Souls deceased," say they, " still living be,
        Why do they not return to bring us news
        Of that strange world, where they such wonders see ?

Fond men ! if we believe that men do live
Answer. Under the zenith of both frozen poles ;
        Though none come thence, advertisement to give ;
        Why bear we not the like faith of our Souls ?

The Soul hath, here on earth, no more to do,
    Than we have business in our mother's womb ;
    What child doth covet to return thereto ?
    Although all children, first from thence do come !

But as Noah's pigeon which returned no more,
    Did shew she footing found, for all the flood;
    So when good Souls, departed through death's door,
    Come not again; it shews their dwelling good.

And doubtless such a Soul as up doth mount,
    And doth appear before her Maker's face,
    Holds this vile world in such a base account,
    As She looks down and scorns this wretched place.

But such as are detruded down to hell;
    Either for shame, they still themselves retire,
    Or tied in chains, they in close prison dwell,
    And cannot come, although they much desire.

"Well, well," say these vain spirits, "though vain it is
5. Objection.   To think our Souls to heaven or hell do go;
    Politic men have thought it not amiss,
    To spread this *lie*, to make men virtuous so!"

Do *you*, then, think this moral Virtue, good?
Answer.   I think you do! even for your private gain;
    For commonwealths by Virtue ever stood;
    And common good, the private doth contain.

If then this Virtue, you do love so well,
    Have you no means, her practice to maintain?
    But you this lie must to the people tell,
    "That good Souls live in joy, and ill in pain."

Must Virtue be preservèd by a lie?
    Virtue and Truth do ever best agree.
    By this, it seems to be a verity,
    Since the effects so good and virtuous be.

For as the Devil, father is of lies,
    So Vice and Mischief do his lies ensue.
    Then this good doctrine did he not devise,
    But made this Lie which saith, "It is not true!"

For how can that be false, which every tongue,
Of every mortal man, affirms for true;
Which truth hath, in all ages, been so strong,
As loadstone-like, all hearts it ever drew.

The
General
Consent of
all.

For not the Christian or the Jew alone ;
The Persian, or the Turk acknowledge this :
This mystery to the wild Indian known,
And to the Cannibal and Tartar, is.

This rich Assyrian drug grows everywhere,
As common in the North, as in the East !
This doctrine doth not enter by the ear,
But, of itself, is native in the breast !

None that acknowledge GOD, or Providence,
Their Soul's eternity did ever doubt;
For all religion takes her root from hence,
Which no poor naked nation lives without.

For since the world for Man created was,
(For only Man, the use thereof doth know)
If Man do perish like a withered grass,
How doth GOD's wisdom order things below ?

And if that wisdom still wise ends propound,
Why made He Man, of other creatures king ?
When (if he perish here !) there is not found,
In all the world so poor and vile a thing ?

If Death do quench us quite ; we have great wrong;
Since for our service, all things else were wrought :
That daws, and trees, and rocks should last so long,
When we must in an instant pass to nought.

But, blest be that Great Power ! that hath us blest
With longer life, than heaven or earth can have ;
Which hath infused into one mortal breast,
Immortal Powers, not subject to the grave.

For though the Soul do seem her grave to bear,
 And in this world is almost buried quick;
 We have no cause the Body's death to fear,
 " For when the shell is broke, out comes a chick. "

For as the Soul's *essential* Powers are three,

Three
kinds of
Life
answerable
to the three
powers of
the Soul.

 The Quick'ning Power, the Power of Sense, and
  Reason ;
 Three kinds of Life to her designèd be,
 Which perfect these three Powers, in their due
  season.

The first Life in the mother's womb is spent,
 Where She her Nursing Power doth only use ;
 Where, when She finds defect of nourishment,
 Sh' expels her body, and this world She views.

This, we call Birth ! but if the child could speak,
 He, Death would call it ! and of Nature, 'plain
 That She should thrust him out naked and weak;
 And in his passage, pinch him with such pain.

Yet, out he comes ! and in this world is placed,
 Where all his Senses in perfection be ;
 Where he finds flowers to smell, and fruits to taste,
 And sounds to hear, and sundry forms to see.

When he hath passed some time upon this Stage,
 His Reason, then, a little seems to wake,
 Which though She spring, when Sense doth fade with
  age,
 Yet can She here, no perfect practice make.

Then doth th' aspiring Soul, the Body leave,
 Which we call Death.   But were it known to all,
 What Life our Souls do, by this death, receive ;
 Men would it, Birth ! or Gaol Delivery ! call.

In this third Life, Reason will be so bright,
    As that her Spark will like the sunbeams shine;
    And shall, of GOD enjoy the real sight,
    Being still increased by influence divine.

O ignorant poor **Man!** what dost thou bear,
An acclamation! Locked up within the casket of thy breast;
    What jewels, and what riches hast thou there.
    What heavenly treasure in so weak a chest!

Look in thy Soul! and thou shalt beauties find,
    Like those which drowned NARCISSUS in the flood;
    Honour and Pleasure both are in thy Mind,
    And all that in the world is counted Good.

Think of her worth! and think that GOD did mean
    This worthy Mind should worthy things embrace!
    Blot not her beauties, with thy thoughts unclean;
    Nor her, dishonour with thy Passions base.

Kill not her Quick'ning Power with surfeitings!
    Mar not her Sense with sensualities!
    Cast not her serious Wit on idle things!
    Make not her free Will slave to vanities!

And when thou thinkest of her Eternity;
    Think not that Death against her nature is;
    Think it a Birth! and, when thou goest to die,
    Sing like a swan, as if thou wentst to bliss!

And if thou, like a child, didst fear before,
    Being in the dark, when thou didst nothing see;
    Now I have brought thee Torch-light, fear no more.
    Now, when thou diest; thou canst not hoodwinked be.

And thou, my Soul! which turn'st thy curious eye,
    To view the beams of thine own form divine;
    Know, that thou canst know nothing perfectly,
    While thou are *clouded* with this flesh of mine.

Take heed of *overweening*! and compare
    Thy peacock's feet, with thy gay peacock's train;
    Study the *best* and *highest* things that are;
    But of thyself, an humble thought retain!

Cast down thyself! and only strive to raise
    The glory of thy Maker's sacred name!
    Use all thy powers, that Blessed Power to praise,
    Which gives thee power to Be, and Use the same.

FINIS.

HYMNS OF
ASTRÆA, IN
ACROSTIC
VERSE.

LONDON:
Printed for I. S.
1599.

[Hymns of ASTRÆA.]

HYMN I.

Of ASTRÆA.

E ARLY, before the day doth spring,
L et us awake, my Muse! and sing!
I t is no time to slumber!
S o many joys this Time doth bring,
A s time will fail to number.

B ut, whereto shall we bend our Lays?
E ven up to heaven, again to raise
T he Maid! which, thence descended,
H ath brought again the Golden Days
A nd all the world amended.

R udeness itself, She doth refine!
E ven like an Alchemist divine,
G ross Times of Iron turning
I nto the purest form of Gold;
N ot to corrupt, till heaven wax old
A nd be refined with burning.

HYMN II.

To ASTRÆA

E TERNAL Virgin! Goddess true!
L et me presume to sing to you!
I OVE, even great JOVE hath leisure
S ometimes, to hear the vulgar crew;
A nd hears them, oft, with pleasure.

B lessed ASTREA! I, in part,
E njoy the blessings you impart!
T he Peace! the milk and honey!
H umanity! and civil Art!
A richer dower than money.

R ight glad am I, that now I live,
E ven in these days, whereto you give
G reat happiness and glory!
I f after you, I should be born;
N o doubt, I should my birthday scorn,
A dmiring your sweet Story.

HYMN III.

To the Spring.

E ARTH now is green, and heaven is blue!
L ively Spring, which makes all new.
I olly Spring doth enter.
S weet young sunbeams do subdue
A ngry, agèd Winter.

B lasts are mild, and seas are calm!
E very meadow flows with balm!
T he earth wears all her riches!
H armonious birds sing such a psalm
A s ear and heart bewitches!

R eserve, sweet Spring! this Nymph of ours,
E ternal garlands of thy flowers!
G reen garlands never wasting!
I n her shall last our State's fair Spring,
N ow and for ever flourishing,
A s long as heaven is lasting.

HYMN IV.

To the month of May.

E ACH day of thine, sweet month of May!
L ove makes a solemn Holy Day.
I will perform like duty!
S ince thou resemblest, every way,
A STRÆA, Queen of Beauty.

B oth you, fresh beauties do partake!
E ither's aspect, doth Summer make,
T houghts of young Love awaking!
H earts you both, do cause to ache;
A nd yet be pleased with aching.

R ight dear art thou! and so is She!
E ven like attractive sympathy
G ains unto both, like dearness.
I ween this made Antiquity
N ame thee, Sweet May of Majesty!
A s being both like in clearness.

HYMN V.

To the Lark.

E ARLY, cheerful, mounting Lark!
L ight's gentle Usher! Morning's Clerk!
I n merry notes delighting;
S tint awhile thy song, and hark,
A nd learn my new inditing!

B ear up this Hymn! to heaven, it bear!
E ven up to heaven, and sing it there!
T o heaven, each morning bear it!
H ave it set to some sweet sphere,
A nd let the angels hear it!

R enowned ASTRÆA, that great name!
(E xceeding great in worth and fame,
G reat worth hath so renowned it)
I t is ASTRÆA's name, I praise!
N ow then, sweet Lark! do thou it raise;
A nd in high heaven resound it!

HYMN VI.

To the Nightingale.

E **VERY** night, from even till morn,
L ove's Chorister amid the thorn,
I   s now so sweet a singer !
S o sweet, as for her Song, I scorn.
A **POLLO**'s voice and finger.

B ut, Nightingale ! sith you delight
E ver to watch the starry night,
T ell all the stars of heaven !
H eaven never had a star so bright
A s now to earth is given !

R oyal **ASTRÆA** makes our day
E ternal, with her beams ! nor may
G ross darkness overcome her !
I   now perceive, why some do write,
" N o country hath so short a night
A s England hath in summer."

HYMN VII.

To the Rose.

E **YE** of the garden ! Queen of Flowers !
L **OVE**'s cup, wherein he nectar pours !
I   ngendered first of nectar.
S weet nurse-child of the Spring's young Hours !
A nd Beauty's fair Character !

B est jewel that the earth doth wear !
E ven when the brave young sun draws near,
T o her hot love pretending ;
H imself likewise, like form doth bear,
A t rising and descending.

R ose, of the Queen of Love beloved !
E ngland's great Kings (divinely moved)
G ave Roses in their banner :
I   t shewed, that Beauty's Rose indeed,
N ow in this Age should them succeed,
A nd reign in more sweet manner.

HYMN VIII.

To all the Princes of Europe.

E urope! the Earth's sweet Paradise!
L et all thy Kings (that would be wise
I n Politic Devotion)
S ail hither, to observe her eyes,
A nd mark her heavenly motion!

B rave Princes of this civil Age!
E nter into this pilgrimage!
T his Saint's tongue is an Oracle!
H er eye hath made a Prince a page ;
A nd works, each day, a miracle!

R aise but your looks to her, and see
E ven the true beams of Majesty!
G reat Princes, mark her duly!
I f all the world you do survey,
N o forehead spreads so bright a ray ;
A nd notes a Prince, so truly!

HYMN IX.

To FLORA.

E mpress of Flowers!   Tell, where away
L ies your sweet Court, this merry May?
I n Greenwich garden alleys!
S ince there the Heavenly Powers do play,
A nd haunt no other valleys.

B eauty, Virtue, Majesty,
E loquent Muses, three times three,
T he new fresh Hours and Graces
H ave pleasure in this place to be,
A bove all other places.

R oses and lilies did them draw,
E re they, divine Astræa saw:
G ay flowers, they sought for pleasure.
I nstead of gathering Crowns of Flowers,
N ow, gather they Astræa's dowers,
A nd bear to heaven, that treasure.

HYMN X.

To the Month of September.

E ACH month hath praise in some degree,
L et May to others seem to be
I n Sense, the sweetest season;
S eptember! thou are best to me!
A nd best doth please my Reason.

B ut neither for their corn, nor wine;
E xtol I, those mild days of thine!
T hough corn and wine might praise thee;
H eaven gives thee honour more divine
A nd higher fortunes raise thee!

R enowned art thou, sweet Month! for this.
E mong thy days, her birthday is!
G race, Plenty, Peace, and Honour
I n one fair hour with her were born!
N ow since, they still her crown adorn,
A nd still attend upon her.

HYMN XI.

To the Sun.

E YE of the world! Fountain of light!
L ife of day, and death of night!
I humbly seek thy kindness!
S weet! dazzle not my feeble sight,
A nd strike me not with blindness!

B ehold me mildly from that face
E ven where thou now dost run thy race,
T he sphere where now thou turnest,
H aving, like PHÆTON changed thy place,
A nd yet hearts only burnest.

R ed in her right cheek, thou dost rise
E xalted after, in her eyes;
G reat glory, there, thou shewest!
I n th'other cheek, when thou descendest,
N ew redness unto it thou lendest!
A nd so thy Round, thou goest!

.

HYMN XII.

To her Picture.

E XTREME was his audacity,
L ittle his skill, that finished thee!
I am ashamed and sorry,
S o dull her counterfeit should be ;
A nd She, so full of glory!

B ut here are colours, red and white ;
E ach line, and each proportion right :
T hese lines, this red and whiteness,
H ave wanting yet a life and light,
A majesty and brightness.

R ude counterfeit! I then did err ;
E ven now, when I would needs infer
G reat boldness in thy maker!
I did mistake! He was not bold,
N or durst his eyes, her eyes behold :
A nd this made him mistake her.

HYMN XIII.

Of her Mind.

E ARTH, now adieu! My ravished thought
L ifted to heaven, sets thee at nought!
I nfinite is my longing,
S ecrets of angels to be taught,
A nd things to heaven belonging!

B rought down from heaven, of angels' kind,
E ven now, do I admire her Mind!
T his is my contemplation!
H er clear sweet Spirit, which is refined
A bove humane creation!

R ich sunbeam of th' Eternal Light!
E xcellent Soul! How shall I write?
G ood angels make me able!
I cannot see but by your eye ;
N or but by your tongue, signify
A thing so admirable.

HYMN XIV.

Of the Sunbeams of her Mind.

E xceeding glorious is this Star!
L et us behold her beams afar
I n a side line reflected!
S ight bears them not, when near they are
A nd in right lines directed.

B ehold her in her virtue's beams,
E xtending sun-like to all realms!
T he sun none views too nearly.
H er well of goodness, in these streams,
A ppears right well and clearly.

R adiant virtues! if your light
E nfeeble the best judgement's sight;
G reat splendour above measure
I s in the Mind, from whence you flow!
N o wit may have access to know
A nd view so bright a treasure.

HYMN XV.

Of her Wit.

E ye of that Mind most quick and clear,
L ike heaven's Eye, which from his sphere,
I nto all things pryeth;
S ees through all things everywhere,
A nd all their natures trieth.

B right image of an angel's wit,
E xceeding sharp and swift like it,
T hings instantly discerning;
H aving a nature infinite,
A nd yet increased by learning.

R ebound upon thyself thy light!
E njoy thine own sweet precious sight!
G ive us but some reflection!
I t is enough for us if we,
N ow in her speech, now policy;
A dmire thine high perfection!

H Y M N   X V I.

Of her Will.

E ver well affected Will,
L oving goodness, loathing ill!
I nestimable treasure!
S ince such a power hath power to spill,
A nd save us, at her pleasure.

B e thou our law, sweet Will! and say
E ven what thou wilt, we will obey!
T his law, if I could read it.
H erein would I spend night and day,
A nd study still to plead it.

R oyal Free Will, and only free!
E ach other will is slave to thee!
G lad is each will to serve thee!
I n thee such princely power is seen;
N o spirit but takes thee, for her Queen!
A nd thinks she must observe thee!

H Y M N   X V I I.

Of her Memory.

E xcellent jewels would you see?
L ovely ladies! Come with me!
I will (for love I owe you)
S hew you as rich a treasury
A s East or West can shew you!

B ehold! (if you can judge of it)
E ven that great Storehouse of her Wit!
T hat beautiful large table,
H er Memory! wherein is writ
A ll knowledge admirable.

R ead this fair book, and you shall learn
E xquisite skill, if you discern;
G ain heaven, by this discerning!
I n such a memory divine,
N ature did form the Muses nine,
A nd PALLAS, Queen of Learning.

HYMN XVIII.

Of her Phantasy.

E xquisite curiosity !
L ook on thyself, with judging eye !
I f ought be faulty, leave it !
S o delicate a Phantasy
A s this, will straight perceive it,

B ecause her temper is so fine,
E ndued with harmonies divine ;
T herefore if discord strike it,
H er true proportions do repine,
A nd sadly do mislike it.

R ight otherwise, a pleasure sweet,
E ver she takes in actions meet,
G racing with smiles such meetness :
I n her fair forehead beams appear,
N o Summer's day is half so clear !
A dorned with half that sweetness !

HYMN XIX.

Of the Organs of her Mind.

E clipsed She is, and her bright rays
L ie under veils ; yet many ways
I s her fair form revealed !
S he diversely herself conveys,
A nd cannot be concealed.

B y instruments, her powers appear
E xceedingly well tuned and clear !
T his Lute is still in measure,
H olds still in tune, even like a sphere,
A nd yields the world sweet pleasure !

R esolve me, Muse ! how this thing is ?
E ver a body like to this,
G ave heaven to earthly creature ?
I am but fond this doubt to make !
N o doubt, the angels, bodies take
A bove our common nature !

HYMN XX.

Of the Passions of her Heart.

E XAMINE not th' inscrutable Heart,
L ight Muse! of Her, though She in part
I mpart it to the subject!
S earch not! although from heaven thou art!
A nd this a heavenly object.

B ut since She hath a heart, we know
E ver some Passions thence do flow,
T hough ever ruled with honour.
H er judgement reigns!   They wait below,
A nd fix their eyes upon her!

R ectified so, they, in their kind,
E ncrease each virtue of her Mind,
G overned with mild tranquility.
I n all the regions under heaven,
N o State doth bear itself so even,
A nd with so sweet facility.

HYMN XXI.

Of the innumerable Virtues of her Mind.

E RE thou proceed in these sweet pains,
L earn Muse! how many drops it rains
I n cold and moist December!
S um up May flowers! and August's grains!
A nd grapes of mild September!

B ear the sea's sand in Memory!
E arth's grasses! and the stars in sky!
T he little moats, which mounted
H ang in the beams of PHŒBUS' eye,
A nd never can be counted!

R ecount these numbers, numberless,
E re thou, her virtue canst express!
G reat wits, this count will cumber!
I nstruct thyself in numbering schools!
N ow Courtiers use to beg for fools;
A ll such as cannot number.

HYMN XXII.

Of her Wisdom.

E AGLE-eyed Wisdom ! Life's loadstar !
L ooking near, on things afar !
I OVE's best beloved daughter !
S hews to her spirit all that are !
A s JOVE himself hath taught her.

B y this straight rule, She rectifies
E ach thought, that in her heart doth rise ;
T his is her clear true Mirror !
H er Looking Glass, wherein She spies
A ll forms of Truth and Error.

R ight Princely virtue, fit to reign !
E nthronised in her spirit remain,
G uiding our fortunes ever !
I f we this Star once cease to see ;
N o doubt our State will shipwrecked be,
A nd torn and sunk for ever.

HYMN XXIII.

Of her Justice.

E XILED ASTRÆA is come again !
L o here She doth all things maintain
I n number, weight, and measure !
S he rules us, with delightful pain,
A nd we obey with pleasure !

B y Love, She rules more than by Law !
E ven her great Mercy breedeth awe ;
T his is her sword and sceptre !
H erewith She hearts did ever draw,
A nd this guard ever kept her.

R eward doth sit in her right hand !
E ach Virtue, thence takes her garland,
G athered in Honour's garden !
I n her left hand (wherein should be
N. ought but the sword) sits Clemency !
A nd conquers Vice with pardon.

HYMN XXIV.

Of her Magnanimity.

E ven as her State, so is her Mind
L ifted above the vulgar kind !
I t treads proud Fortune under !
S unlike, it sits above the wind ;
A bove the storms, and thunder.

B rave Spirit ! Large Heart ! admiring nought !
E steeming each thing, as it ought !
T hat swelleth not, nor shrinketh !
H onour is always in her thought ;
A nd of great things, She thinketh !

R ocks, pillars, and heaven's axletree
E xemplify her Constancy !
G reat changes never change her !
I n her sex, fears are wont to rise ;
N ature permits, Virtue denies,
A nd scorns the face of danger !

HYMN XXV.

Of her Moderation.

E mpress of Kingdoms, though She be ;
L arger is her Sovereignty,
I f She herself do govern !
S ubject unto herself is She ;
A nd of herself, true Sovereign !

B eauty's Crown, though She do wear ;
E xalted into Fortune's Chair ;
T hroned like the Queen of Pleasure :
H er virtues still possess her ear,
A nd counsel her to Measure !

R eason (if She incarnate were)
E ven Reason's self could never bear
G reatness with Moderation !
I n her, one temper still is seen.
N o liberty claims She as Queen !
A nd shows no alteration !

HYMN XXVI.

E nvy, go weep! My Muse and I
L augh thee to scorn! Thy feeble eye
I s dazzled with the glory
S hining in this gay Poesy,
A nd little golden Story!

B ehold, how my proud quill doth shed
E ternal nectar on her head!
T he pomp of Coronation
H ath not such power, her fame to spread,
A s this my admiration!

R espect my pen, as free and frank;
E xpecting nor reward, nor thank!
G reat wonder only moves it!
I never made it mercenary!
N or should my Muse, this burden carry
A s hired; but that she loves it!

FINIS.

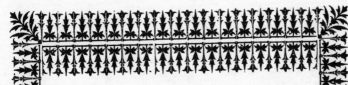

SIX IDILLIA,

THAT IS,

SIX SMALL, OR PETTY, POEMS,

OR ÆGLOGUES,

chosen out of the right famous Sicilian Poet

THEOCRITUS,

And translated into English verse.

Dum defluat amnis.

PRINTED

At Oxford by IOSEPH BARNES.

1588.

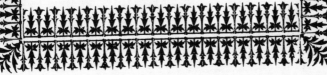

E. D.

*Libenter hic, et omnis exantlabitur
Labor, in tuæ spem gratiæ.*
[HORACE, *Epodes* i. 23-24.]

SIX IDILLIA

chosen out of the famous Sicilian Poet

THEOCRITUS,

and translated into English verse.

THE EIGHTH IDILLION.

Argument.

MENALCAS a Shepherd and DAPHNIS a Neatherd, two Sicilian Lads,
contending who should sing best, pawn their Whistles ; and choose
a Goatherd to be their Judge : who giveth sentence on DAPHNIS
his side.   The thing is imagined to be done in the Isle of Sicily, by
the sea-shore.   Of whose singing, this Idillion is called *Bucoliastæ*,
that is, " Singers of a Neatherd's Song."

BUCOLIASTÆ.

DAPHNIS, MENALCAS, Goatherd.

ITH lovely Neatherd DAPHNIS on the hills,
 they say,
Shepherd MENALCAS met upon a summer's
 day :
Both youthful striplings, both had yellow
 heads of hair ;
In whistling both, and both in singing
 skilful were.

MENALCAS first, beholding DAPHNIS, thus bespake:

MENALCAS.

" Wilt thou in singing, Neatherd DAPHNIS, undertake
To strive with me ?   For I affirm that, at my will,
I can thee pass ! "   Thus DAPHNIS answered on the hill.

DAPHNIS.

" Whistler MENALCAS, thou shalt never me excel
In singing, though to death with singing thou should'st swell ! "

MENALCAS.

" Then wilt thou see, and something for the victor wage ? "

DAPHNIS.

" I will both see, and something for the victor gage ! "

MENALCAS.

" What therefore shall we pawn, that for us may be fit ? "

DAPHNIS.

" I'll pawn a calf ; a wennell lamb lay thou to it ! "

MENALCAS.

" I'll pawn no lamb : for both my Sire and Mother fell
Are very hard ; and all my sheep at e'en they tell."

DAPHNIS.

" What then ?   What shall he gain that wins the victory ? "

MENALCAS.

" A gallant Whistle which I made with notes thrice three,
Joined with white wax, both e'en below and e'en above ;
This will I lay !   My father's things I will not move ! "

DAPHNIS.

" And I a Whistle have with notes thrice three a row,
Joined with white wax, both e'en below and e'en above.
I lately framed it : for this finger yet doth ache
With pricking, which a splinter of the reed did make.
But who shall be our Judge, and give us audience ? "

MENALCAS.

" What if we call this Goatherd here, not far from hence,
Whose dog doth bark hard by the kids ? "   The lusty boys
Did call him, and the Goatherd came to hear their toys.
The lusty boys did sing, the Goatherd judgment gave.
MENALCAS first, by lot, unto his Whistle brave,
Did sing a Neatherd's Song ; and Neatherd DAPHNIS then
Did sing, by course : but first MENALCAS thus began :

MENALCAS.

" Ye Groves and Brooks divine, if on his reed
MENALCAS ever sang a pleasant Lay ;
Fat me these lambs !   If DAPHNIS here will feed
His calves, let him have pasture too I pray ! "

DAPHNIS.

" Ye pleasant Springs and Plants, would DAPHNIS had
As sweet a voice as have the nightingales !
Feed me this herd ! and if the Shepherd's lad
MENALCAS comes, let him have all the dales ! "

MENALCAS.

" 'Tis ever Spring; there meads are ever gay;
There strout the bags; there sheep are fatly fed,
When DAPHNE comes!   Go she away;
Then both the Shepherd there, and grass are dead."

DAPHNIS.

" There both the ewes, and goats, bring forth their twins;
There bees do fill their hives; there oaks are high;
Where MILO treads!   When he away begins
To go, both Neatherd and the neat wax dry."

MENALCAS.

" O husband of the goats!   O wood so high!
O kids! come to this brook, for he is there!
Thou with the broken horns tell MILO shy,
That PROTEUS kept sea-calves, though god he were."

DAPHNIS.

" Nor PELOPS' kingdom may I crave, nor gold;
Nor to outrun the winds upon a lea:
But in this cave I'll sing, with thee in hold,
Both looking on my sheep, and on the sea."

MENALCAS.

" A tempest marreth trees; and drought, a spring:
Snares unto fowls, to beasts nets, are a smart;
Love spoils a man.   O JOVE, alone his sting
I have not felt; for thou a lover art!"

Thus sang these boys, by course, with voices strong;
MENALCAS then began a latter song:

MENALCAS.

" Wolf, spare my kids ! and spare my fruitful sheep !
And hurt me not ! though but a lad, these flocks I guide.
Lampur my dog, art thou indeed so sound asleep ?
Thou should'st not sleep while thou art by thy master's side !
My sheep, fear not to eat the tender grass at will !
Nor when it springeth up again, see that you fail !
Go to, and feed apace, and all your bellies fill !
That part your lambs may have ; and part, my milking pail."

Then DAPHNIS in his turn sweetly began to sing :

DAPHNIS.

" And me, not long ago, fair DAPHNE whistly eyed
As I drove by ; and said, I was a paragon :
Nor then indeed to her I churlishly replied ;
But, looking on the ground, my way still held I on.
Sweet is a cow-calf's voice, and sweet her breath doth smell ;
A bull calf, and a cow, do low full pleasantly.
'Tis sweet in summer by a spring abroad to dwell !
Acorns become the oak ; apples, the apple-tree ;
And calves, the kine ; and kine, the Neatherd much set out."

Thus sung these youths. The Goatherd thus did end the
    doubt :

Goatherd.

" O DAPHNIS, what a dulcet mouth and voice thou hast !
'Tis sweeter thee to hear than honey-combs to taste !
Take thee these Pipes, for thou in singing dost excel !
If me, a Goatherd, thou wilt teach to sing so well ;
This broken-hornèd goat, on thee bestow I will !
Which to the very brim, the pail doth ever fill."

So then was DAPHNIS glad, and lept and clapt his hands;
And danced as doth a fawn, when by the dam he stands.
MENALCAS grieved, the thing his mind did much dismay:
And sad as Bride he was, upon the marriage day.

Since then among the Shepherds, DAPHNIS chief was had!
And took a Nymph to wife when he was but a lad.

DAPHNIS his Emblem.

Me tamen urit Amor.

MENALCAS his Emblem.

At hæc DAPHNE forsan probet.

Goatherd's Emblem.

Est minor nemo nisi comparatus.

THE ELEVENTH IDILLION.

Argument.

THEOCRITUS wrote this Idillion to NICIAS a learned Physician:
wherein he sheweth—by the example of POLYPHEMUS a giant in
Sicily, of the race of the CYCLOPS, who loved the Water Nymph
GALATEA—that there is no medicine so sovereign against Love as
is Poetry. Of whose Love Song, as this Idillion, is termed
CYCLOPS; so he was called CYCLOPS, because he had but one eye,
that stood like a circle in the midst of his forehead.

CYCLOPS.

 NICIAS, there is no other remedy for Love,
  With ointing, or with sprinkling on, that ever I
   could prove,
  Beside the Muses nine! This pleasant medicine
   of the mind
Grows among men; and seems but light, yet very hard to find:
As well I wote you know; who are in physic such a Leech,
And of the Muses so beloved. The cause of this my speech
A CYCLOPS is, who lived here with us right wealthily;
That ancient POLYPHEM, when first he loved GALATE
(When, with a bristled beard, his chin and cheeks first clothed
  were):
He loved her not with roses, apples, or with curlèd hair;
But with the Furies' rage. All other things he little plied.
Full often to their fold, from pastures green, without a guide,
His sheep returnèd home: when all the while he singing lay
In honour of his Love, and on the shore consumed away
From morning until night; sick of the wound, fast by the heart,
Which mighty VENUS gave, and in his liver stuck the dart.

For which, this remedy he found, that sitting oftentimes
Upon a rock and looking on the sea, he sang these rhymes :

" O GALATEA fair, why dost thou shun thy lover true ?
More tender than a lamb, more white than cheese when it is
　　　new,
More wanton than a calf, more sharp than grapes unripe, I find.
You use to come when pleasant sleep, my senses all do bind :
But you are gone again when pleasant sleep doth leave mine
　　　eye ;
And as a sheep you run, that on the plain a wolf doth spy.

" I then began to love thee, GALATE, when first of all
You, with my mother, came to gather leaves of crowtoe
　　　[*hyacinth*] small
Upon our hill ; when I, as Usher, squired you all the way.
Nor when I saw thee first, nor afterwards, nor at this day,
Since then could I refrain : but you, by Jove ! nought set
　　　thereby !

" But well I know, fair Nymph, the very cause why thus
　　　you fly.
Because upon my front, one only brow, with bristles strong
From one ear to the other ear is stretchèd all along :
'Neath which, one eye ; and on my lips, a hugy nose, there
　　　stands.
Yet I, this such a one, a thousand sheep feed on these lands ;
And pleasant milk I drink, which from the strouting bags is
　　　presst.
Nor want I cheese in summer, nor in autumn of the best,
Nor yet in winter time.　My cheese racks ever laden are ;
And better can I pipe than any CYCLOPS may compare.
O apple sweet ! of thee, and of myself I use to sing,
And that at midnight oft.　For thee ! eleven fawns up I
　　　bring,

All great with young : and four bears' whelps, I nourish up
    for thee !
But come thou hither first, and thou shalt have them all of me.
And let the bluish coloured sea beat on the shore so nigh,
The night with me in cave, thou shalt consume more pleasantly !
There are the shady bays, and there tall cypress trees do
    sprout :
And there is ivy black, and fertile vines are all about.
Cool water there I have, distilled of the whitest snow,
A drink divine, which out of woody Etna mount doth flow.
In these respects, who in the sea and waves would rather be ?

  " But if I seem as yet too rough and savage unto thee,
Great store of oaken wood I have, and never-quenchèd fire ;
And I can well endure my soul to burn with thy desire,
With this my only eye, than which I nothing think more
    trim :
Now woe is me, my mother bore me not with fins to swim !
That I might dive to thee ; that I thy dainty hand might kiss,
If lips thou wouldst not let. Then would I lilies bring iwis,
And tender poppy-toe that bears a top like rattles red ,
And these in summer time : but others are in winter bred,
So that I cannot bring them all at once. Now certainly
I'll learn to swim of some or other stranger passing by,
That I may know what pleasure 'tis in waters deep to dwell.

  "Come forth, fair GALATE! and once got out, forget thee well
(As I do, sitting on this rock) home to return again !
But feed my sheep with me, and for to milk them take the
    pain !
And cheese to press, and in the milk the rennet sharp to
    strain !
My mother only wrongeth me ; and her I blame, for she
Spake never yet to thee one good, or lovely, word of me :
And that, although she daily sees how I away do pine.
But I will say, 'My head and feet do ache,' that she may
    whine,

And sorrow at the heart: because my heart with grief is swoll'n.

"O CYCLOPS, CYCLOPS! whither is thy wit and reason flown?
If thou would'st baskets make ; and cut down brouzing from
    the tree,
And bring it to thy lambs, a great deal wiser thou should'st be !
Go, coy some present Nymph !   Why dost thou follow flying
    wind ?
Perhaps another GALATE, and fairer, thou shalt find !
For many Maidens in the evening tide with me will play, ⎫
And all do sweetly laugh, when I stand heark'ning what ⎪
    they say : ⎬
And I somebody seem, and in the earth do bear a sway." ⎭

Thus POLYPHEMUS singing, fed his raging love of old ;
Wherein he sweeter did, than had he sent her sums of gold.

POLYPHEM's Emblem.

Ubi Dictamum inveniam ?

THE SIXTEENTH IDILLION.

Argument.

The style of this Poem is more lofty than any of the rest, and THEOCRITUS wrote it to HIERO, King of Syracuse in Sicily. Wherein he reproveth the nigardise of Princes and Great Men towards the Learned, and namely [*especially*] Poets : in whose power it is to make men famous to all posterity. Towards the end, he praiseth HIERO ; and prayeth that Sicily may be delivered by his prowess from the invasions of the Carthaginians. This Idillion is named HIERO in respect of the person to whom it was written ; or *Charites*, that is, " Graces," in respect of the matter whereof it treateth.

CHARITES, or HIERO.

POETS have still this care, and still the Muses have
    this care ;
    To magnify the gods with Songs, and men that
      worthy are.
The Muses they are goddesses, and gods with praise they
    crown ;
But we are mortal men, and mortal men let us renown !
  But who, of all the men under the cope of heaven that dwell,
By opening of his doors, our Graces entertains so well
That unrewarded quite he doth not send them back again ?
They in a chafe, all barefoot, home to me return with pain :
And me they greatly blame, and that they went for nought
    they grudge ;
And all too weary, in the bottom of an empty hutch,
Laying their heads upon their knees full cold, they still remain :
Where they do poorly dwell, because they home returned in
    vain.

Of all that living are, who loves a man that speaketh well?
I know not one.   For now a days for deeds that do excel
Men care not to be praised : but all are overcome with gain.
For every man looks round, with hand in bosom, whence
    amain
Coin he may get : whose rust rubbed off, he will not give
    again.
But straightway thus he says, " The leg is further than the
    knee,
Let me have gold enough ; the gods to Poets pay their fee!"
Who would another hear, " Enough for all, one HOMER is ;
Of poets he is Prince : yet gets he nought of me iwis ! "

Madmen, what gain is this, to hoard up bags of gold
    within?
This is not money's use, nor hath to wise men ever been !
But part is due unto ourselves, part to the Poet's pen ;
And many kinsfolk must be pleasured, and many men :
And often to the gods thou must do solemn sacrifice.
Nor must thou keep a sparing house : but when, in friendly
    wise,
Thou hast receivèd strangers at thy board ; when they will
    thence,
Let them depart !   But chiefly Poets must thou reverence !
That after thou art hidden in thy grave, thou mayest hear
    well !
Nor basely mayest thou mourn when thou in Acheron dost
    dwell !
Like to some ditcher vile, whose hands with work are hard
    and dry ;
Who from his parents poor, bewails his life in beggary.

In King ANTIOCHUS his Court, and King ALEVAS' too
To distribute the monthly bread a many had to do.
The Scopedans had many droves of calves, which in their
    stalls

'Mong oxen lowed; and shepherds kept, in the Cranonian
 dales,
Infinite flocks to bear the hospital [*hospitable*] CREONDAN's⎫
 charge.⎪
No pleasure should these men enjoy of their expenses large,⎬
When once their souls they had embarked in the Infernal⎪
 Barge;⎭
But leaving all this wealth behind, in wretched misery
Among the dead, without renown, for ever they should lie:
Had not SIMONIDES the Chian Poet, with his pen
And with his lute of many strings so famous made these men
To all posterity. The very horses were renowned;
Which, from their races swift returned, with olive garlands
 crowned.

 Whoever should have known the Lycian Princes and their
 race,
Or them of Troy, of CIGNUS [*CYCNUS*] with his woman's
 coloured face:
Had not the Poets sung the famous Wars of them of old?

 Nor yet ULYSSES (who, for ten years space on seas was rolled,
By sundry sorts of men; and who at last went down to Hell
As yet alive; and from the CYCLOPS' den escapèd well)
Had got such lasting fame: and drowned should lie in
 silence deep
Swineherd EUMÆUS, and PHILÆTUS who had to keep
A herd of neat; LAERTES eke himself had been unknown—
If far and wide their names, great HOMER's verses had not
 blown.

 Immortal fame to mortal men, the Muses nine do give:
But dead men's wealth is spent and quite consumed of them
 that live.
But all one pain[s] it is, to number waves upon the banks,
Whereof great store, the wind from sea doth blow to land in
 ranks;
Or for to wash a brick with water clear till it be white:

As for to move a man whom avarice doth once delight.
Therefore " Adieu ! " to such a one for me ! and let him have
Huge silver heaps at will, and more and more still let him crave!
But I, Goodwill of Men, and Honour, will prefer before
A many mules of price, or many horses kept in store.
Therefore I ask, To whom shall I be welcome with my train
Of Muses nine? whose ways are hard, if JOVE guides not the
    rein.

The heavens yet have not left to roll both months and years
    on reels ;
And many horses yet shall turn about the Chariot's wheels :
The man shall rise that shall have need of me to set him out ;
Doing such deeds of arms as AJAX, or ACHILLES stout,
Did in the field of Simois, where ILUS' bones do rest.
And now the Carthaginians, inhabiting the West,
Who in the utmost end of Liby' dwell, in arms are prest :
And now the Syracuseans their spears do carry in rhe rest ;
Whose left arms laden are with targets made of willow tree.
'Mongst whom King HIERO, the ancient Worthies' match, I see
In armour shine ; whose plume doth overshade his helmet
    bright.

O JUPITER, and thou MINERVA fierce in fight,
And thou PROSERPINA (who, with thy mother, has renown
By Lysimelia streams, in Ephyra that wealthy town),
Out of our island drive our enemies, our bitter fate,
Along the Sardine sea ! that death of friends they may relate
Unto their children and their wives ! and that the towns
    opprest
By enemies, of th'old inhabitants may be possesst !
That they may till the fields ! and sheep upon the downs
    may bleat
By thousands infinite, and fat ! and that the herds of neat
As to their stalls they go, may press the ling'ring traveller !
Let grounds be broken up for seed, what time the grasshopper

Watching the shepherds by their flocks, in boughs close
    singing lies !
And let the spiders spread their slender webs in armories ;
So that of War, the very name may not be heard again !

But let the Poets strive, King HIERO's glory for to strain
Beyond the Scythean sea ; and far beyond those places where
SEMIRAMIS did build those stately walls, and rule did bear.
'Mongst whom, I will be one : for many other men beside,
JOVE's daughters love ; whose study still shall be, both far
    and wide,
Sicilian Arethusa, with the people, to advance ;
And warlike HIERO. Ye Graces! (who keep resiance [*residence*]
In the Thessalian Mount Orchomenus ; to Thebes of old
So hateful, though of you beloved) to stay I will be bold,
Where I am bid to come : and I with them will still remain,
That shall invite me to their house, with all my Muses' train.
Nor you, will I forsake ! For what to men can lovely be
Without your company ? The Graces always be with me !

Emblem.

Si nihil attuleris, ibis HOMERE foras.

THE EIGHTEENTH IDILLION.

Argument.

Twelve noble Spartan Virgins are brought in singing, in the evening, at the chamber door of MENELAUS and HELENA on their Wedding Day. And first they prettily jest with the Bridegroom, then they praise HELENA, last they wish them both joy of their marriage. Therefore this Idillion is entitled *HELEN's Epithalamion* that is " HELEN's Wedding Song."

HELEN's Epithalamion.

N Sparta, long ago, where MENELAUS wore the
  crown,
   Twelve noble Virgins, daughters to the greatest in
   the town,
All dight upon their hair in crowtoe [*hyacinth*] garlands
  fresh and green,
Danced at the chamber door of HELENA the Queen :
What time this MENELAUS, the younger son of ATREUS,
Did marry with this lovely daughter of Prince TYNDARUS ;
And therewithal, at eve, a Wedding Song they jointly sang,
With such a shuffling of their feet that all the palace rang.

" Fair Bridegroom, do you sleep ? Hath slumber all your
  limbs possesst ?
What, are you drowsy ? or hath wine your body so oppresst
That you are gone to bed ? For if you needs would take
  your rest,
You should have ta'en a season meet. Mean time, till it be day
Suffer the Bride with us, and with her mother dear, to play !
For, MENELAUS, She, at evening and at morning tide.

From day to day, and year to year, shall be thy loving Bride.

"O happy Bridegroom, sure some honest man did sneeze
    to thee,
When thou to Sparta came, to meet with such a one as She!
Among the demi-gods thou only art accounted meet ⎫
To be the Son-in-law to JOVE! for underneath one sheet ⎬
His daughter lies with thee! Of all that tread on ground with ⎭
    feet
There is not such a one in Greece! Now sure some goodly
    thing
She will thee bear; if it be like the mother that she bring.

For we, her peers in age, whose course of life is e'en the same;
Who, at Eurotas' streams, like men, are oilèd to the game:
And four times sixty Maids, of all the women youth
    we are;
Of these none wants a fault, if her with HELEN we compare.
Like as the rising morn shews a grateful lightening,
When sacred night is past; and Winter now lets loose the
    Spring:
So glittering HELEN shined among her Maids, lusty and tall.
As is the furrow in a field that far outstretcheth all;
Or in a garden is a cypress tree; or in a trace,
A steed of Thessaly; so She to Sparta was a grace.
No damsel with such works as She, her baskets used to fill;
Nor in a divers coloured web, a woof of greater skill
Doth cut off from the loom; nor any hath such Songs and
    Lays
Unto her dainty harp, in DIAN's and MINERVA's praise,
As HELEN hath: in whose bright eyes all Loves and Graces
    be.

"O fair, O lovely Maid! a Matron is now made of thee!
But we will, every Spring, unto the leaves in meadow go
To gather garlands sweet; and there, not with a little woe,

Will often think of thee, O HELEN! as the suckling lambs
Desire the strouting bags and presence of their tender dams.
We all betimes for thee, a wreath of melitoe will knit;
And on a shady plane for thee will safely fasten it.
And all betimes for thee, under a shady plane below,
Out of a silver box the sweetest ointment will bestow.
And letters shall be written in the bark that men may see,
And read, DO HUMBLE REVERENCE, FOR I AM
   HELEN's TREE!

   "Sweet Bride, good night! and thou, O happy Bridegroom,
      now good night!
LATONA send your happy issue! who is most of might
In helping youth; and blissful VENUS send you equal love
Betwixt you both! and JOVE give lasting riches from above,
Which from your noble selves, unto your noble imps may
   fall!
Sleep on, and breathe into your breasts desires mutual!
But in the morning, wake! Forget it not in any wise!
And we will then return; as soon as any one shall rise
And in the chamber stir, and first of all lift up the head!
HYMEN! O HYMEN! now be gladsome at this marriage
   bed!"

                     Emblem.

               Usque adeo latet utilitas.

THE TWENTY-FIRST IDILLION.

Argument.

A Neatherd is brought chafing that EUNICA, a Maid of the city, disdained to kiss him. Whereby it is thought that THEOCRITUS
seemeth to check them that think this kind of writing in Poetry
to be too base and rustical. And therefore this Poem is termed
Neatherd.

NEATHERD.

UNICA scorned me, when her I would have sweetly
   kist
   And railing at me said, " Go with a mischief,
    where thou list!
Thinkest thou, a wretched Neatherd, me to kiss! I have no will
After the country guise to smouch! Of city lips I skill!
My lovely mouth, so much as in thy dream, thou shalt not
  touch!
How dost thou look! How dost thou talk! How play'st
  thou the slouch!
How daintily thou speak'st! What Courting words thou
  bringest out!
How soft a beard thou hast! How fair thy locks hang round
  about!
Thy lips are like a sick man's lips! thy hands, so black they be!
And rankly thou dost smell! Away, lest thou defilest me!"
  Having thus said, she spattered on her bosom twice or thrice;
And, still beholding me from top to toe in scornful wise,
She muttered with her lips; and with her eyes she looked aside,
And of her beauty wondrous coy she was; her mouth she
  wryed,
And proudly mocked me to my face. My blood boiled in
  each vein,
And red I wox for grief as doth the rose with dewy rain.
Thus leaving me, away she flang! Since when, it vexeth me
That I should be so scorned of such a filthy drab as She.

" Ye shepherds, tell me true, am not I as fair as any swan ?
Hath of a sudden any god made me another man ?
For well I wot, before a comely grace in me did shine,
Like ivy round about a tree, and decked this beard of mine.
My crispèd locks, like parsley, on my temples wont to spread ;
And on my eyebrows black a milk white forehead glisterèd :
More seemly were mine eyes than are MINERVA's eyes, I know.
My mouth for sweetness passèd cheese ; and from my mouth
       did flow
A voice more sweet than honeycombs. Sweet is my Roundelay
When on the whistle, flute, or pipe, or cornet I do play.
And all the women on our hills do say that I am fair,
And all do love me well : but these that breathe the city air
Did never love me yet. And why ? The cause is this I know.
That I a Neatherd am. They hear not how in vales below,
Fair BACCHUS kept a herd of beasts. Nor can these nice
       ones tell
How VENUS, raving for a Neatherd's love, with him did dwell
Upon the hills of Phrygia ; and how she loved again
ADONIS in the woods, and mourned in woods when he was
       slain.
Who was ENDYMION ? Was he not a Neatherd ? Yet the
       Moon
Did love this Neatherd so, that, from the heavens descending
       soon,
She came to Latmos grove where with the dainty lad she lay.
And RHEA, thou a Neatherd dost bewail ! and thou, all day,
O mighty JUPITER ! but for a shepherd's boy didst stray !
EUNICA only, deigned not a Neatherd for to love :
Better, forsooth, than CYBEL, VENUS, or the Moon above !
And VENUS, thou hereafter must not love thy fair ADONE
In city, nor on hill ! but all the night must sleep alone ! "

Emblem.

Habitarunt Dii quoque sylvas.

THE THIRTY-FIRST IDILLION.

Argument.

The conceit of this Idillion is very delicate. Wherein it is imagined how VENUS did send for the Boar who in hunting slew ADONIS, a dainty youth whom she loved : and how the Boar answering for himself that he slew him against his will, as being enamoured on him, and thinking only to kiss his naked thigh ; she forgave him. The Poet's drift is to shew the power of Love, not only in men, but also in brute beasts : although in the last two verses, by the burning of the Boar's amorous teeth, he intimateth that extravagant and unorderly passions are to be restrained by reason.

ADONIS.

HEN VENUS first did see
  ADONIS dead to be ;
  With woeful tattered hair
  And cheeks so wan and sear,
The wingèd Loves she bade,
The Boar should straight be had.
Forthwith like birds they fly,
And through the wood they hie ;
The woeful beast they find,
And him with cords they bind.
One with a rope before
Doth lead the captive Boar :
Another on his back
Doth make his bow to crack.
The beast went wretchedly,
For VENUS horribly
He feared ; who thus him curst :
  " Of all the beasts the worst,
Didst thou this thigh so wound ?
Didst thou my Love confound ? "

K   10

The beast thus spake in fear
"VENUS, to thee I swear!
By thee, and husband thine,
And by these bands of mine,
And by these hunters all,
Thy husband fair and tall,
I mindèd not to kill!
But, as an image still,
I him beheld for love:
Which made me forward shove
His thigh, that naked was;
Thinking to kiss, alas,
And that hath hurt me thus.

"Wherefore these teeth, VENUS!
Or punish, or cut out:
Why bear I in my snout
These needless teeth about!
If these may not suffice;
Cut off my chaps likewise!"

To ruth he VENUS moves,
And she commands the Loves,
His bands for to untie.

After he came not nigh
The wood; but at her will
He followed VENUS still.
And coming to the fire,
He burnt up his desire.

Emblem.

*Raris forma viris, secula prospice
Impunita fuit.*

FINIS.

The Affectionate

Shepheard.

Containing the Complaint of *Daphnis* for
the loue of *Ganymede*.

Amor plus mellis, quam fellis, est.

LONDON,

Printed by Iohn Danter for T. G. and E. N.
and are to bee fold in Saint Dunftones
Church-yeard in Fleetftreet,
1594.

To the Right Excellent
and most beautifull Lady, the Ladie
PENELOPE RITCH.

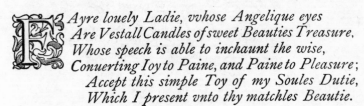

Ayre louely Ladie, vvhose Angelique eyes
Are Vestall Candles of sweet Beauties Treasure,
Whose speech is able to inchaunt the wise,
Conuerting Ioy to Paine, and Paine to Pleasure;
Accept this simple Toy of my Soules Dutie,
Which I present vnto thy matchles Beautie.

And albeit the gift be all too meane,
Too meane an Offring for thine Iuorie Shrine;
Yet must thy Beautie my iust blame susteane,
Since it is mortall, but thy selfe diuine.
Then (Noble Ladie) take in gentle vvorth,
This new-borne Babe which here my Muse brings forth.

Your Honours most affectionate
and perpetually deuoted Shepheard:
DAPHNIS.

The Teares of an
affectionate Shepheard sicke

for Loue.

O R

The Complaint of *Daphnis* for the Loue

of *Ganimede*.

 Carce had the morning Starre hid from the
light   [spangled,
Heauens crimson Canopie with stars be-
But I began to rue th'vnhappy sight
Of that faire Boy that had my hart in-
tangled;
Cursing the   Time,   the   Place,   the
sense, the sin;
I came, I saw, I viewd, I slipped in.

If it be sinne to loue a sweet-fac'd Boy,
(Whose amber locks trust vp in golden tramels
Dangle adowne his louely cheekes with ioy,
When pearle and flowers his faire haire enamels)
If it be sinne to loue a louely Lad;
Oh then sinne I, for whom my soule is sad.

His Iuory-white and Alabaster skin
Is staind throughout with rare Vermillion red,
Whose twinckling starrie lights do neuer blin
To shine on louely *Venus* (Beauties bed :)
But as the Lillie and the blushing Rose,
So white and red on him in order growes.

Vpon a time the Nymphs bestird them-selues
To trie who could his beautie soonest win:
But he accounted them but all as Elues,
Except it were the faire Queene *Guendolen,*
   Her he embrac'd, of her was beloued,
   With plaints he proued, and with teares he moued.

But her an Old-Man had beene sutor too,
That in his age began to doate againe;
Her would he often pray, and often woo,
When through old-age enfeebled was his Braine:
   But she before had lou'd a lustie youth
   That now was dead, the cause of all her ruth.

And thus it hapned, Death and *Cupid* met
Vpon a time at swilling *Bacchus* house,
Where daintie cates vpon the Board were set,
And Goblets full of wine to drinke carouse:
   Where Loue and Death did loue the licor so,
   That out they fall and to the fray they goe.

And hauing both their Quiuers at their backe
Fild full of Arrows; Th'one of fatall steele,
The other all of gold; Deaths shaft was black,
But Loues was yellow: Fortune turnd her wheele;
   And from Deaths Quiuer fell a fatall shaft,
   That vnder *Cupid* by the winde was waft.

And at the same time by ill hap there fell
Another Arrow out of *Cupids* Quiuer;
The which was carried by the winde at will,
And vnder Death the amorous shaft did shiuer:
   They being parted, Loue tooke vp Deaths dart,
   And Death tooke vp Loues Arrow (for his part.)

Thus as they wandred both about the world,
At last Death met with one of feeble age:
Wherewith he drew a shaft and at him hurld
The vnknowne Arrow; (with a furious rage)
   Thinking to strike him dead with Deaths blacke dart,
   But he (alas) with Loue did wound his hart.

This was the doting foole, this was the man
That lou'd faire *Guendolena* Queene of Beautie;
Shee cannot shake him off, doo what she can,
For he hath vowd to her his soules last duety:
   Making him trim vpon the holy-daies;
   And crownes his Loue with Garlands made of Baies.

Now doth he stroke his Beard; and now (againe)
He wipes the driuel from his filthy chin;
Now offers he a kisse; but high Disdaine
Will not permit her hart to pity him:
   Her hart more hard than Adamant or steele,
   Her hart more changeable than Fortunes wheele.

But leaue we him in loue (vp to the eares)
And tell how Loue behau'd himselfe abroad;
Who seeing one that mourned still in teares
(a young-man groaning vnder Loues great Load)
   Thinking to ease his Burden, rid his paines:
   For men haue griefe as long as life remaines.

Alas (the while) that vnawares he drue
The fatall shaft that Death had dropt before;
By which deceit great harme did then issue,
Slaying his face with blood and filthy goare.
   His face, that was to *Guendolen* more deere
   Than loue of Lords, of any lordly Peere.

This was that faire and beautifull young-man,
Whom *Guendolena* so lamented for;
This is that Loue whom she doth curse and ban,
Because she doth that dismall chaunce abhor:
   And if it were not for his Mothers sake,
   Euen *Ganimede* himselfe she would forsake.

Oh would shee would forsake my *Ganimede*,
Whose sugred loue is full of sweete delight,
Vpon whose fore-head you may plainely reade
Loues Pleasure, grau'd in yuorie Tables bright:
   In whose faire eye-balls you may clearely see
   Base Loue still staind with foule indignitie.

Oh would to God he would but pitty mee,
That loue him more than any mortall wight;
Then he and I with loue would soone agree,
That now cannot abide his Sutors sight.
     O would to God (so I might haue my fee)
     My lips were honey, and thy mouth a Bee.

Then shouldst thou sucke my sweete and my faire flower
That now is ripe, and full of honey-berries :
Then would I leade thee to my pleasant Bower
Fild full of Grapes, of Mulberries, and Cherries ;
     Then shouldst thou be my Waspe or else my Bee,
     I would thy hiue, and thou my honey bee.

I would put amber Bracelets on thy wrests,
Crownets of Pearle about thy naked Armes :
And when thou sitst at swilling *Bacchus* feasts
My lips with charmes should saue thee from all harmes :
     And when in sleepe thou tookst thy chiefest Pleasure,
     Mine eyes should gaze vpon thine eye-lids Treasure.

And euery Morne by dawning of the day,
When *Phœbus* riseth with a blushing face,
Siluanus Chappel-Clarkes shall chaunt a Lay,
And play thee hunts-vp in thy resting place :
     My Coote thy Chamber, my bosome thy Bed ;
     Shall be appointed for thy sleepy head.

And when it pleaseth thee to walke abroad,
(Abroad into the fields to take fresh ayre :)
The Meades with *Floras* treasure should be strowde,
(The mantled meaddowes, and the fields so fayre.)
     And by a siluer Well (with golden sands)
     Ile sit me downe, and wash thine yuory hands.

And in the sweltring heate of summer time,
I would make Cabinets for thee (my Loue :)
Sweet-smelling Arbours made of Eglantine
Should be thy shrine, and I would be thy Doue.
     Coole Cabinets of fresh greene Laurell boughs
     Should shadow vs, ore-set with thicke-set Eughes.

Or if thou list to bathe thy naked limbs,
Within the Christall of a Pearle-bright brooke,
Paued with dainty pibbles to the brims;
Or cleare, wherein thyselfe thy selfe mayst looke;
   Weele goe to *Ladon*, whose still trickling noyse,
   Will lull thee fast asleepe amids thy ioyes.

Or if thoult goe vnto the Riuer side,
To angle for the sweet fresh-water fish:
Arm'd with thy implements that will abide
(Thy rod, hooke, line) to take a dainty dish;
   Thy rods shall be of cane, thy lines of silke,
   Thy hooks of siluer, and thy bayts of milke.

Or if thou lou'st to heare sweet Melodie,
Or pipe a Round vpon an Oaten Reede,
Or make thy selfe glad with some myrthfull glee,
Or play them Musicke whilst thy flocke doth feede;
   To *Pans* owne Pipe Ile helpe my louely Lad,
   (*Pans* golden Pype) which he of *Syrinx* had.

Or if thou dar'st to climbe the highest Trees
For Apples, Cherries, Medlars, Peares, or Plumbs,
Nuts, Walnuts, Filbeards, Chest-nuts, Ceruices,
The hoary Peach, when snowy winter comes;
   I haue fine Orchards full of mellowed frute;
   Which I will giue thee to obtain my sute.

Not proud *Alcynous* himselfe can vaunt,
Of goodlier Orchards or of brauer Trees
Than I haue planted; yet thou wilt not graunt
My simple sute; but like the honey Bees
   Thou suckst the flowre till all the sweet be gone;
   And lou'st mee for my Coyne till I haue none.

Leaue *Guendolen* (sweet hart) though she be faire
Yet is she light; not light in vertue shining:
But light in her behauiour, to impaire
Her honour in her Chastities declining;
   Trust not her teares, for they can watonnize,
   When teares in pearle are trickling from her eyes.

If thou wilt come and dwell with me at home;
My sheep-cote shall be strowd with new greene rushes:
Weele haunt the trembling Prickets as they rome
About the fields, along the hauthorne bushes;
   I haue a pie-bald Curre to hunt the Hare:
   So we will liue with daintie forrest fare.

Nay more than this, I haue a Garden-plot,
Wherein there wants nor hearbs, nor roots, nor flowers;
(Flowers to smell, roots to eate, hearbs for the pot,)
And dainty Shelters when the Welkin lowers:
   Sweet-smelling Beds of Lillies and of Roses,
   Which Rosemary banks and Lauender incloses.

There growes the Gilliflowre, the Mynt, the Dayzie
(Both red and white,) the blew-veynd-Violet:
The purple Hyacinth, the Spyke to please thee,
The scarlet dyde Carnation bleeding yet;
   The Sage, the Sauery, and sweet Margerum,
   Isop, Tyme, and Eye-bright, good for the blinde and dumbe.

The Pinke, the Primrose, Cowslip, and Daffadilly,
The Hare-bell blue, the crimson Cullumbine,
Sage, Lettis, Parsley, and the milke-white Lilly,
The Rose, and speckled flowre cald Sops in wine,
   Fine pretie King-cups, and the yellow Bootes,
   That growes by Riuers, and by shallow Brookes.

And manie thousand moe (I cannot name)
Of hearbs and flowers that in gardens grow,
I haue for thee; and Coneyes that be tame,
Yong Rabbets, white as Swan, and blacke as Crow,
   Some speckled here and there with daintie spots:
   And more I haue two mylch and milke-white Goates.

All these, and more, Ile giue thee for thy loue;
If these, and more, may tyce thy loue away:
I haue a Pidgeon-house, in it a Doue,
Which I loue more than mortall tongue can say:
   And last of all, Ile giue thee a little Lambe
   To play withall, new weaned from her Dam.

But if thou wilt not pittie my Complaint,
My Teares, nor Vowes, nor Oathes, made to thy Beautie:
What shall I doo ? But languish, die, or faint,
Since thou dost scorne my Teares, and my Soules Duetie :
　　And Teares contemned, Vowes and Oaths must faile;
　　For where Teares cannot, nothing can preuaile.

Compare the loue of faire Queene *Guendolin*
With mine, and thou shalt [s]ee how she doth loue thee:
I loue thee for thy qualities diuine,
But She doth loue another Swaine aboue thee :
　　I loue thee for thy gifts, She for hir pleasure ;
　　I for thy Vertue, She for Beauties treasure.

And alwaies (I am sure) it cannot last,
But sometime Nature will denie those dimples:
In steed of Beautie (when thy Blossom's past)
Thy face will be deformed, full of wrinckles:
　　Then She that lou'd thee for thy Beauties sake,
　　When Age drawes on, thy loue will soone forsake.

But I that lou'd thee for thy gifts diuine,
In the December of thy Beauties waning,
Will still admire (with ioy) those louely eine,
That now behold me with their beauties baning :
　　Though Ianuarie will neuer come againe,
　　Yet Aprill yeres will come in showers of raine.

When will my May come, that I may embrace thee ?
When will the hower be of my soules ioying ?
Why dost thou seeke in mirthe still to disgrace mee ?
Whose mirth's my health, whose griefe's my harts annoying.
　　Thy bane my bale, thy blisse my blessednes,
　　Thy ill my hell, thy weale my welfare is.

Thus doo I honour thee that loue thee so,
And loue thee so, that so doo honour thee,
Much more than anie mortall man doth know,
Or can discerne by Loue or Iealozie :
　　But if that thou disdainst my louing euer;
　　Oh happie I, if I had loued neuer. *Finis.*

　　　　Plus fellis quam mellis Amor.

The second Dayes Lamentation of

the *Affectionate Shepheard.*

 Ext Morning when the golden Sunne was risen,
And new had bid good morrow to the Mountaines;
When Night her siluer light had lockt in prison,
Which gaue a glimmering on the christall
 Fountaines :
  Then ended sleepe : and then my cares began,
  Eu'n with the vprising of the siluer Swan.

O glorious Sunne quoth I, (viewing the Sunne)
That lightenst euerie thing but me alone :
Why is my Summer season almost done ?
My Spring-time past, and Ages Autumne gone ?
 My Haruest's come, and yet I reapt no corne :
 My loue is great, and yet I am forlorne.

Witnes these watrie eyes my sad lament
(Receauing cisternes of my ceaseles teares),
Witnes my bleeding hart my soules intent,
Witnes the weight distressed *Daphnis* beares :
 Sweet Loue, come ease me of thy burthens paine ;
 Or els I die, or else my hart is slaine.

And thou loue-scorning Boy, cruell, vnkinde ;
Oh let me once againe intreat some pittie :
May be thou wilt relent thy marble minde,
And lend thine eares vnto my dolefull Dittie :
 Oh pittie him, that pittie craues so sweetly ;
 Or else thou shalt be neuer named meekly.

If thou wilt loue me, thou shalt be my Boy,
My sweet Delight, the Comfort of my minde,
My Loue, my Doue, my Sollace, and my Ioy :
But if I can no grace nor mercie finde,
 Ile goe to *Caucasus* to ease my smart,
 And let a Vulture gnaw vpon my hart.

Yet if thou wilt but show me one kinde looke
(A small reward for my so great affection)
Ile graue thy name in Beauties golden Booke,
And shrowd thee vnder *Hellicons* protection ;
    Making the Muses chaunt thy louely prayse :
    (For they delight in Shepheards lowly layes.)

And when th'art wearie of thy keeping Sheepe
Vpon a louely Downe, (to please thy minde)
Ile giue thee fine ruffe-footed Doues to keepe,
And pretie Pidgeons of another kinde :
    A Robbin-red-brest shall thy Minstrell bee,
    Chirping thee sweet, and pleasant Melodie.

Or if thou wilt goe shoote at little Birds
With bow and boult (the Thrustle-cocke and Sparrow)
Such as our Countrey hedges can afford's ;
I haue a fine bowe, and an yuorie arrow :
    And if thou misse, yet meate thou shalt [not] lacke,
    Ile hang a bag and bottle at thy backe.

Wilt thou set springes in a frostie Night,
To catch the long-billd Woodcocke and the Snype ?
(By the bright glimmering of the Starrie light)
The Partridge, Phæsant, or the greedie Grype ?
    Ile lend thee lyme-twigs, and fine sparrow calls,
    Wherewith the Fowler silly Birds inthralls.

Or in a mystie morning if thou wilt
Make pit-falls for the Larke and Pheldifare ;
Thy prop and sweake shall be both ouer-guilt ;
With *Cyparissus* selfe thou shalt compare
    For gins and wyles, the Oozels to beguile ;
    Whilst thou vnder a bush shalt sit and smile.

Or with Hare-pypes (set in a muset hole)
Wilt thou deceaue the deep-earth-deluing Coney ?
Or wilt thou in a yellow Boxen bole,
Taste with a woodden splent the sweet lythe honey ?
    Clusters of crimson Grapes Ile pull thee downe ;
    And with Vine-leaues make thee a louely Crowne.

Or wilt thou drinke a cup of new-made Wine
Froathing at top, mixt with a dish of Creame;
And Straw-berries, or Bil-berries in their prime,
Bath'd in a melting Sugar-Candie streame :
    Bunnell and Perry I haue for thee (alone)
    When Vynes are dead, and all the Grapes are gone.

I haue a pleasant noted Nightingale,
(That sings as sweetly as the siluer Swan)
Kept in a Cage of bone; as white as Whale,
Which I with singing of *Philemon* wan :
    Her shalt thou haue, and all I haue beside;
    If thou wilt be my Boy, or else my Bride.

Then will I lay out all my Lardarie
(Of Cheese, of Cracknells, Curds and Clowted-creame)
Before thy male-content ill-pleasing eye :
But why doo I of such great follies dreame ?
    Alas, he will not see my simple Coate;
    For all my speckled Lambe, nor milk-white Goate.

Against my Birth-day thou shalt be my guest :
Weele haue Greene-cheeses and fine Silly-bubs;
And thou shalt be the chiefe of all my feast.
And I will giue thee two fine pretie Cubs,
    With two young Whelps, to make thee sport withall,
    A golden Racket, and a Tennis-ball.

A guilded Nutmeg, and a race of Ginger,
A silken Girdle, and a drawn-worke Band,
Cuffs for thy wrists, a gold Ring for thy finger,
And sweet Rose-water for thy Lilly-white hand,
    A Purse of silke, bespangd with spots of gold,
    As braue a one as ere thou didst behold.

A paire of Kniues, a greene Hat and a Feather,
New Gloues to put vpon thy milk-white hand
Ile giue thee, for to keep thee from the weather;
With Phœnix feathers shall thy Face be fand,
    Cooling those Cheekes, that being cool'd wexe red,
    Like Lillyes in a bed of Roses shed.

Why doo thy Corall lips disdaine to kisse,
And sucke that Sweete, which manie haue desired?
That Baulme my Bane, that meanes would mend my misse :
Oh let me then with thy sweete Lips b'inspired ;
    When thy Lips touch my Lips, my Lips will turne
    To Corall too, and being cold yce will burne.

Why should thy sweete Loue-locke hang dangling downe,
Kissing thy girdle-steed with falling pride ?
Although thy Skin be white, thy haire is browne :
Oh let not then thy haire thy beautie hide ;
    Cut off thy Locke, and sell it for gold wier :
    (The purest gold is tryde in hottest fier).

Faire-long-haire-wearing *Absolon* was kild,
Because he wore it in a brauerie :
So that whiche gracde his Beautie, Beautie spild,
Making him subiect to vile slauerie,
    In being hangd : a death for him too good,
    That sought his owne shame, and his Fathers blood.

Againe, we read of old King *Priamus*,
(The haplesse syre of valiant *Hector* slaine)
That his haire was so long and odious
In youth, that in his age it bred his paine :
    For if his haire had not been halfe so long,
    His life had been, and he had had no wrong.

For when his stately Citie was destroyd
(That Monument of great Antiquitie)
When his poore hart (with griefe and sorrow cloyd)
Fled to his Wife (last hope in miserie ;)
    Pyrrhus (more hard than Adamantine rockes)
    Held him and halde him by his aged lockes.

These two examples by the way I show,
To proue th'indecencie of mens long haire :
Though I could tell thee of a thousand moe,
Let these suffice for thee (my louely Faire)
    Whose eye's my starre ; whose smiling is my Sunne ;
    Whose loue did ende before my ioys begunne.

Fond Loue is blinde, and so art thou (my Deare)
For thou seest not my Loue, and great desart;
Blinde Loue is fond, and so thou dost appeare;
For fond, and blinde, thou greeust my greeuing hart:
   Be thou fond-blinde, blinde-fond, or one, or all:
   Thou art my Loue, and I must be thy thrall.

Oh lend thine yuorie fore-head for Loues Booke,
Thine eyes for candles to behold the same;
That when dim-sighted ones therein shall looke
They may discerne that proud disdainefull Dame;
   Yet claspe that Booke, and shut that Cazement light;
   Lest th'one obscurde, the other shine too bright.

Sell thy sweet breath to th'daintie Musk-ball-makers;
Yet sell it so as thou mayst soone redeeme it:
Let others of thy beauty be pertakers;
Els none but *Daphnis* will so well esteeme it:
   For what is Beauty except it be well knowne?
   And how can it be knowne, except first showne?

Learne of the Gentlewomen of this Age,
That set their Beauties to the open view,
Making Disdaine their Lord, true Loue their Page;
A Custome Zeale doth hate, Desert doth rue:
   Learne to looke red, anon waxe pale and wan,
   Making a mocke of Loue, a scorne of man.

A candle light, and couer'd with a vaile,
Doth no man good, because it giues no light;
So Beauty of her beauty seemes to faile,
When being not seene it cannot shine so bright.
   Then show thy selfe and know thy selfe withall,
   Lest climing high thou catch too great a fall.

Oh foule Eclipser of that fayre sun-shine,
Which is intitled Beauty in the best;
Making that mortall, which is els diuine,
That staines the fayre which Womens steeme not least:
   Get thee to Hell againe (from whence thou art)
   And leaue the Center of a Woman's hart.

Ah be not staind, (sweet Boy) with this vilde spot,
Indulgence Daughter, Mother of mischaunce;
A blemish that doth euery beauty blot;
That makes them loath'd, but neuer doth aduaunce
    Her Clyents, fautors, friends; or them that loue her;
    And hates them most of all, that most reproue her.

Remember Age, and thou canst not be prowd,
For age puls downe the pride of euery man;
In youthfull yeares by Nature tis allowde
To haue selfe-will, doo Nurture what she can ;
    Nature and Nurture once together met,
    The Soule and shape in decent order set.

Pride looks aloft, still staring on the starres,
Humility looks lowly on the ground;
Th'one menaceth the Gods with ciuill warres,
The other toyles til he haue Vertue found:
    His thoughts are humble, not aspiring hye;
    But Pride looks haughtily with scornefull eye.

Humillity is clad in modest weedes,
But Pride is braue and glorious to the show;
Humillity his friends with kindnes feedes,
But Pride his friends (in neede) will neuer know:
    Supplying not their wants, but them disdaining;
    Whilst they to pitty neuer neede complayning.

Humillity in misery is relieu'd,
But Pride in neede of no man is regarded;
Pitty and Mercy weepe to see him grieu'd
That in distresse had them so well rewarded:
    But Pride is scornd, contemnd, disdaind, derided,
    Whilst Humblenes of all things is prouided.

Oh then be humble, gentle, meeke, and milde ;
So shalt thou be of euery mouth commended;
Be not disdainfull, cruell, proud, (sweet childe)
So shalt thou be of no man much condemned;
    Care not for them that Vertue doo despise;
    Vertue is loathde of fooles; loude of the wise.

O faire Boy trust not to thy Beauties wings,
They cannot carry thee aboue the Sunne:
Beauty and wealth are transitory things,
(For all must ende that euer was begunne)
    But Fame and Vertue neuer shall decay;
    For Fame is toombles, Vertue liues for aye.

The snow is white, and yet the pepper's blacke,
The one is bought, the other is contemned:
Pibbles we haue, but store of Ieat we lacke;
So white comparde to blacke is much condemned:
    We doo not praise the Swanne because shees white,
    But for she doth in Musique much delite.

And yet the siluer-noted Nightingale,
Though she be not so white is more esteemed;
Sturgion is dun of hew, white is the Whale,
Yet for the daintier Dish the first is deemed;
    What thing is whiter than the milke-bred Lilly?
    Thou knowes it not for naught, what man so silly?

Yea what more noysomer vnto the smell
Than Lillies are? what's sweeter than the Sage?
Yet for pure white the Lilly beares the Bell
Till it be faded through decaying Age;
    House-Doues are white, and Oozels Blacke-birds bee;
    Yet what a difference in the taste, we see.

Compare the Cow and Calfe, with Ewe and Lambe;
Rough hayrie Hydes, with softest downy Fell;
Hecfar and Bull, with Weather and with Ramme,
And you shall see how far they doo excell;
    White Kine with blacke, blacke Coney-skins with gray,
    Kine, nesh and strong; skin, deare and cheape alway.

The whitest siluer is not alwaies best,
Lead, Tynne, and Pewter are of base esteeme;
The yellow burnisht gold, that comes from th'East,
And West (of late inuented), may beseeme
    The worlds ritch Treasury, or *Mydas* eye;
    (The Ritch mans God, poore mans felicitie.)

Bugle and Ieat, with snow and Alablaster
I will compare : White Dammasin with blacke ;
Bullas and wheaton Plumbs, (to a good Taster,)
The ripe red Cherries haue the sweetest smacke ;
   When they be greene and young, th'are sowre and naught ;
   But being ripe, with eagerness th'are baught.

Compare the Wyld-cat to the brownish Beauer,
Running for life, with hounds pursued sore ;
When Hunts-men of her pretious Stones bereaue her
(Which with her teeth sh'had bitten off before) :
   Restoratiues, and costly curious Felts
   Are made of them, and rich imbroydred Belts.

To what vse serues a peece of crimbling Chalke ?
The Agget stone is white, yet good for nothing :
Fie, fie, I am asham'd to heare thee talke ;
Be not so much of thine owne Image doating :
   So faire *Narcissus* lost his loue and life.
   (Beautie is often with itselfe at strife).

Right Diamonds are of a russet hieu,
The brightsome Carbuncles are red to see too,
The Saphyre stone is of a watchet blue,
(To this thou canst not chuse but soone agree too):
   Pearles are not white but gray, Rubies are red :
   In praise of Blacke, what can be better sed ?

For if we doo consider of each mortall thing
That flyes in welkin, or in waters swims,
How euerie thing increaseth with the Spring,
And how the blacker still the brighter dims :
   We cannot chuse, but needs we must confesse,
   Sable excels milk-white in more or lesse.

As for example, in the christall cleare
Of a sweete streame, or pleasant running Riuer,
Where thousand formes of fishes will appeare,
(Whose names to thee I cannot now deliuer :)
   The blacker still the brighter haue disgrac'd,
   For pleasant profit, and delicious taste.

Salmon and Trout are of a ruddie colour,
Whiting and Dare is of a milk-white hiew :
Nature by them (perhaps) is made the fuller,
Little they nourish, be they old or new :
   Carp, Loach, Tench, Eeles (though black and bred in mud)
   Delight the tooth with taste, and breed good blud.

Innumerable be the kindes, if I could name them ;
But I a Shepheard, and no Fisher am :
Little it skills whether I praise or blame them,
I onely meddle with my Ew and Lamb :
   Yet this I say, that blacke the better is,
   In birds, beasts, frute, stones, flowres, herbs, mettals, fish.

And last of all, in blacke there doth appeare
Such qualities, as not in yuorie ;
Black cannot blush for shame, looke pale for fear,
Scorning to weare another liuorie.
   Blacke is the badge of sober Modestie,
   The wonted weare of ancient Grauetie.

The learned Sisters sute themselues in blacke,
Learning abandons white, and lighter hues :
Pleasure and Pride light colours neuer lacke ;
But true Religion doth such Toyes refuse :
   Vertue and Grauity are sisters growne,
   Since blacke by both, and both by blacke are knowne.

White is the colour of each paltry Miller,
White is the Ensigne of each comman Woman ;
White, is white Vertues for blacke Vyces Piller ;
White makes proud fooles inferiour vnto no man :
   White, is the white of Body, blacke of Minde,
   (Vertue we seldome in white Habit finde.)

Oh then be not so proud because th'art fayre,
Vertue is onely the ritch gift of God :
Let not selfe-pride thy vertues name impayre,
Beate not greene youth with sharpe Repentance Rod :
   (A Fiend, a Monster, and mishapen Diuel ;
   Vertues foe, Vyces friend, the roote of euill.)

Apply thy minde to be a vertuous man,
Auoyd ill company (the spoyle of youth ;)
To follow Vertues Lore doo what thou can
(Whereby great profit vnto thee ensu[e]th :)
  Reade Bookes, hate Ignorance, (the foe to Art,
  The Damme of Errour, Enuy of the hart).

Serue *Ioue* (vpon thy knees) both day and night,
Adore his Name aboue all things on Earth :
So shall thy vowes be gracious in his sight,
So little Babes are blessed in their Birth :
  Thinke on no worldly woe, lament thy sin ;
  (For lesser cease, when greater griefes begin).

Sweare no vaine oathes ; heare much, but little say ;
Speake ill of no man, tend thine owne affaires,
Bridle thy wrath, thine angrie mood delay ;
(So shall thy minde be seldome cloyd with cares :)
  Be milde and gentle in thy speech to all,
  Refuse no honest gaine when it doth fall.

Be not beguild with words, proue not vngratefull,
Releeue thy Neighbour in his greatest need,
Commit no action that to all is hatefull,
Their want with welth, the poore with plentie feed:
  Twit no man in the teeth with what th'hast done ;
  Remember flesh is fraile, and hatred shunne.

Leaue wicked things, which Men to mischiefe moue,
(Least crosse mis-hap may thee in danger bring,)
Craue no preferment of thy heauenly *Ioue*,
Nor anie honor of thy earthly King :
  Boast not thy selfe before th'Almighties sight,
  (Who knowes thy hart, and anie wicked wight).

Be not offensiue to the peoples eye,
See that thy praiers harts true zeale affords,
Scorne not a man that's falne in miserie,
Esteeme no tatling tales, nor babling words;
  That reason is exiled alwaies thinke,
  When as a drunkard rayles amidst his drinke.

Vse not thy louely lips to loathsome lyes,
By craftie meanes increase no worldly wealth;
Striue not with mightie Men (whose fortune flies)
With temp'rate diet nourish wholesome health:
　　Place well thy words, leaue not thy frend for gold;
　　First trie, then trust; in ventring be not bold.

In *Pan* repose thy trust; extoll his praise
(That neuer shall decay, but euer liues):
Honor thy Parents (to prolong thy dayes),
Let not thy left hand know what right hand giues:
　　From needie men turn not thy face away,
　　(Though Charitie be now yclad in clay).

Heare Shepheards oft (thereby great wisdome growes),
With good aduice a sober answere make:
Be not remoou'd with euery winde that blowes,
(That course doo onely sinfull sinners take).
　　Thy talke will shew thy fame or els thy shame;
　　(As pratling tongue doth often purchase blame).

Obtaine a faithfull frend that will not faile thee,
Thinke on thy Mothers paine in her child-bearing,
Make no debate, least quickly thou bewaile thee,
Visit the sicke with comfortable chearing:
　　Pittie the prisner, helpe the fatherlesse,
　　Reuenge the Widdowes wrongs in her distresse.

Thinke on thy graue, remember still thy end,
Let not thy winding-sheete be staind with guilt,
Trust not a fained reconciled frend,
More than an open foe (that blood hath spilt)
　　(Who tutcheth pitch, with pitch shalbe defiled),
　　Be not with wanton companie beguiled.

Take not a flattring woman to thy wife,
A shameles creature, full of wanton words,
(Whose bad, thy good; whose lust will end thy life,
Cutting thy hart with sharpe two edged swords:)
　　Cast not thy minde on her whose lookes allure,
　　But she that shines in Truth and Vertue pure.

Praise not thy selfe, let other men commend thee;
Beare not a flattring tongue to glauer anie,
Let Parents due correction not offend thee:
Rob not thy neighbor, seeke the loue of manie;
  Hate not to heare good Counsell giuen thee,
  Lay not thy money vnto Vsurie.

Restraine thy steps from too much libertie,
Fulfill not th'enuious mans malitious minde;
Embrace thy Wife, liue not in lecherie;
Content thyselfe with what Fates haue assignde:
  Be rul'd by Reason, Warning dangers saue;
  True Age is reuerend worship to thy graue.

Be patient in extreame Aduersitie,
(Man's chiefest credit growes by dooing well,)
Be no high-minded in Prosperity;
Falshood abhorre, nor lying fable tell.
  Giue not thy selfe to Sloth, (the sinke of Shame,
  The moath of Time, the enemie to Fame.)

This leare I learned of a Bel-dame Trot,
(When I was yong and wylde as now thou art):
But her good counsell I regarded not;
I markt it with my eares, not with my hart:
  But now I finde it too–too true (my Sonne),
  When my Age-withered Spring is almost done.

Behold my gray head, full of siluer haires,
My wrinckled skin, deepe furrowes in my face:
Cares bring Old-Age, Old-Age increaseth cares;
My Time is come, and I haue run my Race:
  Winter hath snow'd vpon my hoarie head,
  And with my Winter all my ioys are dead.

And thou loue-hating Boy, (whom once I loued),
Farewell, a thousand-thousand times farewell;
My Teares the Marble Stones to ruth haue moued;
My sad Complaints the babling Ecchoes tell:
  And yet thou wouldst take no compassion on mee,
  Scorning that crosse which Loue hath laid vpon mee.

The hardest steele with fier doth mend his misse,
Marble is mollifyde with drops of Raine ;
But thou (more hard than Steele or Marble is)
Doost scorne my Teares, and my true loue disdaine,
　　Which for thy sake shall euerlasting bee,
　　Wrote in the Annalls of Eternitie.

By this, the Night (with darknes ouer-spred)
Had drawne the curtaines of her cole-blacke bed ;
And *Cynthia* muffling her face with a clowd,
(Lest all the world of her should be too prowd)
　　Had taken *Conge* of the sable Night,
　　(That wanting her cannot be halfe so bright ;)

When I poore forlorne man and outcast creature
(Despairing of my Loue, despisde of Beautie)
Grew male-content, scorning his louely feature,
That had disdaind my euer-zealous dutie :
　　I hy'd me homeward by the Moone-shine light ;
　　Forswearing Loue, and all his fond delight.

FINIS.

The Shepherds Content

OR

The happines of a harmless life.

Written upon Occasion of the

former Subject.

O F all the kindes of common Countrey life,
  Me thinkes a Shepheards life is most Con-
    tent;
His State is quiet Peace, deuoyd of strife;
His thoughts are pure from all impure
    intent,
His Pleasures rate sits at an easie rent:
    He beares no mallice in his harmles hart,
    Malicious meaning hath in him no part.

He is not troubled with th'afflicted minde,
His cares are onely ouer silly Sheepe;
He is not vnto Iealozie inclinde,
(Thrice happie Man) he knowes not how to weepe;
Whil'st I the Treble in deepe sorrowes keepe;
  I cannot keepe the Meane; for why (alas)
  Griefes haue no meane, though I for meane doe passe.

No Briefes nor Semi-Briefes are in my Songs,
Because (alas) my griefe is seldome shoot;
My Prick-Song's alwayes full of Largues and Longs,
(Because I neuer can obtaine the Port
Of my desires: Hope is a happie Fort.)
  Prick-song (indeed) because it pricks my hart;
  And Song, because sometimes I ease my smart.

The mightie Monarch of a royall Realme,
Swaying his Scepter with a Princely pompe ;
Of his desires cannot so steare the Healme,
But sometime falls into a deadly dumpe,
When as he heares the shrilly-sounding Trumpe
  Of Forren Enemies, or home-bred Foes ;
   His minde of griefe, his hart is full of woes.

Or when bad subiects gainst their Soueraigne
(Like hollow harts) vnnaturally rebell,
How carefull is he to suppresse againe
Their desperate forces, and their powers to quell
With loyall harts, till all (againe) be well :
  When (being subdu'd) his care is rather more
   To keepe them vnder, than it was before.

Thus is he neuer full of sweete Content,
But either this or that his ioy debars :
Now Noble-men gainst Noble-men are bent,
Now Gentlemen and others fall at iarrs :
Thus is his Countrey full of ciuill warrs ;
  He still in danger sits, still fearing Death :
   For Traitors seeke to stop their Princes breath.

The whylst the other hath no enemie,
Without it be the Wolfe and cruell Fates
(Which no man spare): when as his disagree
He with his sheep-hooke knaps them on the pates,
Schooling his tender Lambs from wanton gates :
  Beasts are more kinde then Men, Sheepe seeke not blood
   But countrey caytiues kill their Countreyes good.

The Courtier he fawn's for his Princes fauour,
In hope to get a Princely ritch Reward ;
His tongue is tipt with honey for to glauer ;
Pride deales the Deck whilst Chance doth choose the Card,
Then comes another and his Game hath mard ;
  Sitting betwixt him, and the morning Sun :
   Thus Night is come before the Day is done.

Some Courtiers carefull of their Princes health,
Attends his Person with all dilligence
Whose hand's their hart ; whose welfare is their wealth,
Whose safe Protection is their sure Defence,
For pure affection, not for hope of pence :
    Such is the faithfull hart, such is the minde,
    Of him that is to Vertue still inclinde.

The skilfull Scholler, and braue man at Armes,
First plies his Booke, last fights for Countries Peace ;
Th'one feares Obliuion, th'other fresh Alarmes ;
His paines nere ende, his trauailes neuer cease ;
His with the Day, his with the Night increase :
    He studies how to get eternall Fame ;
    The Souldier fights to win a glorious Name.

The Knight, the Squire, the Gentleman, the Clowne,
Are full of crosses and calamities ;
Lest fickle Fortune should begin to frowne,
And turne their mirth to extreame miseries :
Nothing more certaine than incertainties ;
    Fortune is full of fresh varietie :
    Constant in nothing but inconstancie.

The wealthie Merchant that doth crosse the Seas,
To *Denmarke*, *Poland*, *Spaine*, and *Barbarie* ;
For all his ritches, liues not still at ease ;
Sometimes he feares ship-spoyling Pyracie,
Another while deceipt and treacherie
    Of his owne Factors in a forren Land ;
    Thus doth he still in dread and danger stand.

Well is he tearmd a Merchant-Venturer,
Since he doth venter lands, and goods, and all :
When he doth trauell for his Traffique far,
Little he knowes what fortune may befall,
Or rather what mis-fortune happen shall :
    Sometimes he splits his Ship against a rocke ;
    Loosing his men, his goods, his wealth, his stocke.

And if he so escape with life away,
He counts himselfe a man most fortunate,
Because the waues their rigorous rage did stay,
(When being within their cruell powers of late,
The Seas did seeme to pittie his estate)
 But yet he neuer can recouer health,
 Because his ioy was drowned with his wealth.

The painfull Plough-swaine, and the Husband-man
Rise vp each morning by the breake of day,
Taking what toyle and drudging paines they can,
And all is for to get a little stay ;
And yet they cannot put their care away :
 When Night is come, their cares begin afresh,
 Thinking vpon their Morrowes busines.

Thus euerie man is troubled with vnrest,
From rich to poore, from high to low degree :
Therefore I thinke that man is truly blest,
That neither cares for wealth nor pouertie,
But laughs at Fortune and her foolerie ;
 That giues rich Churles great store of golde and fee,
 And lets poore Schollers liue in miserie,

O fading Branches of decaying Bayes
Who now will water your dry-wither'd Armes ?
Or where is he that sung the louely Layes
Of simple Shepheards in their Countrey-Farmes ?
Ah he is dead, the cause of all our harmes :
 And with him dide my ioy and sweete delight ;
 And cleare to Clowdes, the Day is turnd to Night.

SYDNEY. The Syren of this latter Age ;
SYDNEY. The Blasing-starre of England's glory ;
SYDNEY. The Wonder of wise and sage ;
SYDNEY. The Subiect of true Vertues story ;
 This Syren, Starre, this Wonder, and this Subiect ;
 In dumbe, dim, gone, and mard by Fortunes Obiect.

And thou my sweete *Amintas* vertuous minde,
Should I forget thy Learning or thy Loue;
Well might I be accounted but vnkinde,
Whose pure affection I so oft did proue:
Might my poore Plaints hard stones to pitty moue;
   His losse should be lamented of each Creature,
   So great his Name, so gentle was his Nature.

But sleepe his soule in sweet Elysium,
(The happy Hauen of eternall rest :)
And let me to my former matter come,
Prouing by Reason, Shepheard's life is best,
Because he harbours Vertue in his Brest;
   And is content (the chiefest thing of all)
   With any fortune that shall him befall.

He sits all Day lowd-piping on a Hill,
The whilst his flocke about him daunce apace,
His hart with ioy, his eares with Musique fill:
Anon a bleating Weather beares the Bace,
A Lambe the Treble; and to his disgrace
   Another answers like a middle Meane:
   Thus euery one to beare a Part are faine.

Like a great King he rules a little Land,
Still making Statutes, and ordayning Lawes;
Which if they breake, he beates them with his Wand:
He doth defend them from the greedy Iawes
Of rau'ning Woolues, and Lyons bloudy Pawes.
   His Field, his Realme; his Subiects are his Sheepe;
   Which he doth still in due obedience keepe.

First he ordaines by Act of Parlament,
(Holden by custome in each Countrey Towne),
That if a sheepe (with any bad intent)
Presume to breake the neighbour Hedges downe,
Or haunt strange Pastures that be not his owne;
   He shall be pounded for his lustines,
   Vntill his Master finde out some redres.

Also if any proue a Strageller
From his owne fellowes in a forraine field,
He shall be taken for a wanderer,
And forc'd himselfe immediatly to yeeld,
Or with a wyde-mouth'd Mastiue Curre be kild.
    And if not claimd within a twelue-month's space,
    He shall remaine with Land-lord of the place.

Or if one stray to feede far from the rest,
He shall be pincht by his swift pye-bald Curre;
If any by his fellowes be opprest,
The wronger (for he doth all wrong abhorre)
Shall be well bangd so long as he can sturre.
    Because he did anoy his harmeles Brother,
    That meant not harme to him nor any other.

And last of all, if any wanton Weather,
With briers and brambles teare his fleece in twaine,
He shall be forc'd t'abide cold frosty weather,
And powring showres of ratling stormes of raine,
Till his new fleece begins to grow againe:
    And for his rashnes he is doom'd to goe
    without a new Coate all the Winter throw.

Thus doth he keepe them, still in awfull feare,
And yet allowes them liberty inough;
So deare to him their welfare doth appeare,
That when their fleeces gin to waxen rough,
He combs and trims them with a Rampicke bough,
    Washing them in the streames of siluer *Ladon*,
    To cleanse their skinnes from all corruption.

Another while he wooes his Country Wench,
(With Chaplets crownd, and gaudy girlonds dight)
Whose burning Lust her modest eye doth quench,
Standing amazed at her heauenly sight,
(Beauty doth rauish Sense with sweet Delight)
    Clearing *Arcadia* with a smoothed Browe
    When Sun-bright smiles melts flakes of driuen snowe.

Thus doth he frollicke it each day by day,
And when Night comes drawes homeward to his Coate,
Singing a Iigge or merry Roundelay ;
(For who sings commonly so merry a Noate,
As he that cannot chop or change a groate)
   And in the winter Nights (his chiefe desire)
   He turns a Crabbe or Cracknell in the fire.

He leads his Wench a Country Horn-pipe Round,
About a May-pole on a Holy-day ;
Kissing his louely Lasse (with Garlands Crownd)
With whooping heigh-ho singing Care away ;
Thus doth he passe the merry month of May :
   And all th'yere after in delight and ioy,
   (Scorning a King) he cares for no annoy.

What though with simple cheere he homely fares ?
He liues content, a King can doo no more ;
Nay not so much, for Kings haue manie cares :
But he hath none ; except it be that sore
Which yong and old, which vexeth ritch and poore,
   The pangs of Loue.   O ! who can vanquish Loue ?
   That conquers Kingdomes, and the Gods aboue ?

Deepe-wounding Arrow, hart-consuming Fire ;
Ruler of·Reason, slaue to tyraunt Beautie ;
Monarch of harts, Fuell of fond desire,
Prentice to Folly, foe to faind Duetie.
Pledge of true Zeale, Affections moitie ;
   If thou kilst where thou wilt, and whom it list thee,
   (Alas) how can a silly Soule resist thee ?

By thee great *Collin* lost his libertie,
By thee sweet *Astrophel* forwent his ioy ;
By thee *Amyntas* wept incessantly,
By thee good *Rowland* liu'd in great annoy ;
O cruell, peeuish, vylde, blind-seeing Boy :
   How canst thou hit their harts, and yet not see ?
   (If thou be blinde, as thou art faind to bee).

A Shepheard loues no ill, but onely thee;
He hath no care, but onely by thy causing:
Why doost thou shoot thy cruell shafts at mee?
Giue me some respite, some short time of pausing:
Still my sweet Loue with bitter lucke th'art sawcing:
    Oh, if thou hast a minde to shew thy might;
    Kill mightie Kings, and not a wretched wight.

Yet (O Enthraller of infranchizd harts)
At my poor hart if thou wilt needs be ayming,
Doo me the fauour, show me both thy Darts,
That I may chuse the best for my harts mayming,
(A free consent is priuiledgd from blaming:)
    Then pierce his hard hart with thy golden Arrow,
    That thou my wrong, that he may rue my sorrow.

But let mee feele the force of thy lead Pyle,
What should I doo with loue when I am old?
I know not how to flatter, fawne, or smyle;
Then stay thy hand, O cruell Bow-man hold:
For if thou strik'st me with thy dart of gold,
    I sweare to thee (by Ioues immortall curse)
    I haue more in my hart, than in my purse.

The more I weepe, the more he bends his Bow,
For in my hart a golden Shaft I finde:
(Cruell, vnkinde) and wilt thou leaue me so?
Can no remorce nor pittie moue thy minde?
Is Mercie in the Heauens so hard to finde?
    Oh, then it is no meruaile that on earth
    Of kinde Remorce there is so great a dearth.

How happie were a harmles Shepheards life,
If he had neuer knowen what Loue did meane;
But now fond Loue in euery place is rife,
Staining the purest Soule with spots vncleane,
Making thicke purses, thin: and fat bodies, leane:
    Loue is a fiend, a fire, a heauen, a hell;
    Where pleasure, paine, and sad repentance dwell.

There are so manie *Danaes* nowadayes,
That loue for lucre; paine for gaine is sold:
No true affection can their fancie please,
Except it be a *Ioue*, to raine downe gold
Into their laps, which they wyde open hold:
   If *legem pone* comes, he is receau'd,
   When *Vix haud habeo* is of hope bereau'd.

Thus haue I showed in my Countrey vaine
The sweet Content that Shepheards still inioy;
The mickle pleasure, and the little paine
That euer doth awayte the Shepheards Boy:
His hart is neuer troubled with annoy.
   He is a King, for he commands his Sheepe;
   He knowes no woe, for he doth seldome weepe.

He is a Courtier, for he courts his Loue:
He is a Scholler, for he sings sweet Ditties:
He is a Souldier, for he wounds doth proue;
He is the fame of Townes, the shame of Citties;
He scornes false Fortune, put true Vertue pitties.
   He is a Gentleman, because his nature
   Is kinde and affable to euerie Creature.

Who would not then a simple Shepheard bee,
Rather than be a mightie Monarch made?
Since he inioyes such perfect libertie,
As neuer can decay, nor neuer fade:
He seldome sits in dolefull Cypresse shade,
   But liues in hope, in ioy, in peace, in blisse:
   Ioying all ioy with this content of his.

But now good-fortune lands my little Boate
Vpon the shoare of his desired rest:
Now I must leaue (awhile) my rurall noate,
To thinke on him whom my soule loueth best;
He that can make the most vnhappie blest:
   In whose sweete lap Ile lay me downe to sleepe,
   And neuer wake till Marble-stones shall weepe.

FINIS.

SONNET.

OE here behold these tributarie Teares
 Paid to thy faire, but cruell tyrant Eyes;
Loe here the blossome of my youthfull
  yeares,
 Nipt with the fresh of thy Wraths winter,
  dyes,

Here on Loues Altar I doo offer vp
This burning hart for my Soules sacrifice;
Here I receaue this deadly-poysned Cu[p]
Of *Circe* charm'd; wherein deepe Magicke lyes.

Then Teares (if thou be happie Teares indeed),
And Hart (if thou be lodged in his brest),
And Cup (if thou canst helpe despaire with speed);
Teares, Hart, and Cup conjoyne to make me blest:
 Teares moue, Hart win, Cup cause, ruth, loue, desire,
 In word, in deed, by moane, by zeale, by fire.

FINIS.

THE COMPLAINT
OF CHASTITIE.

Briefely touching the cause of the
death of *Matilda Fitzwalters* an English
Ladie; sometime loued of King *Iohn*,
after poysoned. The Storie is at large
written by *Michael Dreyton*.

Ou modest Dames, inricht with Chastitie.
Maske your bright eyes with *Vestaes* sable
   Vaile,
Since few are left so faire or chast as shee;
(Matter for me to weepe, you to bewaile):
For manie seeming so, of Vertue faile;
   Whose louely Cheeks (with rare ver-
     million tainted)
   Can neuer blush because their faire is
     painted.

O faire-foule Tincture, staine of Woman-kinde,
Mother of Mischiefe, Daughter of Deceate,
False traitor to the Soule, blot to the Minde,
Vsurping Tyrant of true Beauties seate,
Right Cousner of the eye, lewd Follies baite,
   The flag of filthines, the sinke of shame,
   The Diuells dye, dishonour of thy name.

Monster of Art, Bastard of bad Desier,
Il-worshipt Idoll, false Imagerie,
Ensigne of Vice, to thine owne selfe a lier,
Silent Inchaunter, mindes Anatomie,
Sly Bawd to Lust, Pandor to Infamie,
    Slaunder of Truth, Truth of Dissimulation;
    Staining our Clymate more than anie Nature.

What shall I say to thee? thou scorne of Nature,
Blacke spot of sinne, vylde lure of lecherie;
Iniurious Blame to euerie faemale creature,
Wronger of time, Broker of trecherie,
Trap of greene youth, false Womens witcherie,
    Hand-maid of pride, high-way to wickednesse;
    Yet path-way to Repentance, nere the lesse.

Thou dost entice the minde to dooing euill,
Thou setst dissention twixt the man and wife;
A Saint in show, and yet indeed a deuill:
Thou art the cause of euerie common strife;
Thou art the life of Death, the death of Life!
    Thou doost betray thyselfe to Infamie,
    When thou art once discernd by the eye.

Ah, little knew *Matilda* of thy being,
Those times were pure from all impure complection;
Then Loue came at Desert, Desert of seeing,
Then Vertue was the mother of Affection,
(But Beautie now is vnder no subiection),
    Then women were the same that men did deeme,
    But now they are the same they doo not seeme.

What fæmale now intreated of a King
With gold and iewels, pearles and precious stones,
Would willingly refuse so sweete a thing?
Onely for a little show of Vertue ones?
Women haue kindnes grafted in their bones.
    Gold is a deepe-perswading Orator,
    Especially where few the fault abhor.

But yet shee rather deadly poyson chose,
(Oh cruell Bane of most accursed Clime ;)
Than staine that milk-white Mayden-virgin Rose,
Which shee had kept vnspotted till that time :
And not corrupted with this earthly slime
   Her soule shall liue : inclosd eternally,
   In that pure shrine of Immortality.

This is my Doome : and this shall come to passe,
For what are Pleasures but still-vading ioyes ?
Fading as flowers, brittle as a glasse,
Or Potters Clay ; crost with the least annoyes ;
All thinges in this life are but trifling Toyes :
   But Fame and Vertue neuer shall decay,
   For Fame is Toomblesse, Vertue liues for aye !

FINIS.

Hellens Rape.

OR

A light Lanthorne for light Ladies.

Written in English Hexameters.

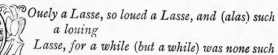

L *Ouely a Lasse, so loued a Lasse, and (alas) such
a louing
Lasse, for a while (but a while) was none such
a sweet bonny Loue-Lasse
As Helen, Mænelaus louing, lou'd, loulie a
loue-lasse,
Till spightfull Fortune from a loue-lasse made
her a loue-lesse*
*Wife.   From a wise woman to a witles vvanton abandond,
When her mate (vnawares) made warres in Peloponessus,
Adultrous Paris (then a Boy) kept sheepe as a shepheard
On Ida Mountaine, vnknowne to the King for a Keeper
Of sheep, on Ida Mountaine, as a Boy, as a shepheard :
Yet such sheep he kept, and was so seemelie a shepheard,
Seemlie a Boy, so seemlie a youth, so seemlie a Younker,
That on Ida was not such a Boy, such a youth, such a Younker.
Sonne now reconcil'd to the Father, fained a letter
Sent him by Iupiter (the greatest God in Olympus)
For to repaire with speede to the brauest Græcian Hauen,*

And to redeeme againe Hesyone *latelie reuolted*
From Troy *by* Aiax, *whom she had newly betrothed.*
Well, so well he told his tale to his Aunt Amaryllis
That Amaryllis, *(his Aunt,) obtaind aid of his aged*
Syre, that he sent him a ship, and made Capten of Argus.
Great store went to Greece with lust-bewitched Alexis,
Telamour, *and* Tydias : *with these he sliceth the salt seas,*
The salt seas slicing, at length he comes to the firme land,
Firme land an auntient Iland cald old Lacedæmon.
Argus *(eye full Earle) when first the ken of a Castle*
He had spide bespake : (to the Mate, to the men, to the Mates-man,
Lo behold of Greece (quoth he) the great Cytadella.
(Ycleaped Menela) *so tearmed of* Deliaes *Husband :*
Happie Helen, *Womens most woonder, beautifull* Helen.
Oh would God (quoth he) with a flattring Tongue he repeated :
Oh would God (quoth he) that I might deserue to be husband
To such a happie huswife, to such a beautifull Helen.
This he spake to intice the minde of a lecherous young-man :
But what spurres need now, for an vntam'd Titt to be trotting :
Or to add old Oile to the flame, new flaxe to the fier :
Paris *heard him hard, and gaue good eare to his hearkening :*
And then his loue to a lust, his lust was turnd to a fier,
Fier was turnd to a flame, and flame was turnd to a burning
Brand : and mothers Dreame was then most truelie resolued.
Well so far th'are come, that now th'are come to the Castle,
Castle all of stone, yet euery stone vvas a Castle :
Euerie foote had a Fort, and euerie Fort had a fountaine,
Euerie fountaine a spring, and euerie spring had a spurting
Streame : so strong without, vvithin, so stately a building,
Neuer afore vvas seene ; If neuer afore Polyphœbe
Was seene : vvas to be seene, if nere to be seene vvas Olympus.
Flovvers vvere framd of flints, Walls, Rubies, Rafters of Argent :
Pauement of Chrisolite, Windows contriu'd of a Cristall :
Vessels were of gold, with gold was each thing adorned :
Golden Webs more worth than a vvealthy Souldan *of Egypt,*
And her selfe more vvorth than a vvealthy Souldan *of Egypt :*

And her selfe more worth than all the wealth shee possessed;
Selfe? indeede such a selfe, as thundring Ioue *in* Olympus,
Though he were father could finde in his hart to be husband.
Embassage ended, to the Queene of faire Lacedæmon;
(Happie King of a Queene so faire, of a Countrey so famous)
Embassage ended, a Banquet braue was appointed:
Sweet Repast for a Prince, fine Iunkets fit for a Kings sonne.
Biskets and Carrawayes, Comfets, Tart, Plate, Ielley, Ginger-
      bread,
Lymons and Medlars: and Dishes moe by a thousand.
First they fell to the feast, and after fall to a Dauncing,
And from a Dance to a Trance, from a Trance they fell to a falling,
Either in other armes, and either in armes of another.
Pastime ouer-past, and Banquet duely prepared,
Deuoutly pared: Each one hies home to his owne home,
Saue Lord and Ladie; Young Lad, but yet such an old Lad,
In such a Ladies lappe, at such a slipperie by-blow,
That in a vvorld so vvilde, could not be found such a wilie
Lad: in an Age so old, could not be found such an old lad:
Old lad, and bold lad, such a Boy, such a lustie Iuuentus:
Well to their vvorke they goe, and both they iumble in one Bed:
Worke so well they like, that they still like to be vvorking:
For Aurora *mounts before he leaues to be mounting:*
And Astræa *fades before she faints to be falling:*
*(*Helen *a light Huswife, now a lightsome starre in* Olympus.)*

FINIS.

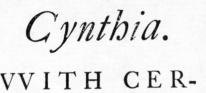

Cynthia.

VVITH CER-

taine Sonnets, and

the Legend of

Cassandra.

Quod cupio nequeo.

At London,

Printed for Humfrey

Lownes, and are to bee

sold at the VVest doore

of Paules. 1 5 9 5 .

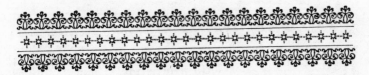

To the Right Honorable, and
most noble-minded Lorde,
William Stanley, Earle of
Darby, &c.

Ight Honorable, the dutifull affection I beare to your manie vertues, is cause, that to manifest my loue to your Lordship, I am constrained to shew my simplenes to the world. Many are they that admire your worth, of the which number, I (though the meanest in abilitie, yet with the formost in affection) am one that most desire to serue, and onely to serue your Honour.

Small is the gift, but great is my good-will; the which, by how much the lesse I am able to expresse it, by so much the more it is infinite. Liue long: and inherit your Predecessors vertues, as you doe their dignitie and estate. This is my wish: the which your honorable excellent giftes doe promise me to obtaine: and whereof these few rude and vnpollished lines, are a true (though an vndeseruing) testimony. If my ability were better, the signes should be greater; but being as it is, your honour must take me as I am, not as I should be. My yeares being so young, my perfection cannot be greater: But howsoeuer it is, yours it is; and I my selfe am yours; in all humble seruice, most ready to be commaunded.

Richard Barnefeilde.

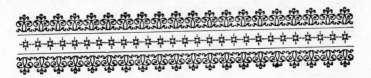

To the curteous Gentlemen Readers.

Gentlemen; the last Terme [*i.e., November* 1594] there came forth a little toy of mine, intituled, *The affectionate Shepheard* : In the which, his Country *Content* found such friendly fauor, that it hath incouraged me to publish my second fruites. *The affectionate Shepheard* being the first : howsoeuer undeseruedly (I protest) I haue beene thought (of some) to haue beene the authour of two Books heretofore. I neede not to name them, because they are two-well knowne already : nor will I deny them, because they are dislik't ; but because they are not mine. This protestation (I hope) will satisfie th'indifferent : as for them that are maliciously enuious, as I cannot, so I care not to please. Some there were, that did interpret *The affectionate Shepheard*, otherwise then (in truth) I meant, touching the subiect thereof, to wit, the loue of a Shepheard to a boy ; a fault, the which I will not excuse, because I neuer made. Onely this, I will vnshaddow my conceit : being nothing else, but an imitation of *Virgill*, in the second Eglogue of *Alexis*. In one or two places (in this Booke) I vse the name of *Eliza* pastorally : wherein, lest any one should misconster my meaning (as I hope none will) I haue here briefly discouered my harmeles conceipt as concerning that name : whereof once (in a simple Shepheards deuice) I wrot this Epigramme.

> *One name there is, which name aboue all other*
> *I most esteeme, as time and place shall proue :*
> *The one is* Vesta, *th'other* Cupids *Mother,*
> *The first my Goddesse is, the last my loue ;*
> *Subiect to Both I am : to that by berth ;*
> *To this for beautie ; fairest on the earth.*

Thus, hoping you will beare with my rude conceit of *Cynthia*, (if for no other cause, yet, for that it is the first imitation of the verse of that excellent Poet, Maister *Spencer*, in his *Fayrie Queene*) I will leaue you to the reading of that, which I so much desire may breed your Delight.

Richard Barnefeild.

T. T. in commendation of the
Authour his worke.

Hylom that in a shepheards gray coate masked,
(Where masked loue the nonage of his skill)
Reares new Eagle-winged pen, new tasked,
To scale the by-clift Muse sole-pleasing hill :
Dropping sweete Nectar poesie from his quill,
Admires faire C Y N T H I A with his iuory pen
Faire C Y N T H I A lou'd, fear'd, of Gods and men.

Downe sliding from that cloudes ore-pearing mounteine :
Decking with double grace the neighbour plaines, [fountain,
Drawes christall dew, from P E G A S E foote-sprung
Whose flower set banks, delights, sweet choice containes :
Nere yet discouerd to the country swaines :
  Heere bud those branches, which adorne his turtle,
  With loue made garlands, of heart-bleeding Mirtle.

Rays'd from the cynders, of the thrice-sact towne :
I L L I O N S sooth-telling S Y B I L L I S T appeares,
Eclipsing P H O E B U S loue, with scornefull frowne,
Whose tragicke end, affords warme-water teares,
(For pitty-wanting P A C O E, none forbeares)
  Such period haps, to beauties price ore-priz'd :
  Where I A N V S-faced loue, doth lurke disguiz'd.

Nere-waining C Y N T H I A yeelds thee triple thankes,
Whose beames vnborrowed darke the worlds faire eie
And as full streames that euer fill their bankes,
So those rare Sonnets, where wits ripe doth lie,
With Troian Nimph, doe soare thy fame to skie.
  And those, and these, contend thy Muse to raise
  (Larke mounting Muse) with more then common praise.

To his Mistresse.

Right Starre of Beauty, fairest Faire aliue,
Rare president of peerelesse chastity;
(In whom the Muses and the Graces striue,
VVhich shall possesse the chiefest part of thee:)
Oh let these simple lines accepted bee:
   VVhich here I offer at thy sacred shrine:
   Sacred, because sweet Beauty is diuine.

And though I cannot please each curious eare,
With sugred Noates of heauenly Harmonie:
Yet if my loue shall to thy selfe appeare,
No other Muse I will inuoke but thee:
And if thou wilt my faire *Thalia* be,
   Ile sing sweet Hymnes and praises to thy name,
   In that cleare Temple of eternall Fame.

But ah (alas) how can mine infant Muse
(That neuer heard of *Helicon* before)
Performe my promise past: when they refuse
Poore Shepheards Plaints? yet will I still adore
Thy sacred Name, al though I write no more:
   Yet hope I shall, if this accepted bee:
   If not, in silence sleepe eternally.

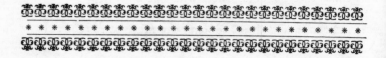

CYNTHIA.

Ow was the Welkyn all inuelloped
  With duskie Mantle of the sable Night:
  And CYNTHIA lifting vp her drouping
    head,
  Blusht at the Beautie of her borrowed
    light,
  When Sleepe now summon'd euery
    mortal wight.
Then loe (me thought) I saw or seem'd to see,
  An heauenly Creature like an Angell bright,
  That in great haste came pacing towards me:
Was neuer mortall eye beheld so faire a Shee.

Thou lazie man (quoth she) what mak'st thou heere
  (Luld in the lap of Honours Enimie?)
  I heere commaund thee now for to appeare
  (By vertue of IOVES mickle Maiestie)
  In yonder Wood. (Which with her finger shee
  Out-poynting) had no sooner turn'd her face,
  And leauing mee to muze what she should bee,
  Yuanished into some other place:
But straite (me thought) I saw a rout of heauenlie Race.

Downe in a Dale, hard by a Forrest side,
  (Vnder the shaddow of a loftie Pine,)
  Not far from whence a trickling streame did glide,
  Did nature by her secret art combine,
  A pleasant Arbour, of a spreading Vine:
  Wherein Art stroue with nature to compaire,
  That made it rather seeme a thing diuine
  Being scituate all in the open Aire:
A fairer nere was seene, if any seene so faire.

There might one see, and yet not see (indeede)
  Fresh *Flora* flourishing in chiefest Prime,
  Arrayed all in gay and gorgeous weede,
  The Primrose and sweet-smelling Eglantine,
  As fitted best beguiling so the time:
  And euer as she went she strewd the place,
  Red-roses mixt with Daffadillies fine,
  For Gods and Goddesses, that in like case
In this same order sat, with il-beseeming grace.

First, in a royall Chaire of massie gold,
  (Bard all about with plates of burning steele)
  Sat *Iupiter* most glorious to behold,
  And in his hand was placed Fortunes wheele:
  The which he often turn'd, and oft did reele.
  And next to him, in griefe and gealouzie,
  (If sight may censure what the heart doth feele)
  In sad lament was placed *Mercurie*;
That dying seem'd to weep, and weeping seem'd to die.

On th'other side, aboue the other twaine,
  (Delighting as it seem'd to sit alone)
  Sat *Mulciber*; in pride and high disdaine,
  Mounted on high vpon a stately throne,
  And euen with that I heard a deadly grone:
  Muzing at this, and such an vncouth sight,
  (Not knowing what shoulde make that piteous mone)
  I saw three furies, all in Armour dight,
With euery one a Lampe, and euery one a light.

I deemed so; nor was I much deceau'd,
  For poured forth in sensuall Delight,
  There might I see of Sences quite bereau'd
  King *Priams* Sonne, that *Alexander* hight
  (Wrapt in the Mantle of eternall Night.)
  And vnder him, awaiting for his fall,
  Sate Shame, here Death, and there sat fel Despight,
  That with their Horrour did his heart appall:
Thus was his Blisse to Bale, his Hony turn'd to gall.

In which delight feeding mine hungry eye,
  Of two great Goddesses a sight I had,
  And after them in wondrous Iollity,
  (As one that inly ioy'd, so was she glad)
  The Queene of Loue full royallie yclad,
  In glistring Gold, and peerelesse precious stone,
  There might I spie: and her Companion had,
  Proud *Paris*, Nephew to *Laomedon*,
That afterward did cause the Death of many a one.

By this the formost melting all in teares,
  And rayning downe resolued Pearls in showers,
  Gan to approach the place of heauenly Pheares,
  And with her weeping, watring all their Bowers,
  Throwing sweet Odors on those fading flowers,
  At length, she them bespake thus mournfullie.
  High *Ioue* (quoth she) and yee Cœlestiall powers,
  That here in Iudgement sit twixt her and mee,
Now listen (for a while) and iudge with equitie.

Sporting our selues to day, as wee were woont
  (I meane, I, *Pallas*, and the Queene of Loue.)
  Intending with *Diana* for to hunt,
  On *Ida* Mountaine top our skill to proue,
  A golden Ball was trindled from aboue,
  And on the Rinde was writ this Poesie,
  PVLCHERIMÆ for which a while we stroue,
  Each saying shee was fairest of the three,
When loe a shepheards Swaine not far away we see.

I spi'd him first, and spying thus bespake,
  Shall yonder Swaine vnfolde the mysterie?
  Agreed (quoth *Venus*) and by *Stygian* Lake,
  To whom he giues the ball so shall it bee:
  Nor from his censure will I flie, quoth shee,
  (Poynting to *Pallas*) though I loose the gole.
  Thus euery one yplac'd in her degree,
  The Shepheard comes, whose partial eies gan role,
And on our beuties look't, and of our beuties stole.

I promis'd wealth, *Minerua* promised wit,
  (Shee promis'd wit to him that was vnwise,)
  But he (fond foole) had soone refused it,
  And minding to bestow that glorious Prize,
  On *Venus*, that with pleasure might suffize
  His greedie minde in loose lasciuiousnes:
  Vpon a sudden, wanting goode aduice,
  Holde heere (quoth he) this golden Ball possesse,
Which *Paris* giues to thee for meede of worthines,

Thus haue I shew'd the summe of all my sute,
  And as a Plaintiffe heere appeale to thee,
  And to the rest. Whose folly I impute
  To filthie lust, and partialitie,
  That made him iudge amisse: and so doo we
  (Quoth *Pallas*, *Venus*,) nor will I gaine-say,
  Although it's mine by right, yet willinglie,
  I heere disclaime my title and obey:
When silence being made, *Ioue* thus began to saie.

Thou *Venus*, art my darling, thou my deare,
  (*Minerua*,) shee, my sister and my wife:
  So that of all a due respect I beare,
  Assign'd as one to end this doubtfull strife,
  (Touching your forme, your fame, your loue, your life)
  Beauty is vaine much like a gloomy light,
  And wanting wit is counted but a trife,
  Especially when Honour's put to flight:
Thus of a louely, soone becomes a loathly sight.

VVit without wealth is bad, yet counted good,
  wealth wanting wisdom's worse, yet deem'd as wel,
  From whence (for ay) doth flow, as from a flood,
  A pleasant Poyson, and a heauenly Hell,
  where mortall men do couet still to dwell.
  Yet one there is to Vertue so inclin'd,
  That as for Maiesty she beares the Bell,
  So in the truth who tries her princelie minde,
Both Wisdom, Beauty, Wealth, and all in her shall find.

In Westerne world amids the Ocean maine,
  In compleat Vertue shining like the Sunne,
  In great Renowne a maiden Queene doth raigne,
  Whose royall Race, in Ruine first begun,
  Till Heauens bright Lamps dissolue shall nere be done :
  In whose faire eies Loue linckt with vertues been,
  In euerlasting Peace and Vnion.
  Which sweet Consort in her full well beseeme
Of Bounty, and of Beauty fairest Fayrie Queene.

And to conclude, the gifts in her yfound,
  Are all so noble, royall, and so rare,
  That more and more in her they doe abound ;
  In her most peerelesse Prince without compare,
  Endowing still her minde with vertuous care :
  That through the world (so wide) the flying fame,
  (And Name that Enuies selfe cannot impaire,)
  Is blown of this faire Queen, this gorgeous dame,
Fame borrowing al men's mouths to royalize the same.

And with this sentence *Iupiter* did end,
  This is the Pricke (quoth he), this is the praies,
  To whom, this as a Present I will send,
  That shameth *Cynthia* in her siluer Raies,
  If so you three this deed doe not displease.
  Then one, and all, and euery one of them,
  To her that is the honour of her daies,
  A second *Iudith* in I E R V S A L E M.
To her we send this Pearle, this Iewell, and this Iem.

Then call'd he vp the winged *Mercury*,
  (The mighty Messenger of Gods enrold,)
And bad him hither hastily to hie,
Whom tended by her Nymphes he should behold,
  (Like Pearles ycouched all in shining gold.)
And euen with that, from pleasant slumbring sleepe,
  (Desiring much these wonders to vnfold)
I wak'ning, when *Aurora* gan to peepe,
Depriu'd so soone of my sweet Dreame, gan almost weepe.

The Conclusion.

Hus, sacred Virgin, Muse of chastitie,
  This difference is betwixt the Moone and thee :
  Shee shines by Night ; but thou by Day do'st
    shine :
Shee Monthly changeth ; thou dost nere decline :
And as the Sunne, to her, doth lend his light,
So hee, by thee, is onely made so bright :
Yet neither Sun, nor Moone, thou canst be named,
Because thy light hath both their beauties shamed :
  Then, since an heauenly Name doth thee befall,
  Thou V I R G O art : (if any Signe at all).

FINIS.

[*SONNETS.*]

SONNET. I.

Porting at fancie, setting light by loue,
  There came a theefe, and stole away my
   heart,
  (And therefore robd me of my chiefest
   part)
  Yet cannot Reason him a felon proue.
  For why his beauty (my hearts thiefe)
   affirmeth,
 Piercing no skin (the bodies fensiue wall)
 And hauing leaue, and free consent withall,
Himselfe not guilty, from loue guilty tearmeth,
Conscience the Iudge, twelue Reasons are the Iurie,
  They finde mine eies the be[a]utie t' haue let in,
  And on this verdict giuen, agreed they bin,
VVherefore, because his beauty did allure yee,
  Your Doome is this : in teares still to be drowned,
  VVhen his faire forehead with disdain is frowned.

SONNET. II.

B[a]uty and Maiesty are falne at ods,
    Th'one claimes his cheeke, the other claimes
        his chin;
    Then Vertue comes, and puts her title in.
(Quoth she) I make him like th'immortall Gods.
(Quoth Maiestie) I owne his lookes, his Brow,
    His lips, (quoth Loue) his eies, his faire is mine.
    And yet (quoth Maiesty) he is not thine,
I mixe Disdaine with Loues congealed Snow.
I, but (quoth Loue) his lockes are mine (by right)
    His stately gate is mine (quoth Maiestie,)
    And mine (quoth Vertue) is his Modestie.
Thus as they striue about this heauenly wight,
    At last the other two to Vertue yeeld,
    The lists of Loue, fought in faire Beauties field.

SONNET. III.

He Stoicks thinke, (and they come neere the truth,)
    That vertue is the chiefest good of all,
    The Academicks on *Idea* call.
    The Epicures in pleasure spend their youth,
The Perrepatetickes iudge felicitie,
    To be the chiefest good aboue all other,
    One man, thinks this: and that conceaues another:
So that in one thing very few agree.
Let Stoicks haue their Vertue if they will,
    And all the rest their chiefe-supposed good,
    Let cruell Martialists delight in blood,
And Mysers ioy their bags with gold to fill:
    My chiefest good, my chiefe felicity,
    Is to be gazing on my loues faire eie.

SONNET. IIII.

Wo stars there are in one faire firmament,
　　(Of some intitled *Ganymedes* sweet face),
　　VVhich other stars in brightnes doe disgrace,
As much as *Po* in clearenes passeth *Trent*.
Nor are they common natur'd stars : for why,
　These stars when other shine vaile their pure light,
　And when all other vanish out of sight,
They adde a glory to the worlds great eie.
By these two stars my life is onely led,
　In them I place my ioy, in them my pleasure,
　Loue's piercing Darts, and Natures precious treasure
With their sweet foode my fainting soule is fed :
　Then when my sunne is absent from my sight
　How can it chuse (with me) but be dark night ?

SONNET. V.

T is reported of faire *Thetis* Sonne,
　　(*Achilles* famous for his chiualry,
　　His noble minde and magnanimity,)
That when the Troian wars were new begun,
Whos'euer was deepe-wounded with his speare,
　Could neuer be recured of his maime,
　Nor euer after be made whole againe :
Except with that speares rust he holpen were.
Euen so it fareth with my fortune now,
　Who being wounded with his piercing eie,
　Must either thereby finde a remedy,
Or els to be releeu'd, I know not how.
　Then if thou hast a minde still to annoy me,
　Kill me with kisses, if thou wilt destroy me.

R. Barnfield.
Jan. 1595.

SONNET. VI.

Weet Corrall lips, where Nature's treasure lies,
 The balme of blisse, the soueraigne salue of
  sorrow,
 The secret touch of loues heart-burning arrow,
Come quench my thirst or els poor *Daphnis* dies.
One night I dream'd (alas twas but a Dreame)
 That I did feele the sweetnes of the same,
 Where-with inspir'd, I young againe became,
And from my heart a spring of blood did streame,
But when I wak't, I found it nothing so,
 Saue that my limbs (me thought) did waxe more strong
 And I more lusty far, and far more yong.
This gift on him rich Nature did bestow.
 Then if in dreaming so, I so did speede,
 What should I doe, if I did so indeede ?

SONNET. VII.

Weet *Thames* I honour thee, not for thou art
 The chiefest Riuer of the fairest Ile,
 Nor for thou dost admirers eies beguile,
 But for thou hold'st the keeper of my heart,
For on thy waues, (thy Christal-billow'd waues,)
 My fairest faire, my siluer Swan is swimming :
 Against the sunne his pruned feathers trimming :
Whilst *Neptune* his faire feete with water laues,
Neptune, I feare not thee, not yet thine eie,
 And yet (alas) *Apollo* lou'd a boy,
 And *Cyparissus* was *Siluanus* ioy.
No, no, I feare none but faire *Thetis*, I,
 For if she spie my Loue, (alas) aie me,
 My mirth is turn'd to extreame miserie.

SONNET. VIII.

Ometimes I wish that I his pillow were,
 So might I steale a kisse, and yet not seene,
 So might I gaze vpon his sleeping eine,
 Although I did it with a panting feare :
But when I well consider how vaine my wish is,
 Ah foolish Bees (thinke I) that doe not sucke
 His lips for hony ; but poore flowers doe plucke
Which haue no sweet in them : when his sole kisses,
Are able to reuiue a dying soule.
 Kisse him, but sting him not, for if you doe,
 His angry voice your flying will pursue :
But when they heare his tongue, what can controule,
 Their back-returne ? for then they plaine may see,
 How hony-combs from his lips dropping bee.

SONNET. IX.

Iana (on a time) walking the wood,
 To sport herselfe, of her faire traine forlorne,
 Chaunc't for to pricke her foote against a thorne,
 And from thence issu'd out a streame of blood.
No sooner shee was vanisht out of sight,
 But loues faire Queen came there away by chance,
 And hauing of this hap a glym'ring glance,
She put the blood into a christall bright,
When being now come vnto mount *Rhodope*,
 With her faire hands she formes a shape of Snow,
 And blends it with this blood ; from whence doth grow
A louely creature, brighter than the Dey.
 And being christned in faire *Paphos* shrine,
 She call'd him *Ganymede* : as all diuine.

R. Barnfield.
Jan. 1595.

SONNET. X.

Hus was my loue, thus was my *Ganymed*,
 (Heauens ioy, worlds wonder, natures fairest
  work,
 In whose aspect Hope and Dispaire doe lurke)
Made of pure blood in whitest snow yshed,
And for sweete *Venus* only form'd his face,
 And his each member delicately framed,
 And last of all faire *Ganymede* him named,
His limbs (as their Creatrix) her imbrace.
But as for his pure, spotles, vertuous minde,
 Because it sprung of chaste *Dianaes* blood,
 (Goddesse of Maides, directresse of all good,)
Hit wholy is to chastity inclinde.
 And thus it is : as far as I can proue,
 He loues to be beloued, but not to loue.

SONNET XI.

Ighing, and sadly sitting by my Loue,
 He ask't the cause of my hearts sorrowing,
 Coniuring me by heauens eternall King
 To tell the cause which me so much did moue.
Compell'd : (quoth I) to thee will I confesse,
 Loue is the cause ; and only loue it is
 That doth depriue me of my heauenly blisse.
Loue is the paine that doth my heart oppresse.
And what is she (quoth he) whom thou dos't loue ?
 Looke in this glasse (quoth I) there shalt thou see
 The perfect forme of my fælicitie.
When, thinking that it would strange Magique proue,
 He open'd it : and taking of the couer,
 He straight perceau'd himselfe to be my Louer.

SONNET. XII.

Ome talke of *Ganymede* th' *Idalian* Boy,
  And some of faire *Adonis* make their boast,
  Some talke of him whom louely *Læda* lost,
  And some of *Ecchoes* loue that was so coy.
They speake by heere-say, I of perfect truth,
  They partially commend the persons named,
  And for them, sweet Encomions haue framed :
I onely t'him haue sacrifized my youth.
As for those wonders of antiquitie,
  And those whom later ages haue inioy'd,
  (But ah what hath not cruell death destroide ?
Death, that enuies this worlds felicitie),
  They were (perhaps) lesse faire then Poets write.
  But he is fairer then I can indite.

SONNET. XIII.

Peake Eccho, tell ; how may I call my loue ? *Loue.*
  But how his Lamps that are so christa-
      line ?   *Eyne.*
  Oh happy starrs that make your heauens diuine :
And happy Iems that admiration moue.
How tearm'st his golden tresses wau'd with aire ? *Haire.*
  Oh louely haire of your more-louely Maister,
  Image of loue, faire shape of Alablaster,
Why do'st thou driue thy Louer to dispaire ?
How do'st thou cal the bed wher beuty grows ?   *Rose.*
  Faire virgine-Rose, whose mayden blossoms couer
  The milke-white Lilly, thy imbracing Louer :
Whose kisses makes thee oft thy red to lose.
  And blushing oft for shame, when he hath kist thee,
  He vades away, and thou raing'st where it list thee.

SONNET. XIIII.

Ere, hold this gloue (this milk-white cheueril gloue)
  Not quaintly ouer-wrought with curious knots,
  Not deckt with golden spangs, nor siluer spots,
  Yet wholsome for thy hand as thou shalt proue.
Ah no; (sweet boy) place this gloue neere thy heart,
  Weare it, and lodge it still within thy brest,
  So shalt thou make me (most vnhappy,) blest.
So shalt thou rid my paine, and ease my smart:
How can that be (perhaps) thou wilt reply,
  A gloue is for the hand not for the heart,
  Nor can it well be prou'd by common art,
Nor reasons rule. To this, thus answere I:
  If thou from gloue do'st take away the g,
  Then gloue is loue: and so I send it thee.

SONNET. XV.

[H] fairest *Ganymede*, disdaine me not,
  Though silly Sheepeheard I, presume to loue thee,
  Though my harsh songs and Sonnets cannot
      moue thee,
Yet to thy beauty is my loue no blot.
Apollo, *Ioue*, and many Gods beside,
  S' daind not the name of cuntry shepheards swains,
  Nor want we pleasure, though we take some pains,
We liue contentedly: a thing call'd pride,
Which so corrupts the Court and euery place,
  (Each place I meane where learning is neglected,
  And yet of late, euen learnings selfe's infected)
I know not what it meanes, in any case:
  Wee onely (when *Molorchus* gins to peepe)
  Learne for to folde, and to vnfold our sheepe.

SONNET. XVI.

Ong haue I long'd to see my Loue againe,
  Still haue I wisht, but neuer could obtaine it ;
  Rather than all the world (if I might gaine it)
Would I desire my loues sweet precious gaine.
Yet in my soule I see him euerie day,
  See him, and see his still sterne countenaunce,
  But (ah) what is of long continuance,
Where Maiestie and Beautie beares the sway?
Sometimes, when I imagine that I see him,
  (As loue is full of foolish fantasies)
  VVeening to kisse his lips, as my loues fee's,
I feele but Aire : nothing but Aire to bee him.
  Thus with *Ixion*, kisse I clouds in vaine :
  Thus with *Ixion*, feele I endles paine.

SONNET. XVII.

Herry-lipt *Adonis* in his snowie shape,
  Might not compare with his pure Iuorie white,
  On whose faire front a Poets pen may write,
Whose rosiate red excels the crimson grape,
His loue-enticing delicate soft limbs,
  Are rarely fram'd t'intrap poore gazing eies :
  His cheekes, the Lillie and Carnation dies,
With louely tincture which *Apolloes* dims.
His lips ripe strawberries in Nectar wet,
  His mouth a Hiue, his tongue a hony-combe,
  Where Muses (like Bees) make their mansion.
His teeth pure Pearle in blushing Correll set.
  Oh how can such a body sinne-procuring,
  Be slow to loue, and quicke to hate, enduring ?

SONNET. XVIII.

Ot *Megabætes* nor *Cleonymus*,
    (Of whom great *Plutarch* makes such mention,
    Praysing their faire with rare inuention)
  As *Ganymede* were halfe so beauteous.
They onely pleas'd the eies of two great Kings,
  But all the worlde at my loue stands amazed,
  Nor one that on his Angels face hath gazed,
But (rauisht with delight) him Presents brings.
Some weaning Lambs, and some a suckling Kyd,
  Some Nuts, and fil-beards, others Peares and Plums,
  Another with a milk-white Heyfar comes;
As lately *Ægons* man (*Damætas*) did:
  But neither he, nor all the Nymphs beside,
  Can win my *Ganymede*, with them t'abide.

SONNET. XIX.

H no; nor I my selfe: though my pure loue
    (Sweete *Ganymede*) to thee hath still beene pure,
    And euen till my last gaspe shall aie endure,
  Could euer thy obdurate beuty moue:
Then cease oh Goddesse sonne (for sure thou art,
  A Goddesse sonne that canst resist desire)
  Cease thy hard heart, and entertaine loues fire,
Within thy sacred breast: by Natures art.
And as I loue thee more then any Creature,
  (Loue thee, because thy beautie is diuine;
  Loue thee, because my selfe, my soule is thine:
Wholie deuoted to thy louelie feature),
  Euen so of all the vowels, I and V,
  Are dearest vnto me, as doth ensue.

SONNET. XX.

But now my Muse toyld with continuall care,
    Begins to faint, and slacke her former pace,
    Expecting fauour from that heauenly grace,
    That maie (in time) her feeble strength repaire.
Till when (sweete youth) th'essence of my soule,
    (Thou that dost sit and sing at my hearts griefe.
    Thou that dost send thy shepheard no reliefe)
Beholde, these lines ; the sonnes of Teares and Dole.
Ah had great *Colin* chiefe of sheepheards all,
    Or gentle *Rowland*, my professed friend,
    Had they thy beautie, or my pennance pend,
Greater had beene thy fame, and lesse my fall :
    But since that euerie one cannot be wittie,
    Pardon I craue of them, and of thee, pitty.

FINIS.

AN ODE.

Ights were short, and daies were long;
Blossoms on the Hauthorn's hung:
Philomæle (Night-Musiques-King)
Tolde the comming of the spring.
Whose sweete siluer-sounding voice
Made the little birds reioice:
Skipping light from spray to spray,
Till *Aurora* shew'd the day.
Scarce might one see, when I might see
(For such chaunces sudden bee)
By a well of Marble-stone
A Shepheard lying all alone.
Weepe he did; and his weeping
Made the fading flowers spring.
Daphnis was his name (I weene)
Youngest Swaine of Summers Queene.
When *Aurora* saw 'twas he.
Weepe she did for companie:
Weepe she did for her sweete sonne
That (when antique *Troy* was wonne)
Suffer'd death by lucklesse fate,
Whom she now laments too late:
And each morning (by Cocks crew)
Showers downe her siluer dew.
Whose teares (falling from their spring)
Giue moysture to each liuing thing,
That on earth increase and grow,

Through power of their friendlie foe.
Whose effect when *Flora* felt,
Teares, that did her bosome melt,
(For who can resist teares often,
But Shee whom no teares can soften ?)
Peering straite aboue the banks,
Shew'd herselfe to giue her thanks.
Wondring thus at Natures worke,
(Wherein many maruailes lurke)
Me thought I heard a dolefull noise,
Consorted with a mournfull voice,
Drawing nie to heare more plaine,
Heare I did, vnto my paine,
(For who is not pain'd to heare
Him in griefe whom heart holdes deare?)
Silly swaine (with griefe ore-gone)
Thus to make his piteous mone.
Loue I did, (alas the while)
Loue I did, but did beguile
My deare loue with louing so,
(VVhom as then I did not know.)
Loue I did the fairest boy,
That these fields did ere enioy.
Loue I did, fair *Ganymed* ;
(*Venus* darling, beauties bed :)
Him I thought the fairest creature ;
Him the quintessence of Nature :
But yet (alas) I was deceiu'd,
(Loue of reason is bereau'd)
For since then I saw a Lasse,
(Lasse) that did in beauty passe,
(Passe) faire *Ganymede* as farre
As *Phœbus* doth the smallest starre.
Loue commaunded me to loue ;
Fancy bade me not remoue
My affection from the swaine

Which he cannot graunt the crauer ?)
Loue at last (though loath) preuailde ;
(Loue) that so my heart assailde ;
Whom I neuer could obtaine :
(For who can obtaine that fauour,
Wounding me with her faire eies,
(Ah how Loue can subtelize,
And deuize a thousand shifts,
How to worke men to his drifts.)
Her it is, for whom I mourne ;
Her, for whom my life I scorne ;
Her, for whom I weepe all day ;
Her, for whom I sigh, and say,
Either She, or els no creature,
Shall enioy my loue : whose feature
Though I neuer can obtaine,
Yet shall my true loue remaine :
Till (my body turn'd to clay)
My poore soule must passe away,
To the heauens ; where (I hope)
Hit shall finde a resting scope :
Then since I loued thee (alone)
Remember me when I am gone.
Scarce had he these last words spoken,
But me thought his heart was broken ;
With great griefe that did abound,
(Cares and griefe the heart confound)
In whose heart (thus riu'd in three)
E L I Z A written I might see :
In Caracters of crimson blood,
(VVhose meaning well I vnderstood.)
Which, for my heart might not behold,
I hyed me home my sheep to folde.

F I N I S.

CASSANDRA.

 PON a gorgious gold embossed bed, [sunne,
With Tissue curtaines drawne against the
(Which gazers eies into amazement led,
So curiously the workmanship was done,)
    Lay faire *Cassandra*, in her snowie smocke,
    Whose lips the Rubies and the pearles
    did locke.

And from her Iuory front hung dangling downe,
A bush of long and louely curled haire ;
VVhose head impalled with a precious Crowne
Of orient Pearle, made her to seeme more faire :
    And yet more faire she hardly could be thought,
    Then Loue and Nature in her face had wrought.

By this, young *Phœbus* rising from the East,
Had tane a view of this rare Paragon :
Wherewith he soone his radiant beames addresst,
And with great ioy her (sleeping) gazed vpon :
    Til at the last, through her light cazements cleare,
    He stole a kisse ; and softly call'd her Deare.

Yet not so softly but (therwith awak't,)
Shee gins to open her faire christall couers,
Wherewith the wounded God, for terror quakt,
(Viewing those darts that kill disdained louers :)
    And blushing red to see himselfe so shamed
    He scorns his Coach, and his owne beauty blamed.

Now with a trice he leaues the azure skies,
(As whilome *Ioue* did at *Europaes* rape,)
And rauisht with her loue-a[l]luring eies,
He turns himselfe into a humane shape :
　　And that his wish the sooner might ensue,
　　He sutes himselfe like one of *Venus* crew.

Vpon his head he wore a Hunters hat
Of crimson veluet, spangd with stars of gold,
Which grac'd his louely face : and ouer that
A siluer hatband ritchly to behold :
　　On his left shoulder hung a loose Tyara,
　　As whilome vs'd faire *Penthesilea.*

Faire *Penthesilea* th'*Amazonian* Queene,
When she to Troy came with her warlike band,
Of braue Viragoes glorious to be seene ;
Whose manlike force no power might withstand :
　　So look't *Apollo* in his louely weedes,
　　As he vnto the Troian Damzell speedes.

Not faire, *Adonis* in his chiefest pride,
Did seeme more faire, then young *Apollo* seemed,
When he through th'aire inuisibly did glide,
T'obtaine his Loue, which he Angelike deemed ;
　　Whom finding in her chamber all alone,
　　He thus begins t'expresse his piteous mone.

O fairest, faire, aboue all faires (quoth hee)
If euer Loue obtained Ladies fauour,
Then shew thy selfe compassionate to me,
Whose head surpriz'd with thy diuine behauior,
　　Yeelds my selfe captiue to thy conqu'ring eies :
　　O then shew mercy, do not tyrannize.

Scarce had *Apollo* vtter'd these last words
(Rayning downe pearle from his immortall eies)
When she for answere, naught but feare affords,
Filling the place with lamentable cries :
　　But *Phœbus* fearing much these raging fits,
　　With sugred kisses sweetely charm'd her lips.

(And tells her softly in her softer eare)
That he a God is, and no mortall creature:
Wherewith abandoning all needlesse feare,
(A common frailtie of weake womans nature)
   She boldly askes him of his deitie,
   Gracing her question with her wanton eie.

Which charge to him no sooner was assignde,
But taking faire *Cassandra* by the hand
(The true bewraier of his secrete minde)
He first begins to let her vnderstand,
   That he from *Demogorgon* was descended:
   Father of th'Earth, of Gods and men commended.

The tenor of which tale he now recites,
Closing each period with a rauisht kisse:
Which kindnes, she vnwillingly requites,
Conioyning oft her Corrall lips to his:
   Not that she lou'd the loue of any one;
   But that she meant to cozen him anone.

Hee briefly t'her relates his pedegree:
The sonne of *Ioue*, sole guider of the sunne,
He that slue *Python* so victoriouslie,
He that the name of wisdomes God hath wonne,
   The God of Musique, and of Poetry:
   Of Phisicke, Learning, and Chirurgery.

All which he eloquently reckons vp,
That she might know how great a God he was:
And being charm'd with *Cupid's* golden cup
He partiallie vnto her praise doth passe,
   Calling her tipe of honour, Queen of beauty:
   To whom all eies owe tributary duety.

I loued once, (quoth hee) aie me I lou'd,
As faire a shape as euer nature framed:
Had she not been so hard t'haue beene remou'd,
By birth a sea-Nymph; cruell *Daphne* named:
   Whom, for shee would not to my will agree,
   The Gods transform'd into a Laurell tree.

Ah therefore be not, (with that word he kist her)
Be not (quot[h] he) so proud as *Daphne* was :
Ne care thou for the anger of my sister,
She cannot, nay she shall not hurt my *Cass* :
   For if she doe, I vow (by dreadfull night)
   Neuer againe to lend her of my light.

This said : he sweetly doth imbrace his loue,
Yoaking his armes about her Iuory necke :
And calls her wanton *Venus* milk-white Doue,
VVhose ruddie lips the damaske roses decke.
   And euer as his tongue compiles her praise,
   Loue daintie Dimples in her cheekes doth raise.

And meaning now to worke her stratagem
Vpon the silly God, that thinks none ill,
She hugs him in her armes, and kisses him ;
(Th'easlyer to intice him to her will.)
   And being not able to maintaine the feeld,
   Thus she begins (or rather seemes) to yeeld.

VVoon with thy words, and rauisht with my beauty,
Loe here *Cassandra* yeelds her selfe to thee,
Requiring nothing for thy vowed duety,
But only firmnesse, Loue, and secrecy :
   Which for that now (euen now) I meane to try thee,
   A boone I craue ; which thou canst not deny me.

Scarce were these honywords breath'd from her lips,
But he, supposing that she ment good-faith,
Her filed tongues temptations interceps ;
And (like a Nouice,) thus to her he saith :
   Aske what thou wilt, and I will giue it thee;
   Health, wealth, long life, wit, art, or dignitie.

Here-with she blushing red, (for shame did adde
A crimson tincture to her palish hew,)
Seeming in outward semblance passing glad,
(As one that th'end of her petition knew)
   She makes him sweare by vgly *Acheron*,
   That he his promise should performe anon.

Which done : relying on his sacred oath,
She askes of him the gift of prophecie :
He (silent) giues consent : though seeming loath
To grant so much to fraile mortalitie :
   But since that he his vowes maie not recall,
   He giues to her the sp'rite propheticall.

But she no sooner had obtain'd her wish,
VVhen straite vnpris'ning her lasciuiuous armes
From his softe bosom (th'aluary of blisse)
She chastely counterchecks loues hote alarmes :
   And fearing lest his presence might offend her,
   She slips aside ; and (absent) doth defend her.

   (*Muliere ne credas, ne mortuæ quidem.*)

Looke how a brightsome Planet in the skie,
(Spangling the Welkin with a golden spot)
Shootes suddenly from the beholders eie,
And leaues him looking there where she is not :
   Euen so amazed *Phœbus* (to descrie her)
   Lookes all about, but no where can espie her.

Not th'hungry Lyon, hauing lost his pray,
With greater furie runneth through the wood,
(Making no signe of momentarie staie,
Till he haue satisfi'd himslfe with blood,)
   Then angry *Phœbus* mounts into the skie :
   Threatning the world with his hot-burning eie.

Now nimbly to his glist'ring Coach he skips,
And churlishlie ascends his loftie chaire,
Yerking his head strong Iades with yron whips,
Whose fearefull neighing ecchoes through the aire,
   Snorting out fierie Sulphure from theire nosethrils :
   Whose deadly damp the worlds poore people kils.

Him leaue me (for a while) amids the heauens,
VVreaking his anger on his sturdie steedes :
Whose speedful course the day and night now eeuens,
(The earth dis-robed of her summer weedes)
   And nowe black-mantled night with her browne vaile,
   Couers each thing that all the world might quaile.

VVhen loe, *Cassandra* lying at her rest,
(Her rest were restlesse thoughts :) it so befell,
Her minde with multitude of cares opprest,
Requir'd some sleepe her passions to expell :
    VVhich when sad *Morpheus* will did vnderstand,
    He clos'd her eie-lids with his leaden hand.

Now sleepeth shee : and as shee sleepes, beholde ;
Shee seemes to see the God whom late shee wronged
Standing before her ; whose fierce looks vnfold,
His hidden wrath (to whom iust ire belonged)
    Seeing, shee sighs, and sighing quak't for feare,
    To see the shaddow of her shame appeare.

Betwixt amaze and dread as shee thus stands,
The fearefull vision drew more neere vnto her :
Aud pynioning her armes in captiue bands
So sure, that mortall wight may not vndoe her,
    He with a bloudy knife (oh cruell part,)
    VVith raging fury stabd her to the heart.

Heerewith awaking from her slumbring sleepe,
(For feare, and care, are enemies to rest :)
At such time as *Aurora* gins to peepe
And shew her selfe ; far orient in the East :
    Shee heard a voice which said : O wicked woman,
    Why dost thou stil the gods to vengeance summon ?

Thou shalt (indeede) fore-tell of things to come ;
And truely, too ; (for why my vowes are past)
But heare the end of *Ioues* eternall doome :
Because thy promise did so little last,
    Although thou tell the truth, (this gift I giue thee)
    Yet for thy falsehood, no man shall beleeue thee.

And (for thy sake) this pennance I impose
Vpon the remnant of all woman kinde,
For that they be such truth professed foes ;
A constant woman shall be hard to finde :
    And that all flesh at my dread name may tremble,
    When they weep most, then shall they most dissemble.

This said *Apollo* then: And since that time
His words haue proved true as Oracles:
Whose turning thoughtes ambitiously doe clime
To heauens height; and world with lightnes fils:
  VVhose sex are subject to inconstancie,
  As other creatures are to destinie.

Yet famous *Sabrine* on thy banks doth rest
The fairest Maide that euer world admired:
Whose constant minde, with heauenly gifts possest
Makes her rare selfe of all the world desired.
  In whose chaste thoughts no vanitie doth enter;
  So pure a minde *Endymions* Love hath lent her.

Queene of my thoughts, but subiect of my verse,
(Divine *Eliza*) pardon my defect:
Whose artlesse pen so rudely doth reherse
Thy beauties worth; (for want of due respect)
  Oh pardon thou the follies of my youth;
  Pardon my faith, my loue, my zeale, my truth.

But to *Cassandra* now: who hauing heard
The cruell sentence of the threatning voice;
At length (too late) begins to waxe affeard,
Lamenting much her vnrepentant choice:
  And seeing her hard hap without reliefe,
  She sheeds salt teares in token of her griefe.

VVhich when *Aurora* saw, and saw t'was shee,
Euen shee her selfe whose far-renowmed fame
Made all the world to wonder at her beauty,
It mou'd compassion in this ruthfull Dame:
  And thinking on her Sonnes sad destinie,
  With mournfull teares she beares her companie.

Great was the mone, which faire *Cassandra* made:
Greater the kindnesse, which *Aurora* shew'd:
VVhose sorrow with the sunne began to fade,
And her moist teares on th'earths green grasse bestow'd:
  Kissing the flowers with her siluer dew,
  VVhose fading beautie, seem'd her case to rew.

Scarce was the louely Easterne Queene departed,
From stately *Ilion* (whose proud-reared wals
Seem'd to controule the cloudes, till *Vulcan* darted
Against their Tower his burning fier-bals)
   When sweet *Cassandra* (leauing her soft bed)
   In seemely sort her selfe apparelled.

And hearing that her honourable Sire,
(Old princely *Pryamus Troy's* aged King)
Was gone into *Ioues* Temple, to conspire
Against the *Greekes,* (whom he to war did bring)
   Shee, (like a Furie), in a bedlam rage,
   Runs gadding thither, his fell wrath t'assuage.

But not preuailing : truely she fore-tolde
The fall of *Troy* (with bold erected face :)
They count her hare-brain'd, mad, and ouer-bold,
To presse in presence in so graue a place :
   But in meane season *Paris* he is gone,
   To bring destruction on faire *Ilion.*

What, ten-yeeres siedge by force could not subuert,
That, two false traitors in one night destroi'd :
Who richly guerdon'd for their bad desert,
VVas of *Æneas* but small time inioi'd :
   VVho, for concealement of *Achilles* loue,
   VVas banished ; from *Ilion* to remoue.

King *Pryam* dead and all the Troians slaine ;
(His sonnes, his friends and deere confederates)
And lots now cast for captiues that remaine,
(Whom Death hath spared for more cruell fates)
   Cassandra then to *Agamemnon* fell,
   With whom a Lemman she disdain'd to dwell.

She, weepes ; he, wooes ; he would, but she would not :
He, tell's his birth ; shee, pleades virginitie :
He saith, selfe-pride doth rarest beauty blot :
(And with that word he kist her louingly :)
   Shee, yeeldingly resists ; he faines to die :
   Shee, fall's for feare ; he, on her feareleslie.

But this braue generall of all the *Greekes*,
VVas quickly foyled at a womans hands,
For who so rashly such incounters seekes,
Of hard mis-hap in danger euer stands :
　　Onely chaste thoughts, vertuous abstinence,
　　Gainst such sweet poyson is the sur'st defence.

But who can shun the force of beauties blow ?
Who is not rauisht with a louely looke ?
Grac'd with a wanton eie, (the hearts dumb show)
Such fish are taken with a siluer hooke :
　　And when true loue cannot these pearles obtaine
　　Vnguentum Album is the only meane.

Farre be it from my thought (diuinest Maid)
To haue relation to thy heauenly hew,
(In whose sweete voice the Muses are imbaid)
No pen can paint thy commendation due :
　　Saue only that pen, which no pen can be,
　　An Angels quill, to make a pen for thee.

But to returne to these vnhappie Louers,
(Sleeping securely in each others armes)
VVhose sugred ioies nights sable mantle couers,
Little regarding their ensuing harmes :
　　VVhich afterward they iointlie both repented :
　　" Fate is fore-seene, but neuer is preuented."

Which saying to be true, this lucklesse Dame
Approued in the sequele of her story :
Now waxing pale, now blushing red (for shame),
She seales her lips with silence (womens glory)
　　Till *Agamemnon* vrging her replies,
　　Thus of his death she truely prophecies.

The day shall come, (quoth she) O dismal daie !
When thou by false *Ægistus* shalt be slaine :
Heere could she tell no more ; but made a stay.
(From further speech as willing to refraine :)
　　Not knowing then, nor little did she thinke,
　　That she with him of that same cup must drinke

But what? (fond man) he laughs her skil to scorne,
And iesteth at her diuination:
Ah to what vnbeliefe are Princes borne?
(The onely ouer-throw of many a Nation:)
  And so it did befall this lucklesse Prince,
  Whom all the world hath much lamented since.

Insteede of teares, he smileth at her tale:
Insteede of griefe, he makes great shew of gladnes:
But after blisse, there euer followes bale;
And after mirth, there alwaies commeth sadnes:
  But gladnesse, blisse, and mirth had so possest him,
  That sadnes, bale, and griefe could not molest him.

Oh cruell *Parcæ* (quoth *Cassandra* then)
Why are you *Parcæ*, yet not mou'd with praier?
Oh small security of mortall men,
That liue on earth, and breathe this vitall aire:
  When we laugh most, then are we next to sorrow;
  The Birds feede vs to-day, we them to-morrow.

But if the first did little moue his minde,
Her later speeches lesse with him preuailed;
Who beinge wholy to selfe-will inclinde,
Deemes her weake braine with lunacy assailed:
  And still the more shee councels him to stay,
  The more he striueth to make haste away.

How on the Seas he scap'd stormes, rocks and sholes,
(Seas that enuide the conquest he had wone,
Gaping like hell to swallow Greekish soules,)
I heere omit; onely suppose it done:
  His storm-tyrde Barke safely brings him to shore,
  His whole Fleete els, or suncke or lost before.

Lift vp thy head, thou ashie-cyndred *Troy*,
See the commaunder of thy traitor foes,
That made thy last nights woe, his first daies ioie,
Now gins his night of ioy and daie of woes:
  His fall be thy delight, thine was his pride:
  As he thee then, so now thou him deride.

He and *Cassandra* now are set on shore,
VVhich he salutes with ioy, she greetes with teares,
Currors are sent that poast to Court before,
Whose tidings fill th'adultrous Queene with feares,
   Who with *Ægistus* in a lust-staind bed,
   Her selfe, her King, her State dishonored.

She wakes the lecher with a loud-strain'd shrike,
Loue-toies they leaue, now doth lament begin :
Ile flie (quoth he) but she doth that mislike,
Guilt vnto guilt, and sinne she ads to sinne :
   Shee meanes to kill (immodest loue to couer)
   A kingly husband, for a caytiue louer.

The peoples ioies, conceiued at his returne,
Their thronging multitudes : their gladsome cries,
Their gleeful hymnes, whiles piles of incense burne :
Their publique shewes, kept at solemnities :
   We passe : and tell how King and Queene did meet,
   Where he with zeale, she him with guile did greet.

He (noble Lord) fearelesse of hidden treason,
Sweetely salutes this weeping Crocodile :
Excusing euery cause with instant reason
That kept him from her sight so long a while :
   She, faintly pardons him ; smiling by Art :
   (For life was in her lookes, death in her hart.)

For pledge that I am pleas'd receiue (quoth shee)
This rich wrought robe, thy *Clytemnestras* toile :
Her ten yeeres worke this day shall honour thee,
For ten yeeres war, and one daies glorious spoile :
   Whil'st thou contendedst there, I heere did this :
   Weare it my loue, my life, my ioy, my blisse.

Scarce had the Syren said what I haue write,
But he (kind Prince) by her milde words misled,
Receiu'd the robe, to trie if it were fit ;
(The robe) that had no issue for his head ;
   Which, whilst he vainly hoped to haue found,
   Ægistus pierst him with a mortal wound.

Oh how the *Troyan* Damzell was amazed
To see so fell and bloudy a Tragedie,
Performed in one Act; she naught but gazed,
Vpon the picture; whom shee dead did see,
  Before her face : whose body she emballms,
  With brennish teares, and sudden deadly qualms.

Faine would she haue fled backe on her swift horse
But *Clytemnestra* bad her be content,
Her time was com'n : now bootelesse vsd she force,
Against so many; whom this Tygresse sent
  To apprehend her : who (within one hower
  Brought backe againe) was lockt within a Tower.

Now is she ioylesse, friendlesse, and (in fine)
Without all hope of further libertie :
Insteed of cates, cold water was her wine,
And *Agamemnons* corps her meate must be,
  Or els she must for hunger starue (poore sole)
  What could she do but make great mone and dole.

So darke the dungeon was, wherein she was,
That neither Sunne (by day) nor Mone (by night)
Did shew themselues : and thus it came to passe.
The Sunne denide to lend his glorious light
  To such a periur'd wight, or to be seene;
  (What neede she light, that ouer-light had bin ?)

Now silent night drew on; when all things sleepe,
Saue theeves, and cares; and now stil mid-night came :
When sad *Cassandra* did naught els but weepe;
Oft calling on her *Agamemnons* name.
  But seeing that the dead did not replie,
  Thus she begins to mourne, lament, and crie.

Oh cruell Fortune (mother of despaire,)
Well art thou christen'd with a cruell name :
Since thou regardest not the wise, or faire,
But do'st bestow thy riches (to thy shame)
  On fooles and lowly swaines, that care not for thee :
  And yet I weepe, and yet thou do'st abhorre me.

Fie on ambition, fie on filthy pride,
The roote of ill, the cause of all my woe :
On whose fraile yce my youth first slipt aside :
And falling downe, receiu'd a fatall blow.
   Ah who hath liu'd to see such miserie
   As I haue done, and yet I cannot die ?

I liu'd (quoth she) to see *Troy* set on fire :
I liu'd to see, renowned *Hector* slaine :
I liu'd to see, the shame of my desire :
And yet I liue, to feel my grieuous paine :
   Let all young maides example take by me,
   To keepe their oathes, and spotlesse chastity.

Happy are they, that neuer liu'd to know
What 'tis to liue in this world happily :
Happy are they which neuer yet felt woe :
Happy are they, that die in infancie :
   Whose sins are cancell'd in their mothers wombe :
   Whose cradle is their graue, whose lap their tomb.

Here ended shee ; and then her teares began,
That (Chorus-like) at euery word downe rained.
VVhich like a paire of christall fountaines ran,
Along her louely cheekes : with roses stained :
   Which as they wither still (for want of raine)
   Those siluer showers water them againe.

Now had the poore-mans clock (shrill chauntcleare)
Twice giuen notice of the Mornes approach,
(That then began in glorie to appeare,
Drawne in her stately colour'd saffron-Coach)
   VVhen shee (poore Lady) almost turn'd to teares,
   Began to teare and rend her golden haires.

Lie there (quoth shee) the workers of my woes
You trifling toies, which my liues staine haue bin :
You, by whose meanes our coines chiefly growes,
Clothing the backe with pride, the soule with sin :
   Lie there (quoth shee) the causers of my care ;
   This said, her robes she all in pieces tare.

Here-with, as weary of her wretched life,
(VVhich shee inioy'd with small felicitie)
She ends her fortune with a fatall knife ;
(First day of ioy, last day of miserie :)
 Then why is death accounted Nature's foe,
 Since death (indeed) is but the end of woe ?

For as by death, her bodie was released
From that strong prison made of lime and stone ;
Euen so by death her purest soule was eased,
From bodies prison, and from endlesse mone :
 VVhere now shee walkes in sweete *Elysium*
 (The place for wrongful Death and Martirdum.)

FINIS.

The Encomion of Lady Pecunia :

OR

The praife of Money.

quærenda pecunia primum est,
Virtus post nummos. Horace.

By *Richard Barnfeild*, Graduate in *Oxford.*

LONDON,

Printed by G. S. for Iohn Iaggard, and are
to be sold at his shoppe neere Temple-barre,
at the Signe of the Hand and starre.
1598.

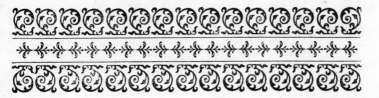

To the Gentlemen Readers.

Entlemen, being incouraged through your gentle acceptance of my *Cynthia*, I haue once more aduentured on your Curtesies: hoping to finde you (as I haue done heretofore) friendly. Being determined to write of somthing, and yet not resolued of any thing, I considered with my selfe, if one should write of Loue (they will say) why, euery one writes of Loue: if of Vertue, why, who regards Vertue? To be short, I could thinke of nothing, but either it was common, or not at all in request. At length I bethought my selfe of a Subiect, both new (as hauing neuer beene written vpon before) and pleasing (as I thought) because Mans Nature (commonly) loues to heare that praised, with whose pressence, hee is most pleased.

Erasmus (the glory of *Netherland*, and the refiner of the Latin Tongue) wrote a whole Booke, in *the prayse of Folly*. Then if so excellent a Scholler, writ in praise of Vanity, why may not I write in praise of that which is profitable? There are no two Countreys, where Gold is esteemed, lesse than in *India*, and more then in *England*: the reason is, because the *Indians* are barbarous, and our Nation ciuill.

I have giuen *Pecunia* the title of a Woman, Both for the termination of the Word, and because (as Women are) shee is lov'd of men. The brauest Voyages in the World, haue beene made for Gold: for it, men haue venterd (by Sea) to the furthest parts of the Earth: In the Pursute whereof, *Englands Nestor* and *Neptune* (*Haukins* and *Drake*) lost their liues. Vpon the Deathes of the which two, of the first I writ this :

The Waters were his Winding sheete, the Sea was made his Toome ;
Yet for his fame the Ocean Sea, was not sufficient roome.

Of the latter this :

England *his hart* ; *his Corps the Waters haue ;*
And that which raysd his fame, became his graue.

The *Prætorians* (after the death of *Pertinax*) in the election of a new Emperour, more esteemed the money of *Iulianus*, then either the vertue of *Seuerus*, or the Valour of *Pessennius*. Then of what great estimation and account, this Lady *Pecunia*, both hath beene in the Worlde, and is at this present, I leaue to your Iudgement. But what speake I so much of her praise in my Epistle, that haue commended her so at large in my Booke ? To the reading wherof, (Gentlemen) I referre you.

[THE AUTHORS FIRST EPISTLE-DEDICATORY (1605).

[Collated with the Bridgwater House copy.]

LEd by the swift report of winged Fame,
     With siluer trumpet, sounding forth your name
     To you I dedicate this merry Muse,
And for my Patron, I your fauour chuse :
She is a Lady, she must be respected :
She is a Queene, she may not be neglected.
     This is the shadow, you the substance haue,
     Which substance now this shadow seems to craue.

RICHARD BARNFIELD.]

The prayse of Lady Pecunia.

Sing not of *Angellica* the faire,
(For whom the Palladine of *Fraunce* fell
   mad)
Nor of sweet *Rosamond*, olde *Cliffords* heire,
(Whose death did make the second *Henry*
   sad)
  But of the fairest Faire *Pecunia*,
  The famous Queene of rich *America*.

Goddesse of Golde, great Empresse of the Earth,
O thou that canst doe all Thinges vnder Heauen :
That doost conuert the saddest minde to Mirth ;
(Of whom the elder Age was quite bereauen)
  Of thee Ile sing, and in thy Prayse Ile write ;
  You *golden Angels* helpe me to indite.

You, you alone, can make my Muse to speake ;
And tell a golden Tale, with siluer Tongue :
You onely can my pleasing silence breake ;
And adde some Musique, to a merry Songue :
  But amongst all the fiue, in Musicks Art,
  I would not sing the *Counter*-tenor part.

The Meane is best, and that I meane to keepe ;
So shall I keepe my selfe from That I meane :
Lest with some Others, I be forc'd to weepe,
And cry *Peccaui*, in a dolefull Scæne.
  But to the matter which I haue in hand,
  The Lady Regent, both by Sea and Land.

When *Saturne* liu'd, and wore the Kingly Crowne,
(And *Ioue* was yet vnborne, but not vnbred)
This Ladies fame was then of no renowne ;
(For Golde was then, no more esteem'd then Lead)
  Then Truth and Honesty were onely vs'd,
  Siluer and Golde were vtterly refus'd.

But when the Worlde grew wiser in Conceit,
And saw how Men in manners did decline,
How Charitie began to loose her heate,
And One did at anothers good repine,
  Then did the Aged, first of all respect her ;
  And vowd from thenceforth, neuer to reiect her.

Thus with the Worlde, her beauty did increase ;
And manie Suters had she to obtaine her :
Some sought her in the Wars, and some in peace ;
But few of youthfull age, could euer gaine her :
  Or if they did, she soone was gone againe ;
  And would with them, but little while remaine.

For why against the Nature of her Sexe,
(That commonlie dispise the feeble Olde)
Shee, loues olde men ; but young men she reiects ;
Because to her, their Loue is quicklie colde :
  Olde men (like Husbands iealous of their Wiues)
  Lock her vp fast, and keepe her as their Liues.

The young man carelesse to maintaine his life,
Neglects her Loue (as though he did abhor her)
Like one that hardly doeth obtaine a wife,
And when he hath her once, he cares not for her :
  Shee, seeing that the young man doeth despyse her,
  Leaues the franke heart, and flies vnto the Myser.

Hee intertaines her, with a ioyfull hart ;
And seemes to rue her vndeserued wrong :
And from his Pressence, she shall neuer part ;
Or if shee doo, he thinkes her Absence long :
  And oftentimes he sends for her againe,
  Whose life without her, cannot long remaine.

And when he hath her, in his owne possession,
He locks her in an iron-barred Chest,
And doubting somewhat, of the like Transgression,
He holds that iron-walled Prison best.
   And least some *rusty* sicknesse should infect her,
   He often visits her, and doeth respect her.

As for the young man (subiect vnto sinne)
No maruell though the Diuell doe distresse him ;
To tempt mans frailtie, which doth neuer linne,
Who many times, hath not a *Crosse* to blesse him :
   But how can hee incurre the Heauens Curse,
   That hath so many *Crosses* in his Purse ?

Hee needes not feare those wicked sprights, that waulke
Vnder the Couerture of cole-blacke Night ;
For why the Diuell still, a *Crosse* doeth baulke,
Because on it, was hangd the Lorde of Light :
   But let not Mysers trust to *siluer Crosses*,
   Least in the End, their gaines be turnd to losses.

But what care they, so they may hoorde vp golde ?
Either for God, or Diuell, or Heauen, or Hell ?
So they may faire *Pecuniaes* face behold ;
And euery Day, their Mounts of Money tell.
   What tho to count their Coyne, they neuer blin,
   Count they their Coyne, and counts not God their sin ?

But what talke I of sinne, to Vsurers ?
Or looke for mendment, at a Mysers hand ?
Pecunia, hath so many followers,
Bootlesse it is, her Power to with-stand.
   King *Couetise*, and *Warinesse* his Wife,
   The Parents were, that first did giue her Life.

But now vnto her Praise I will proceede,
Which is as ample, as the Worlde is wide :
What great Contentment doth her Pressence breede
In him, that can his wealth with Wysdome guide ?
   She is the Soueraigne Queene, of all Delights :
   For her the Lawyer pleades ; the Souldier fights.

For her, the Merchant venters on the Seas :
For her, the Scholler studdies at his Booke :
For her, the Vsurer (with greater ease)
For sillie fishes, layes a siluer hooke :
    For her, the Townsman leaues the Countrey Village :
    For her, the Plowman giues himselfe to Tillage.

For her, the Gentlemen doeth raise his rents :
For her, the Seruingman attends his maister :
For her, the curious head new toyes inuents :
For her, to Sores, the Surgeon layes his plaister.
    In fine for her, each man in his Vocation,
    Applies himselfe, in euerie sev'rall Nation.

What can thy hart desire, but thou mayst haue it,
If thou hast readie money to disburse ?
Then thanke thy Fortune, that so freely gaue it ;
For of all friends, the surest is thy purse.
    Friends may proue false, and leaue thee in thy need ;
    But still thy Purse will bee thy friend indeed.

Admit thou come, into a place vnknowne ;
And no man knowes, of whence, or what thou art :
If once thy faire *Pecunia*, shee be showne,
Thou art esteem'd a man of great Desart :
    And placed at the Tables vpper ende ;
    Not for thine owne sake, but thy faithfull frende.

But if you want your Ladies louely grace,
And haue not wherewithall to pay your shot,
Your Hostis pressently will step in Place,
You are a Stranger (Sir) I know you not :
    By trusting Diuers, I am run in Det ;
    Therefore of mee, nor meate nor Bed you get.

O who can then, expresse the worthie praise,
Which faire *Pecunia* iustly doeth desarue ?
That can the meanest man, to Honor raise ;
And feed the soule, that ready is to starue.
    Affection, which was wont to bee so pure,
    Against a golden Siege, may not endure.

Witnesse the trade of Mercenary sinne;
(Or Occupation, if thou list to tearme it)
Where faire *Pecunia* must the suite beginne;
(As common-tride Experience doeth confirme it)
  Not *Mercury* himselfe, with siluer Tongue,
  Can so inchaunt, as can a golden Songue.

When nothing could subdue the *Phrygian Troy*,
(That Citty through the world so much renowned)
Pecunia did her vtterly destroy:
And left her fame, in darke Obliuion drowned.
  And many Citties since, no lesse in fame,
  For Loue of her, haue yeelded to their shame.

What Thing is then, so well belou'd as money?
It is a speciall Comfort to the minde;
More faire then Women are; more sweet then honey:
Easie to loose, but very harde to finde.
  In fine, to him, whose Purse beginns to faint,
  Golde is a God, and Siluer is a Saint.

The Tyme was once, when Honestie was counted
A Demy god; and so esteem'd of all:
But now *Pecunia* on his Seate is mounted;
Since Honestie in great Disgrace did fall.
  No state, no Calling now, doeth him esteeme;
  Nor of the other ill, doeth any deeme.

The reason is, because he is so poore:
(And who respects the poore, and needie Creature?)
Still begging of his almes, from Doore to Doore:
All ragd, and torne; and eeke deformed in feature.
  In Countinance so changde, that none can know him;
  So weake, and euery vice doeth ouerthrow him.

But faire *Pecunia*, (most diuinely bred)
For sundrie shapes, doth *Proteus* selfe surpasse:
In one Lande, she is suted all in Lead;
And in another, she is clad in Brasse:
  But still within the Coast of *Albion*,
  She euer puts, her best Apparell on.

Siluer and Golde, and nothing else is currant,
In *Englands*, in faire *Englands* happy Land :
All baser sorts of Mettalls, haue no Warrant ;
Yet secretly they *slip*, from hand to hand.
   If any such be tooke, the same is lost,
   And pressently is nayled on a Post.

Which with Quick-siluer, being flourisht ouer,
Seemes to be perfect Siluer, to the showe :
As Woemens paintings, their defects doe couer,
Vnder this false attyre, so doe they goe.
   If on a woollen Cloth, thou rub the same,
   Then will it straight beginne to blush, for shame.

If chafed on thy haire, till it be hot,
If it good Siluer bee, the scent is sweete :
If counterfeit, thy chafing hath begot
A ranke-smelt sauour ; for a Queene vnmeete :
   Pecunia is a Queene, for her Desarts,
   And in the Decke, may goe for *Queene of harts*.

The Queene of harts, because she rules all harts ;
And hath all harts, obedient to her Will :
Whose Bounty, fame vnto the Worlde imparts ;
And with her glory, all the Worlde doeth fill :
   The *Queene of Diamonds*, she cannot bee ;
   There is but one, E L I Z A , thou art shee.

And thou art shee, O sacred Soueraigne ;
Whom God hath helpt with his Al-mighty hand :
Blessing thy People, with thy peacefull raigne ;
And made this little Land, a happy Land :
   May all those liue, that wish long life to thee,
   And all the rest, perish eternally.

Thy tyme was once, when faire *Pecunia,* here
Did basely goe attyred all in Leather :
But since her raigne, she neuer did appeere
But richly clad ; in Golde, or Siluer either :
   Nor reason is it, that her Golden raigne
   With baser Coyne, eclypsed should remaine.

And as the Coyne, she hath repurifyde,
From baser substance, to the purest Mettels:
Religion so, hath shee refinde beside,
From Papistrie, to Truth; which daily settles
   Within her Peoples harts; though some there bee,
   That cleaue vnto their wonted Papistrie.

No flocke of sheepe, but some are still infected.:
No peece of Lawne so pure, but hath some fret:
All buildings are not strong, that are erected:
All Plants proue not, that in good ground are set:
   Some tares are sowne, amongst the choicest seed:
   No garden can be cleansd of euery Weede.

But now to her, whose praise is her pretended,
(Diuine *Pecunia*) fairer then the morne:
Which cannot be sufficiently commended;
Whose Sun-bright Beauty doeth the Worlde adorne,
   Adorns the World, but specially the Purse;
   Without whose pressence, nothing can be worse.

Not faire *Hæsione* (King of *Priams* sister)
Did euer showe more Beauty, in her face,
Then can this louely Lady, if it list her
To showe her selfe; admir'd for comely grace:
   Which neither Age can weare, nor Tyme conclude;
   For why, her Beauty yeerely is renude.

New Coyne is coynd each yeare, within the Tower;
So that her Beauty neuer can decay:
Which to resist, no mortall man hath Power,
When as she doeth her glorious Beames display.
   Nor doeth *Pecunia*, onely please the eie,
   But charms the eare, with heauenly Harmonie.

Lyke to an other *Orpheus*, can she play
Vpon her *treble Harpe*, whose siluer sound
Inchaunts the eare, and steales the hart away:
Nor hardly can deceit, therein be found.
   Although such Musique, some a Shilling cost,
   Yet is it worth but *Nine-pence*, at the most.

Had I the sweet inchaunting Tongue of *Tully*,
That charmd the hearers, lyke the Syrens Song;
Yet could I not describe the Prayses fully,
Which to *Pecunia* iustly doe belong.
   Let it suffice, her Beauty doeth excell:
   Whose praise no Pen can paint, no Tongue can tell.

Then how shall I describe, with artlesse Pen,
The praise of her, whose praise, all praise surmounteth?
Breeding amazement, in the mindes of men:
Of whom, this pressent Age to much accounteth.
   Varietie of Words, would sooner want,
   Then store of plentious matter, would be scant.

Whether yee list, to looke into the Citty:
(Where money tempts the poore Beholders eye)
Or to the Countrey Townes, deuoyde of Pitty:
(Where to the poore, each place doeth almes denye)
   All Thinges for money now, are bought and solde,
   That either hart can thinke, or eie beholde.

Nay more for money (as report doeth tell)
Thou mayst obteine a Pardon for thy sinnes:
The Pope of *Rome*, for money will it sell;
(Whereby thy soule, no small saluation winnes)
   But how can hee, (of Pride the chiefe Beginner)
   Forgiue thy sinnes, that is himselfe a sinner?

Then, sith the Pope is subiect vnto sinne,
No maruell tho, diuine *Pecunia* tempt him,
With her faire Beauty; whose good-will to winne,
Each one contends; and shall we then exempt him.
   Did neuer mortall man, yet looke vpon her,
   But straightwaies he became, enamourd on her.

Yet would I wish, the Wight that loues her so,
And hath obtain'd, the like good-will againe,
To vse her wisely, lest she proue his foe;
And so, in stead of Pleasure, breed his paine.
   She may be kyst; but shee must not be *clypt*:
   Lest such Delight in bitter gall be dypt.

The iuyce of grapes, which is a soueraigne Thing
To cheere the hart, and to reuiue the spirits ;
Being vsde immoderatly (in surfetting)
Rather Dispraise, then commendation merits :
   Euen so *Pecunia*, is, as shee is vsed ;
   Good of her selfe, but bad if once abused.

With her, the Tenant payes his Landlords rent :
On her, depends the stay of euery state :
To her, rich Pressents euery day are sent :
In her, it rests to end all dire Debate :
   Through her, to Wealth, is raisd the Countrey Boore :
   From her, proceedes much proffit to the poore.

Then how can I, sufficiently commend,
Her Beauties worth, which makes the World to wonder ?
Or end her prayse, whose prayses haue no End ?
Whose absence brings the stoutest stomack vnder :
   Let it suffice, *Pecunia* hath no peere ;
   No Wight, no Beauty held ; more faire, more deere.

F I N I S .

His Prayer to Pecunia.

Reat Lady, sith I haue complyde thy Prayse,
(According to my skill and not thy merit :)
And sought thy Fame aboue the starrs to rayse ;
(Had I sweete *Ovids* vaine, or *Virgils* spirit)
   I craue no more but this, for my good will,
   That in my Want, thou wilt supplye me still.

THE

Complaint of Poetrie,

for the Death of Liberalitie.

Viuit post funera virtus.

LONDON,

Printed by G. S. for Iohn Iaggard, and are
to be solde at his shoppe neere Temple-barre,
at the Signe of the Hand and starre.
1 5 9 8.

To his Worshipfull wel-willer, Maister

Edward Leigh, of Grayes Inne.

Mage of that, whose losse is here lamented ;
(In whom, so many vertues are containd)
Daine to accept, what I haue novv presented.
Though Bounties death, herein be not fained,
In your mind, she not reuiue (with speed)
Then will I sweare, that shee is dead indeed.

THE COMPLAINT OF
Poetrie, for the Death of Liberalitie.

Eepe Heauens now, for you haue lost your
    light ;
Ye Sunne and Moone, beare witnes of my
    mone :
The cleere is turnd to clouds ; the day to
    night ;
And all my hope, and all my ioy is gone :
    Bounty is dead, the cause of my annoy ;
    Bounty is dead, and with her dide my ioy.

O who can comfort my afflicted soule ?
Or adde some ende to my increasing sorrowes ?
Who can deliuer me from endlesse dole ?
(Which from my hart eternall torment borrowes.)
    When *Bounty* liu'd, I bore the Bell away ;
    When *Bounty* dide, my credit did decay.

I neuer then, did write one verse in vaine ;
Nor euer went my Poems vnregarded :
Then did each Noble breast, me intertaine,
And for my Labours I was well rewarded :
    But now *Good wordes*, are stept in *Bounties* place,
    Thinking thereby, her glorie to disgrace.

But who can liue with words, in these hard tymes ?
(Although they came from *Iupiter* himselfe ?)
Or who can take such Paiment, for his Rymes ?
(When nothing now, is so esteem'd as Pelfe ?)
   Tis not *Good wordes*, that can a man maintaine ;
   Wordes are but winde ; and winde is all but vaine.

Where is *Mecænas*, Learnings noble Patron ?
(That *Maroes* Muse, with Bountie so did cherish ?)
Or faire *Zenobia*, that worthy Matron ?
(Whose name, for Learnings Loue, shall neuer perish)
   What tho their Bodies, lie full lowe in graue,
   Their fame the worlde; their souls the Heauens haue.

Vile *Auaricia*, how hast thou inchaunted
The Noble mindes, of great and mightie Men ?
Or what infernall furie late hath haunted
Their niggard purses ? (to the learned pen)
   Was it *Augustus* wealth, or noble minde,
   That euerlasting fame, to him assinde ?

If wealth ?   Why *Cræsus* was more rich then hee ;
(Yet *Cræsus* glorie, with his life did end)
It was his Noble mind, that moued mee
To write his praise, and eeke his Acts commend.
   Who ere had heard, of *Alexanders* fame,
   If *Quintus Curtius* had not pend the same ?

Then sith by mee, their deedes haue been declared,
(Which else had perisht with their liues decay)
Who to augment their glories, haue not spared
To crowne their browes, with neuer-fading Bay :
   What Art deserues such Liberalitie,
   As doeth the peerlesse Art of Poetrie ?

But *Liberalitie* is dead and gone :
And *Auarice* vsurps true *Bounties* seat.
For her it is, I make this endlesse mone,
(Whose praises worth no men can well repeat.
   Sweet *Liberalitie* adiew for euer,
   For *Poetrie* againe, shall see thee neuer.

Neuer againe, shall I thy presence see :
Neuer againe, shal I thy bountie tast :
Neuer againe, shal I accepted bee :
Neuer againe, shall I be so embrac't :
    Neuer againe, shall I the bad recall :
    Neuer againe, shall I be lou'd of all :

Thou wast the Nurse, whose Bountie gaue me sucke :
Thou wast the Sunne, whose beames did lend me light :
Thou wast the Tree, whose fruit I still did plucke :
Thou wast the Patron, to maintaine my right :
    Through thee I liu'd ; on thee I did relie ;
    In thee I ioy'd ; and now for thee I die.

What man, hath lately lost a faithfull frend ?
Or Husband, is depriued of his Wife ?
But doth his after-daies in dolour spend ?
(Leading a loathsome, discontented life ?)
    Dearer then friend, or wife, haue I forgone ;
    Then maruell not, although I make such mone.

Faire *Philomela*, cease thy sad complaint ;
And lend thine eares, vnto my dolefull Ditty :
(Whose soule with sorrowe, now begins to faint,
And yet I cannot moue mens hearts to pitty :)
    Thy woes are light, compared vnto mine :
    You waterie Nymphes, to mee your plaints resigne.

And thou *Melpomene*, (the Muse of Death)
That neuer sing'st, but in a dolefull straine ;
Sith cruell Destinie hath stopt her breath,
(Who whilst she liu'd, was Vertues Soueraigne
    Leaue *Hellicon*, (whose bankes so pleasant bee)
    And beare a part of sorrowe now with mee.

The Trees (for sorrowe) shead their fading Leaues,
And weepe out gum, in stead of other teares ;
Comfort nor ioy, no Creature now conceiues,
To chirpe and sing, each little bird forbeares.
    The sillie Sheepe, hangs downe his drooping head,
    And all because, that *Bounty* she is dead.

The greater that I feele my griefe to be,
The lesser able, am I to expresse it ;
Such is the nature of extremitie,
The heart it som-thing eases, to confesse it.
    Therefore Ile wake my muse, amidst her sleeping,
    And what I want in wordes, supplie with weeping.

Weepe still mine eies, a Riuer full of Teares,
To drowne my Sorrowe in, that so molests me ;
And rid my head of cares ; my thoughts of feares :
Exiling sweet Content, that so detests me.
    But ah (alas) my Teares are almost dun,
    And yet my griefe, it is but new begun.

Euen as the Sunne, when as it leaues our sight,
Doth shine with those Antipodes, beneath vs ;
Lending the other worlde her glorious light,
And dismall Darknesse, onely doeth bequeath vs :
    Euen so sweet *Bountie*, seeming dead to mee,
    Liues now to none, but smooth-Tongd Flatterie.

O *Adulation*, Canker-worme of Truth ;
The flattring Glasse of Pride, and Self-conceit :
(Making olde wrinkled Age, appeare like youth)
Dissimulations Maske, and follies Beate :
    Pittie it is, that thou art so rewarded,
    Whilst Truth and Honestie, goe vnregarded.

O that Nobilitie, it selfe should staine,
In being bountifull, to such vile Creatures :
Who, when they flatter most, then most they faine ;
Knowing what humor best, will fit their Natures.
    What man so mad, that knowes himselfe but pore,
    And will beleeue that he hath riches store.

Vpon a time, the craftie Foxe did flatter
The foolish Pye (whose mouth was full of meate)
The Pye beleeuing him, began to chatter,
And sing for ioy, (not hauing list to eate)
    And whil'st the foolish Pye, her meate let fall,
    The craftie Foxe, did runne awaie with all.

Terence describeth vnder *Gnatoes* name,
The right conditions of a Parasyte :
(And with such Eloquence, sets foorth the same,
As doeth the learned Reader much delyght)
    Shewing, that such a Sycophant as *Gnato*,
    In more esteem'd, then twentie such a *Plato*.

Bounty looke backe, vpon thy goods mispent ;
And thinke how ill, thou hast bestow'd thy mony :
Consider not their wordes, but their intent ;
Their hearts are gall, although their tongues be hony :
    They speake not as they thinke, but all is fained,
    And onely to th'intent to be maintained.

And herein happie, I areade the poore ;
No flattring Spanyels, fawne on them for meate :
The reason is, because the Countrey Boore
Hath little enough, for himselfe to eate :
    No man will flatter him, except himselfe ;
    And why ? because hee hath no store of wealth.

But sure it is not *Liberalitie*
That doeth reward these fawning smel-feasts so :
It is the vice of Prodigalitie,
That doeth the Bankers of *Bounty* over-flo :
    Bounty is dead : yea so it needes must bee ;
    Or if aliue, yet is shee dead to mee.

Therefore as one, whose friend is lately dead,
I will bewaile the death, of my deere frend ;
Vppon whose Tombe, ten thousand Teares Ile shead,
Till drearie Death, of mee shall make an end :
    Or if she want a Toombe, to her desart,
    Oh then, Ile burie her within my hart.

But (*Bounty*) if thou loue a Tombe of stone,
Oh then seeke out, a hard and stonie hart :
For were mine so, yet would it melt with mone,
And all because, that I with thee must part.
    Then, if a stonie hart must thee interr,
    Goe finde a Step-dame, or a Vsurer.

And sith there dies no Wight, of great account,
But hath an Epitaph compos'd by mee,
Bounty, that did all other far surmount,
Vpon her Tombe, this Epitaph shall bee :
 Here lies the Wight, that Learning did maintaine,
 And at the last, by A V A R I C E *was slaine.*

Vile *Auarice*, why hast thou kildd my Deare ?
And robd the World, of such a worthy Treasure ?
In whome no sparke of goodnesse doth appeare,
So greedie is thy mind, without all measure,
 Thy death, from Death did merit to release her :
 The Murtherers deseru'd to die, not *Caesar*.

The Merchants wife ; the Tender-hearted Mother
That leaues her loue ; whose Sonne is prest for warre ;
(Resting, the one ; as woefull as the other ;)
Hopes met at length, when ended is the iarre,
 To see her Husband ; see her Sonne again ;
 " Were it not then for Hope, the hart were slaine."

But I, whose hope is turned to despaire
Nere looke to see my dearest Deare againe :
Then *Pleasure* sit thou downe, in *Sorrowes* Chaire,
And (for a while) thy wonted Mirth refraine.
 Bounty is dead, that whylome was my Treasure,
 Bounty is dead, my joy and onely pleasure.

If *Pythias* death, of *Damon* were bewailed ;
Or *Pillades* did rue, *Orestes* ende :
If *Hercules*, for *Hylas* losse were quailed ;
Or *Theseus*, for *Pyrithous* Teares did spende :
 When doe I mourne for *Bounty*, being dead :
 Who liuing, was my hand, my hart, my head.

My hand, to helpe mee, in my greatest need :
My hart, to comfort mee, in my distresse :
My head, whom onely I obeyd, indeed :
If she were such, how can my griefe be lesse ?
 Perhaps my wordes, may pierce the *Parcœ's* eares ;
 If not with wordes, Ile moue them with my teares.

But ah (alas) my Teares are spent in vaine,
(For she is dead, and I am left aliue)
Teares cannot call, sweet *Bounty* backe againe ;
Then why doe I, gainst Fate and Fortune striue ?
   And for her death, thus weepe, lament, and crie;
   Sith euery mortall wight, is borne to die.

But as the woefull mother doeth lament,
Her tender babe, with cruell Death opprest :
Whose life was spotlesse, pure, and innocent,
(And therefore sure, it[s] soule is gone to rest)
   So *Bountie*, which her selfe did vpright keepe,
   Yet for her losse, loue cannot chuse but weepe.

The losse of her, is losse to many a one :
The losse of her, is losse vnto the poore :
And therefore not a losse, to mee alone,
But vnto such, as goe from Doore to Doore.
   Her losse, is losse vnto the fatherlesse ;
   And vnto all, that are in great distresse.

The maimed Souldier, comming from the warre,
The woefull wight, whose house was lately burnd ;
The sillie soule ; the wofull Traueylar ;
And all, whom Fortune at her feet hath spurnd ;
   Lament the losse of *Liberalitie* :
   "Its ease, to haue in griefe some Companie."

The Wife of *Hector* (sad *Andromache*)
Did not bewaile, her husbands death alone :
But (sith he was the *Troians* onely stay)
The wiues of *Troy* (for him) made æquall mone.
   Shee, shead the teares of Loue ; and they of pittie :
   Shee, for her deare dead Lord ; they, for their Cittie.

Nor is the Death of *Liberalitie*,
(Although my griefe be greater than the rest)
Onely lamented, and bewaild of mee ;
(And yet of mee, she was beloued best)
   But, sith she was so bountifull to all,
   She is lamented, both of great and small.

O that my Teares could moue the powres diuine,
That *Bountie* might be called from the dead :
As Pitty pierc'd the hart of *Proserpine* ;
Who (moued with the Teares *Admetus* shead)
   Did sende him backe againe, his louing Wife ;
   Who lost her owne, to saue her husbands life.

Impartiall *Parcæ*, will no prayers moue you ?
Can Creatures so diuine, haue stony harts?
Haplesse are they, whose hap it is to proue you,
For you respect no Creatures good Desarts.
   O *Atropos*, (the cruelst of the three)
   Why hast thou tane, my faithfull friend from mee ?

But ah, she cannot (or shee will not) heare me,
Or if shee doo, yet may not she repent her :
Then come (sweet Death) O why doest thou forbeare me ?
Aye mee ! thy Dart is blunt, it will not enter.
   Oh now I knowe the cause, and reason why ;
   I am immortall, and I cannot dye.

So *Cytheræa* would haue dide, but could not ;
When faire *Adonis* by her side lay slaine :
So I desire the Sisters, what I should not ;
For why (alas) I wish for Death in vaine ;
   Death is their seruant, and obeys their will ;
   And if they bid him spare, he cannot kill.

Oh would I were, as other Creatures are ;
Then would I die, and so my griefe were ended :
But Death (against my will) my life doeth spare ;
(So little with the fates I am befrended)
   Sith, when I would, thou doost my sute denie,
   Vile Tyrant, when thou wilt, I will not die.

And *Bounty*, though her body thou hast slaine,
Yet shall her memorie remaine for euer :
For euer, shall her memorie remaine ;
Whereof no spitefull Fortune can bereaue her.
   Then Sorrowe cease, and wipe thy weeping eye ;
   For Fame shall liue, when all the World shall dye.

FINIS.

THE
Combat, betweene
Conscience and Couetousnesse,
in the minde of Man.

quid non mortalia pectora cogis
Auri sacra fames? Virgil.

LONDON,

Printed by G. S. for Iohn Iaggard, and are
to be solde at his shoppe neere Temple-barre,
at the Signe of the Hand and starre.
1598.

To his Worshipfull good friend,

Maister *Iohn Steuenton*, of *Dothill*, in the County
of *Salop*, Esquire.

Ith Conscience (long since) is exilde the Citty,
   O let her in the Countrey, finde some Pitty :
But if she be exilde, the Countrey too,
   O let her finde, some fauour yet of you.

The Combat betweene Conscience
and Couetousnesse in the
mind of Man.

Ow had the cole-blacke steedes, of pitchie
   Night,
(Breathing out Darknesse) banisht cheer-
   full Light,
And sleepe (the shaddowe of eternall rest)
My seuerall senses, wholy had possest.
When loe, there was presented to my view,
   A vision strange, yet not so strange, as true.
Conscience (me thought) appeared vnto mee,
Cloth'd with good Deedes, with Trueth and Honestie,
Her countinance demure, and sober sad,
Nor any other Ornament shee had.
Then *Couetousnesse* did incounter her,
Clad in a Cassock, lyke a Vsurer,
The Cassock, it was made of poore-mens skinnes,
Lac'd here and there, with many seuerall sinnes :
Nor was it furd, with any common furre ;
Or if it were, himselfe hee was the *fur*.
A Bag of money, in his hande he helde,
The which with hungry eie, he still behelde.
The place wherein this vision first began,
(A spacious plaine) was cald *The Minde of Man*.
The Carle no sooner, *Conscience* had espyde,
But swelling lyke a Toade, (puft vp with pryde)

He straight began against her to inuey :
These were the wordes, which *Couetise* did sey.
Conscience (quoth hee) how dar'st thou bee so bold,
To claime the place, that I by right doe hold ?
Neither by right, nor might, thou canst obtaine it :
By might (thou knowst full well) thou canst not gaine it
The greatest Princes are my followars,
The King in Peace, the Captaine in the Warres :
The Courtier, and the simple Countrey-man :
The Iudge, the Merchant, and the Gentleman :
The learned Lawyer, and the Politician :
The skilfull Surgeon, and the fine Physician :
In briefe, all sortes of men mee entertaine,
And hold mee, as their Soules sole Soueraigne,
And in my quarrell, they will fight and die,
Rather then I should suffer iniurie.
And as for title, interest, and right,
Ile proue its mine by that, as well as might,
Though *Couetousnesse*, were vsed long before,
Yet *Iudas* Treason, made my Fame the more ;
When *Christ* he caused, crucifyde to bee,
For thirtie pence, man solde his minde to mee :
And now adaies, what tenure is more free,
Than that which purchas'd is, with Gold and fee ?

Conscience.

With patience, haue I heard thy large Complaint,
Wherein the Diuell, would be thought a Saint :
But wot ye what, the Saying is of olde ?
One tale is good, vntill anothers tolde.
Truth is the right, that I must stand vpon,
(For other title, hath poore *Conscience* none)
First I will proue it, by Antiquitie,
That thou art but an vp-start, vnto mee ;
Before that thou wast euer thought vpon,
The minde of Man, belongd to mee alone.
For after that the Lord, hath Man created,
And him in blisse-full Paradice had seated ;
(Knowing his Nature was to vice inclynde)
God gaue me vnto man, to rule his mynde,
And as it were, his Gouernour to bee,

To guide his minde, in Trueth, and Honestie.
And where thou sayst, that man did sell his soule ;
That Argument, I quicklie can controule :
It is a fayned fable, thou doost tell,
That, which is not his owne, he cannot sell ;
No man can sell his soule, altho he thought it :
Mans soule is *Christs*, for hee hath dearely bought it.
Therefore vsurping *Couetise*, be gone.
For why, the minde belongs to mee alone.

Couetousnesse.

Alas poore *Conscience*, how thou art deceav'd ?
As though of senses, thou wert quite bereaud.
What wilt thou say (that thinkst thou canst not erre)
If I can proue my selfe the ancienter ?
Though into *Adams* minde, God did infuse thee,
Before his fall, yet man did neuer vse thee.
What was it else, but *Aurice* in *Eue*,
(Thinking thereby, in greater Blisse to liue)
That made her taste, of the forbidden fruite ?
Of her Desier, was not I the roote ?
Did she not couet ? (tempted by the Deuill)
The Apple of the Tree, of good and euill ?
Before man vsed *Conscience*, she did couet :
Therefore by her Transgression, here I proue it,
That *Couetousnesse* possest the minde of man,
Before that any *Conscience* began.

Conscience.

Euen as a counterfeited precious stone,
Seemes to bee far more rich, to looke vpon,
Then doeth the right : But when a man comes neere,
His baseness then, doeth euident appeere :
So *Couetise*, the Reasons thou doost tell,
Seeme to be strong, but being weighed well,
They are indeed, but onely meere Illusions,
And doe inforce but very weake Conclusions.
When as the Lord (fore-knowing his offence)
Had giuen man a Charge, of Abstinence,
And to refraine, the fruite of good and ill :
Man had a *Conscience*, to obey his will,

And neuer would be tempted thereunto,
Vntill the Woeman, shee, did worke *man woe*.
And make him breake, the Lords Commaundement,
Which all Mankinde, did afterward repent :
So that thou seest, thy Argument is vaine,
And I am prov'd, the elder of the twaine.

Couetousnesse.

Fond Wretch, it was not *Conscience*, but feare,
That made the first man (Adam) to forbeare
To tast the fruite, of the forbidden Tree,
Lest, if offending hee were found to bee,
(According as *Iehouah* saide on hye,
For his so great Transgression, hee should dye.)
Feare curbd his minde, it was not *Conscience* then,
(For *Conscience* freely, rules the harts of men)
And is a godly motion of the mynde,
To euerie vertuous action inclynde,
And not enforc'd, through feare of Punishment,
But is to vertue, voluntary bent :
Then (simple Trul) be packing presentlie,
For in this place, there is no roome for thee.

Conscience.

Aye mee (distressed Wight) what shall I doe ?
Where shall I rest ? Or whither shall I goe ?
Vnto the rich ? (woes mee) they, doe abhor me :
Vnto the poore ? (alas) they, care not for me :
Vnto the Olde-man ? hee ; hath mee forgot :
Vnto the Young-man ? yet hee, knowes me not :
Vnto the Prince ? hee ; can dispence with me :
Vnto the Magistrate ? that, may not bee :
Vnto the Court ? for it, I am too base :
Vnto the Countrey ? there, I haue no place :
Vnto the Citty ? thence ; I am exilde :
Vnto the Village ? there ; I am reuilde :
Vnto the Barre ? the Lawyer there, is bribed ?
Vnto the Warre ? there, *Conscience* is derided :
Vnto the Temple ? there, I am disguised :
Vnto the Market ? there, I am dispised :
Thus both the young and olde, the rich and poore,

Against mee (silly Creature) shut their doore.
Then, sith each one seekes my rebuke and shame,
Ile goe againe to Heauen (from whence I came.)
   This saide (me thought) making exceeding mone,
She went her way, and left the Carle alone,
Who vaunting of his late-got victorie,
Aduanc'd himselfe in pompe and Maiestie :
Much like a Cocke, who hauing kild his foe,
Brisks vp himselfe, and then begins to crow.
So *Couetise*, when *Conscience* was departed,
Gan to be proud in minde, and hauty harted :
And in a stately Chayre of state he set him,
(For *Conscience* banisht) there are none to let him.
And being but one entrie, to this Plaine,
(Whereof as king and Lord, he did remaine)
Repentance cald, he causd that to be kept,
Lest *Conscience* should returne, whilst as he slept :
Wherefore he causd it, to be watcht and warded
Both night and Day, and to be strongly guarded :
To keepe it safe, these three he did intreat,
Hardnesse of hart, with *Falshood* and *Deceat :*
And if at any time, she chaunc'd to venter,
Hardnesse of hart, denide her still to enter.
When *Conscience* was exilde the minde of Man,
Then *Couetise*, his gouernment began.
This once being seene, what I had seene before,
(Being onely seene in sleepe) was seene no more ;
For with the sorrowe, which my Soule did take
At sight hereof, foorthwith I did awake.

FINIS.

Poems:

In diuers humors.

Trahit sua quemque voluptas. Virgil.

LONDON,
Printed by **G. S.** for **Iohn Iaggard**, and are
to be solde at his shoppe neere Temple-barre,
at the Signe of the Hand and starre.
1598.

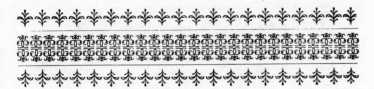

To the learned, and accomplisht Gentleman,

Maister *Nicholas Blackleech*,

of Grayes Inne.

O you, that know the tuch of true Conceat ;
(Whose many gifts I neede not to repeat)
I vvrite these Lines ; fruits of vnriper yeares ;
Wherein my Muse no harder censure feares :
Hoping in gentle Worth, you will them take ;
Not for the gift, but for the giuers sake.

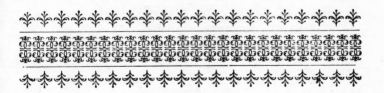

SONNET. I.

To his friend Maister R. L.   In praise of
Musique and Poetrie.

F Musique and sweet Poetrie agree,
   As they must needes (the Sister and the
      Brother)
   Then must the Loue be great, twixt thee
      and mee,
      Because thou lou'st the one, and I the
         other.
   Dowland to thee is deare; whose heauenly tuch
Vpon the Lute, doeth rauish humaine sense:
Spenser to mee; whose deepe Conceit is such,
   As passing all Conceit, needs no defence.
   Thou lou'st to heare the sweete melodious sound,
That *Phœbus* Lute (the Queene of Musique) makes:
And I in deepe Delight am chiefly drownd,
   When as himselfe to singing he betakes.
      One God is God of Both (as Poets faigne)
      One Knight loues Both, and Both in thee remaine.

265

SONNET. II.

Against the Dispraysers of Poetrie.

Haucer is dead; and *Gower* lyes in grave;
  The Earle of *Surrey*, long agoe is gone;
  Sir *Philip Sidneis* soule, the Heauens haue;
  George Gascoigne him beforne, was tomb'd in stone,
    Yet, tho their Bodies lye full low in ground,
(As euery thing must dye, that earst was borne)
Their liuing fame, no Fortune can confound;
Nor euer shall their Labours be forlorne.
    And you, that discommend sweete Poetrie,
(So that the Subiect of the same be good)
Here may you see, your fond simplicitie;
Sith Kings haue fauord it, of royall Blood.
    The King of *Scots* (now liuing) is a Poet,
  As his *Lepanto*, and his *Furies* shoe it.

A Remembrance of some English Poets.

Iue *Spenser* euer, in thy *Fairy Queene*:
  Whose like (for deepe Conceit) was neuer seene.
  Crownd mayst thou bee, vnto thy more renowne,
  (As King of Poets) with a Lawrell Crowne.

And *Daniell*, praised for thy sweet-chast Verse:
Whose Fame is grav'd on *Rosamonds* blacke Herse.
Still mayst thou liue: and still be honored,
For that rare Worke, *The White Rose and the Red.*

And *Drayton*, whose wel-written Tragedies,
And sweete Epistles, soare thy fame to skies.
Thy learned Name, is æquall with the rest;
Whose stately Numbers are so well addrest.

And *Shakespeare* thou, whose hony-flowing Vaine,
(Pleasing the World) thy Praises doth obtaine.
Whose *Venus*, and whose *Lucrece* (sweete, and chaste)
Thy Name in fames immortall Booke haue plac't.
   Liue euer you, at least in Fame liue euer:
  Well may the Bodye dye, but Fame dies neuer.

An Ode.

AS it fell vpon a Day,
  In the merrie Month of May,
  Sitting in a pleasant shade,
  Which a groue of Myrtles made,
Beastes did leape, and Birds did sing,
Trees did grow, and Plants did spring:
Euery thing did banish mone,
Saue the Nightingale alone.
Shee (poore Bird) as all forlorne,
Leand her Breast vp-till a Thorne,
And there sung the dolefulst Ditty,
That to heare it was great Pitty.
Fie, fie, fie, now would she cry
Teru Teru, by and by:
That to heare her so complaine,
Scarce I could from Teares refraine:
For her griefes so liuely showne,
Made me thinke vpon mine owne.
Ah (thought I) thou mournst in vaine;
None takes Pitty on thy paine:
Senslesse Trees, they cannot heere thee;
Ruthlesse Beares, they wil not cheer thee.
King *Pandion,* hee is dead:
All thy friends are lapt in Lead.
All thy fellow Birds doe singe,
Carelesse of thy sorrowing.

Whilst as fickle Fortune smilde,
Thou and I, were both beguilde.
Euerie one that flatters thee,
Is no friend in miserie :
Words are easie, like the winde ;
Faithfull friends are hard to finde :
Euerie man will bee thy friend,
Whilst thou hast wherewith to spend :
But if store of Crownes be scant,
No man will supply thy want.
If that one be prodigall,
Bountifull, they will him call.
And with such-like flattering,
Pitty but hee were a King.
If hee bee adict to vice,
Quickly him, they will intice.
If to Woemen hee be bent,
They haue at Commaundement.
But if Fortune once doe frowne,
Then farewell his great renowne :
They that fawnd on him before,
Vse his company no more.
Hee that is thy friend indeed,
Hee will helpe thee in thy neede :
If thou sorrowe, hee will weepe ;
If thou wake, hee cannot sleepe :
Thus of euerie griefe, in hart,
Hee, with thee, doeth beare a Part.
These are certaine Signes, to knowe
Faithfull friend, from flatt'ring foe.

Written, at the Request of a Gentleman,

vnder a Gentlewoman's Picture.

Uen as *Apelles* could not paint *Campaspes* face
    aright :
Because *Campaspes* Sun-bright eyes did dimme
    Apelles sight :
    Euen so, amazed at her sight, her sight, all sights
        excelling,
Like *Nyobe* the Painter stoode, her sight his sight expelling,
Thus Art and Nature did contend, who should the Victor bee,
Till Art by Nature was supprest, as all the worlde may see.

An Epitaph vpon the Death, of Sir Philip

Sidney, Knight ; Lord-gouernour of Vlissing.

Hat *England* lost, that Learning lov'd, that euery
    mouth commended,
    That fame did prayse, that Prince did rayse, that
        Countrey do defended,
    Here lyes the man : lyke to the Swan, who know-
        ing shee shall die,
Doeth tune her voice vnto the Spheares, and scornes Mortalitie.
Two worthie Earls his vncles were ; a Lady was his Mother ;
A Knight his father ; and himselfe a noble Countesse Brother.
Belov'd, bewaild ; aliue, now dead ; of all, with Teares for euer ;
Here lyes Sir *Philip Sidneis* Corps, whom cruell Death did
    seuer,
He liv'd for her, hee dyde for her ; for whom he dyde, he liued :
O graunt (O God) that wee of her, may neuer be depriued.

An Epitaph vpon the Death of his Aunt,

Mistresse Elizabeth Skrymsher.

Loe here beholde the certaine Ende, of euery liuing
    wight :
No Creature is secure from Death, for Death
    will haue his Right.
He spareth none : both rich and poore, both
    young and olde must die ;
So fraile is flesh, so short is Life, so sure Mortalitie.
When first the Bodye liues to Life, the soule first dies to
    sinne :
And they that loose this earthly Life, a heauenly Life shall
    winne,
If they liue well : as well she liv'd, that lyeth Vnder heere ;
Whose Vertuous Life to all the Worlde, most plainly did
    appeere.
Good to the poore, friend to the rich, and foe to no Degree :
A President of modest Life, and peerelesse Chastitie.
Who louing more, Who more belov'd of euerie honest mynde ?
Who more to Hospitalitie, and Clemencie inclinde
Then she ? that being buried here, lyes wrapt in Earth
    below ;
From whence we came, to whom wee must, and bee as shee
    is now,
A Clodd of Clay : though her pure soule in endlesse Blisse
    doeth rest ;
Ioying all Ioy, the Place of Peace, prepared for the blest :
Where holy Angells sit and sing, before the King of Kings ;
Not mynding worldly Vanities, but onely heauenly Things.
Vnto which Ioy, Vnto which Blisse, Vnto which Place of
    Pleasure,
God graunt that wee may come at last, t' inioy that heauenly
    Treasure.
Which to obtaine, to liue as shee hath done let us endeuor ;
That wee may liue with Christ himselfe, (above) that liues
    for euer.

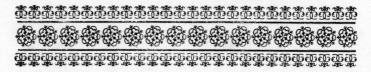

A Comparison of the Life
of Man.

Ans life is vvell compared to a feast,
Furnisht with choice of all Varietie :
To it comes Tyme ; and as a bidden guest
Hee sets him downe, in Pompe and Maiestie ;
The three-folde Age of Man, the Waiters bee,
Then with an earthen voyder (made of clay)
Comes Death, and takes the table clean
away.

FINIS.

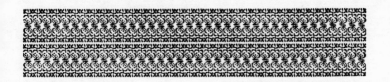

ASTROPHEL.

A Pastoral Elegy upon the death of the most noble and valorous Knight, Sir PHILIP SIDNEY.

Dedicated
to the most beautiful and virtuous Lady
the Countess of ESSEX.

[By EDMUND SPENSER, the Countess of PEMBROKE, and others.]

[Printed as an Appendix to COLIN CLOUT's *come home again,* first printed in 1595 ; but the epistle of which is dated "From my house of Kilcolman, the 27 of December, 1591."]

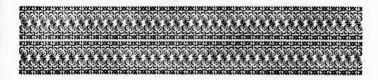

Astrophel.

HEPHERDS that wont, on pipes of oaten reed,
Ofttimes to plain your love's concealèd smart;
And with your piteous lays have learned to breed
Compassion in a country lass's heart:
Hearken, ye gentle shepherds, to my song!
And place my doleful plaint, your plaints emong.

To you alone, I sing this mournful verse,
The mournful'st verse that ever man heard tell:
To you whose softened hearts it may empierce
With dolour's dart, for death of ASTROPHEL.
To you I sing, and to none other wight,
For well I wot my rhymes been rudely dight.

Yet as they been, if any nicer wit
Shall hap to hear, or covet them to read:
Think he, that such are for such ones most fit,
Made not to please the living but the dead:
And if in him, found pity ever place;
Let him be moved to pity such a case.

ASTROPHEL.

A Pastoral Elegy upon the death of
the most noble and valorous Knight,
Sir PHILIP SIDNEY.

GENTLE shepherd born in Arcady,
Of gentlest race that ever shepherd bore;
About the grassy banks of Hœmony,
Did keep his sheep, his little stock and store.
Full carefully he kept them day and night
In fairest fields; and ASTROPHEL he hight.

Young ASTROPHEL! the pride of shepherds' praise.
Young ASTROPHEL! the rustic lasses' love.
Far passing all the pastors of his days
In all that seemly shepherd might behove.
In one thing only failing of the best;
That he was not so happy as the rest.

For from the time that first the nymph his mother
Him forth did bring; and taught, her lambs to feed:
A slender swain, excelling far each other
In comely shape, like her that did him breed:
He grew up fast in goodness and in grace;
And doubly fair wox both in mind and face.

Which daily more and more he did augment
With gentle usage and demeanour mild;
That all men's hearts with secret ravishment
He stole away, and wittingly beguiled.
Ne Spite itself—that all good things doth spill—
Found ought in him, that she could say was ill.

His sports were fair, his joyance innocent,
Sweet without sour, and honey without gall;
And he himself seemed made for merriment,
Merrily masking both in bower and hall.
There was no pleasure nor delightful play
When ASTROPHEL so ever was away.

For he could pipe, and dance, and carol sweet;
Emongst the shepherds in their shearing feast:
As summer's lark that with her song doth greet
The dawning day, forth coming from the East.
And lays of love he also would compose.
Thrice happy she! whom he to praise did choose.

Full many maidens often did him woo,
Them to vouchsafe, emongst his rhymes to name :
Or make for them, as he was wont to do,
For her that did his heart with love inflame ;
For which they promised to dight for him,
Gay chaplets of flowers and garlands trim.

And many a nymph, both of the wood and brook,
Soon as his oaten pipe began to shrill ;
Both crystal wells and shady groves forsook,
To hear the charms of his enchanting skill :
And brought him presents ; flowers, if it were prime :
Or mellow fruit, if it were harvest time.

But he for none of them did care a whit ;
Yet wood-gods for them oft sighed sore :
Ne for their gifts unworthy of his wit,
Yet not unworthy of the country's store.
For One alone he cared, for One he sighed
His life's treasure, and his dear love's delight.

STELLA the fair ! the fairest star in sky :
As fair as VENUS, or the fairest fair.
A fairer star saw never living eye,
Shot her sharp pointed beams through purest air.
Her, he did love ; her, he alone he did honour ;
His thoughts, his rhymes, his songs were all upon her.

To her, he vowed the service of his days ;
On her, he spent the riches of his wit ;
For her, he made hymns of immortal praise :
Of only her ; he sang, he thought, he writ.
Her, and but her, of love he worthy deemed :
For all the rest, but little he esteemed.

Ne her with idle words alone he vowed,
And verses vain—yet verses are not vain :
But with brave deeds, to her sole service vowed ;
And bold achievements, her did entertain.
For both in deeds and words he nurtured was.
Both wise and hardy—too hardy, alas !

In wrestling, nimble ; and in running, swift ;
In shooting, steady ; and in swimming, strong :
Well made to strike, to throw, to leap, to lift,
And all the sports that shepherds are emong.
In every one, he vanquished every one,
He vanquished all, and vanquished was of none.

Besides, in hunting such felicity
Or rather infelicity, he found ;
That every field and forest far away
He sought, where savage beasts do most abound.
No beast so savage, but he could it kill :
No chase so hard, but he therein had skill.

Such skill, matched with such courage as he had,
Did prick him forth with proud desire of praise ;
To seek abroad, of danger nought y'drad,
His mistress' name and his own fame to raise.
What need, peril to be sought abroad ?
Since round about us, it doth make abode.

It fortuned as he, that perilous game
In foreign soil pursued, far away ;
Into a forest wide and waste, he came,
Where store he heard to be of savage prey.
So wide a forest and so waste as this,
Nor famous Ardenne, nor foul Arlo is.

There his well-woven toils and subtle trains
He laid, the brutish nation to enwrap :
So well he wrought with practice and with pains,
That he of them, great troops did soon entrap.
Full happy man ! misweening much, was he ;
So rich a spoil within his power to see.

Eftsoons, all heedless of his dearest hale,
Full greedily into the herd he thrust
To slaughter them and work their final bale,
Lest that his toil should of their troops be burst.
Wide wounds emongst them, many one he made ;
Now with his sharp boar spear, now with his blade.

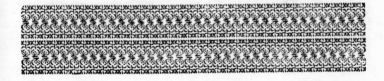

His care was all, how he them all might kill;
That none might 'scape, so partial unto none.
Ill mind! so much to mind another's ill,
As to become unmindful of his own.
But pardon that unto the cruel skies,
That from himself to them, withdrew his eyes.

So as he raged emongst that beastly rout;
A cruel beast of most accursèd brood,
Upon him turned—despair makes cowards stout ;
And with fell tooth, accustomèd to blood,
Launched his thigh with so mischievous might,
That it both bone and muscle rivèd quite.

So deadly was the dint, and deep the wound,
And so huge streams of blood thereout did flow;
That he endurèd not the direful stound
But on the cold dear earth, himself did throw.
The whiles the captive herd his nets did rend,
And having none to let ; to wood did wend.

Ah, where were ye this while, his shepherd peers ?
To whom alive was nought so dear as he.
And ye fair maids, the matches of his years !
Which in his grace, did boast you most to be ?
And where were ye, when he of you had need,
To stop his wound that wondrously did bleed ?

Ah, wretched boy! the shape of drearihead!
And sad ensample of man's sudden end!
Full little faileth, but thou shalt be dead ;
Unpitied, unplained of foe or friend :
Whilst none is nigh, thine eyelids up to close ;
And kiss thy lips like faded leaves of rose.

A sort of shepherds suing of the chase,
As they the forest rangèd on a day ;
By fate or fortune came unto the place,
Whereas the luckless boy yet bleeding lay.
Yet bleeding lay, and yet would still have bled,
Had not good hap those shepherds thither led.

They stopped his wound—too late to stop, it was,
And in their arms then softly did him rear :
Tho, as he willed, unto his lovèd lass,
His dearest love, him dolefully did bear.
The doleful'st bier that ever man did see
Was ASTROPHEL, but dearest unto me.

She, when she saw her love in such a plight,
With curdled blood and filthy gore deformed ;
That wont to be with flowers and garlands dight,
And her dear favours dearly well adorned.
Her face, the fairest face that eye might see,
She likewise did deform, like him to be.

Her yellow locks that shone so bright and long,
As sunny beams in fairest summer's day;
She fiercely tore: and with outrageous wrong,
From her red cheeks, the roses rent away.
And her fair breast, the treasury of joy;
She spoiled thereof, and fillèd with annoy.

His pallid face, impicturèd with death;
She bathèd oft with tears and drièd oft:
And with sweet kisses, sucked the wasting breath
Out of his lips, like lilies pale and soft.
And oft she called to him, who answered nought;
But only by his looks did tell his thought.

The rest of her impatient regret
And piteous moan, the which she for him made;
No tongue can tell, nor any forth can set:
But he whose heart, like sorrow did invade.
At last, when pain his vital powers had spent,
His wasted life her weary lodge forewent.

Which when she saw, she stayèd not a whit,
But after him, did make untimely haste:
Forthwith her ghost out of her corps did flit,
And followed her mate, like turtle chaste.
To prove that death, their hearts cannot divide;
Which living were in love so firmly tied.

The gods, which all things see, this same beheld.
And pitying this pair of lovers true;
Transformèd them, there lying on the field,
Into one flower that is both red and blue.
It first grows red, and then to blue doth fade;
Like ASTROPHEL, which thereinto was madè.

And in the midst thereof a star appears,
As fairly formed as any star in sky;
Resembling STELLA in her freshest years,
Forth darting beams of beauty from her eyes:
And all the day it standeth full of dew,
Which is the tears that from her eyes did flow.

That herb of some, " Starlight " is called by name;
Of others *Penthia*, though not so well:
But thou wherever thou dost find the same,
From this day forth do call it *Astrophel*.
And whensoever thou it up dost take;
Do pluck it softly, for that shepherd's sake.

Hereof when tidings far abroad did pass,
The shepherds all which lovèd him full dear—
And sure, full dear of all he lovèd was—
Did thither flock to see what they did hear.
And when that piteous spectacle they viewed,
The same with bitter tears they all bedewed.

And every one did make exceeding moan,
With inward anguish and great grief opprest;
And every one did weep and wail and moan,
And means devised to show his sorrow best.
That from that hour since first on grassy green,
Shepherds kept sheep; was not like mourning seen.

But first his sister that CLORINDA hight,
The gentlest shepherdess that lives this day;
And most resembling both in shape and sprite,
Her brother dear, began this doleful lay.
Which lest I mar the sweetness of the verse,
In sort as she it sung, I will rehearse.

" YE me! to whom shall I, my case complain,
That may compassion my impatient grief?
Or where shall I unfold my inward pain
That my enriven heart may find relief?
Shall I unto the heavenly powers it show,
Or unto earthly men that dwell below? "

"To heavens! Ah, they, alas, the authors were
And workers of my unremèdied woe;
For they foresee what to us happens here,
And they foresaw, yet suffered this be so.
From them comes good, from them comes also ill;
That which they made, who can them warn to spill?"

" To men!   Ah, they, alas, like wretched be
And subject to the heaven's ordinance ;
Bound to abide whatever they decree,
Their best redress, is their best sufferance.
How then can they, like wretched, comfort me ?
The which no less, need comforted to be."

" Then to myself, will I my sorrow mourn,
Sith none alive like sorrowful remains ;
And to myself, my plaints shall back return,
To pay their usury with doubled pains.
The woods, the hills, the rivers shall resound
The mournful accent of my sorrow's ground."

" Woods, hills and rivers now are desolate ;
Sith he is gone the which them all did grace :
And all the fields do wail their widow-state ;
Sith death, their fairest flower did late deface.
The fairest flower in field that ever grew,
Was ASTROPHEL: that 'was,' we all may rue."

" What cruel hand of cursèd foe unknown,
Hath cropped the stalk which bore so fair a flower ?
Untimely cropped, before it well were grown,
And clean defacèd in untimely hour.
Great loss to all that ever him see,
Great loss to all, but greatest loss to me."

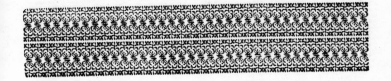

"Break now your garlands, O ye shepherds' lasses!
Sith the fair flower, which them adorned, is gone:
The flower, which them adorned, is gone to ashes,
Never again let lass put garland on.
    Instead of garland, wear sad cypress now;
    And bitter elder, broken from the bough."

"Ne ever sing the love-lays which he made;
Whoever made such lays of love as he?
Ne ever read the riddles, which he said
Unto yourselves, to make you merry glee.
    Your merry glee is now laid all abed,
    Your merry-maker now, alas! is dead."

"Death! the devourer of all world's delight,
Hath robbèd you, and reft from me my joy;
Both you and me and all the world, he quite
Hath robbed of joyance; and left sad annoy.
    Joy of the world! and shepherds' pride was he:
    Shepherds hope never, like again to see."

"Oh, Death! that hast us of such riches reft,
Tell us at least, What hast thou with it done?
What is become of him, whose flower here left;
Is but the shadow of his likeness gone.
    Scarce like the shadow of that which he was:
    Nought like, but that he, like a shade, did pass."

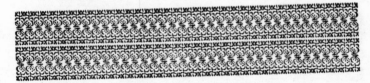

" But that immortal spirit, which was deckt
With all the dowries of celestial grace ;
By sovereign choice from th' heavenly quires select,
And lineally derived from angels' race :
  O what is now of it become aread ?
  Aye me ! can so divine a thing be dead ? "

" Ah, no ! It is not dead, nor can it die ;
But lives for aye in blissful Paradise :
Where like a new-born babe it soft doth lie
In bed of lilies, wrapped in tender wise :
  And compassed all about with roses sweet,
  And dainty violets from head to feet."

" There, thousand birds, all of celestial brood,
To him do sweetly carol day and night ;
And with strange notes, of him well understood,
Lull him asleep in angelic delight :
  Whilst in sweet dream, to him presented be
  Immortal beauties, which no eye may see."

" But he them sees, and takes exceeding pleasure
Of their divine aspects, appearing plain ;
And kindling love in him above all measure
Sweet love, still joyous, never feeling pain.
  For what so goodly form he there doth see,
  He may enjoy, from jealous rancour free."

" There liveth he in everlasting bliss,
Sweet spirit ! never fearing more to die :
Ne dreading harm from any foes of his,
Ne fearing savage beast's more cruelty.
  Whilst we here, wretches ! wail his private lack ;
  And with vain vows do often call him back."

" But live thou there still happy, happy spirit !
And give us leave, thee here thus to lament :
Not thee, that dost thy heaven's joy inherit ;
But our own selves, that here in dole are drent.
  Thus do we weep and wail, and wear our eyes,
  Mourning in others, our own miseries."

Which when she ended had, another swain,
Of gentle wit and dainty sweet device ;
Whom ASTROPHEL full dear did entertain
Whilst here he lived, and held in passing price :
Hight THESTYLIS, began his mournful tourn,
And made the Muses in his song to mourn.

And after him, full many other moe,
As every one in order loved him best ;

'Gan dight themselves t'express their inward woe
With doleful lays unto the tune addrest.
The which I here in order will rehearse,
As fittest flowers to deck his mournful hearse.

The mourning Muse of THESTYLIS.

OME FORTH ye nymphs! come forth! forsake your
  watery bowers!
Forsake your mossy caves; and help me to lament.
Help me to tune my doleful notes to gurgling sound
Of Liffey's tumbling streams.   Come let salt tears of ours,
Mix with his waters fresh.   O come let one consent
Join us to mourn with wailful plaints the deadly wound
Which fatal clap hath made, decreed by higher powers;
The dreary day in which they have from us yrent
The noblest plant that might from East to West be found.
Mourn! mourn great PHILIP's fall! mourn we his woeful end,
Whom spiteful death hath plucked untimely from the tree;
While yet his years in flower did promise worthy fruit.
Ah, dreadful MARS! why didst thou not thy knight defend?
What wrathful mood, what fault of ours hath moved thee,
Of such a shining light to leave us destitute?
Thou with benign aspect sometime didst us behold.
Thou hast in Britons' valour ta'en delight of old,

And with thy presence oft vouchsafed to attribute
Fame and renown to us, for glorious martial deeds :
But now their ireful beams have chilled our hearts with cold.
Thou hast estranged thyself and deignest not our land :
Far off to others now, thy favour, honour breeds ;
And high disdain doth cause thee shun our clime, I fear.
For hadst thou not been wroth, or that time near at hand ;
Thou wouldst have heard the cry that woeful England made:
Eke Zealand's piteous plaints, and Holland's toren hair
Would haply have appeased thy divine angry mind.
Thou shouldst have seen the trees refuse to yield their shade
And wailing to let fall the honour of their head,
And birds in mournful tunes lamenting in their kind.
Up from his tomb, the mighty CORINEUS rose,
Who cursing oft the fates that this mishap had bred,
His hoary locks he tare, calling the heavens unkind.
The Thames was heard to roar, the Rhine, and eke the Meuse,
The Scheldt, the Danow self this great mischance did rue :
With torment and with grief, their fountains pure and clear
Were troubled ; and with swelling floods declared their woes.
The Muses comfortless, the nymphs with pallid hue ;
The sylvan gods likewise came running far and near ;
And all, with hearts bedewed, and eyes cast up on high,
"O help ! O help, ye gods ! " they ghastly 'gan to cry,
"O change the cruel fate of this so rare a wight
And grant that nature's course may measure out his age ! "
The beasts their food forsook, and trembling fearfully,

Each sought his cave or den.   This cry did them so fright.
Out from amid the waves, by storm then stirred to rage,
This cry did cause to rise th'old father OCEAN hoar,
Who grave with eld, and full of majesty in sight,
Spake in this wise, "Refrain," quoth he, "your tears and
    plaints!
Cease these your idle words!   Make vain requests no more!
No humble speech nor moan may move the fixèd stint
Of destiny or death.   Such is His will that paints
The earth with colours fresh, the darkest skies with store
Of starry lights: and though your tears a heart of flint
Might tender make; yet nought herein will they prevail."
   Whiles thus he said, the noble Knight, who 'gan to feel
His vital force to faint, and death with cruel dint
Of direful dart his mortal body to assail:
With eyes lift up to heaven, and courage frank as steel;
With cheerful face where valour lively was exprest,
But humble mind, he said, "O LORD! if ought this frail
And earthly carcass have Thy service sought t'advance;
If my desire have been still to relieve th'opprest;
If Justice to maintain, that valour I have spent
Which Thou me gav'st; or if henceforth I might advance
Thy name, Thy truth: then spare me, LORD! if Thou
    think best;
Forbear these unripe years! But if Thy will be bent,
If that prefixèd time be come which Thou hast set:
Through pure and fervent faith, I hope now to be placed

In th'everlasting bliss; which with Thy precious blood
Thou purchase didst for us." With that a sigh he fet,
And straight a cloudy mist his senses overcast.
His lips waxed pale and wan, like damask rose's bud
Cast from the stalk; or like in field to purple flower
Which languisheth, being shred by culter as it past.
A trembling chilly cold ran through their veins, which were
With eyes brimful of tears to see his fatal hour:
Whose blustering sighs at first their sorrow did declare;
Next, murmuring ensued; at last they not forbear
Plain outcries; all against the heavens that enviously
Deprived us of a sprite so perfect and so rare.
The sun his lightsome beams did shroud, and hide his face
For grief; whereby the earth feared night eternally:
The mountains eachwhere shook, the rivers turned their
      streams;
And th'air 'gan winter-like to rage and fret apace:
And grisly ghosts by night were seen; and fiery gleams
Amid the clouds with claps of thunder, that did seem
To rent the skies; and made both man and beast afraid:
The birds of ill presage this luckless chance foretold
By dernful noise; and dogs with howling made man deem
Some mischief was at hand: for such they do esteem
As tokens of mishap; and so have done of old.

  Ah, that thou hadst but heard his lovely STELLA plain
Her grievous loss, or seen her heavy mourning cheer;
Whilst she, with woe oppressed, her sorrows did unfold.

Her hair hung loose neglect about her shoulders twain :
And from those two bright stars to him sometime so dear,
Her heart sent drops of pearl ; which fell in foison down
'Twixt lily and the rose.   She wrung her hands with pain
And piteously 'gan say, " My true and faithful pheer !
Alas, and woe is me ! why should my fortune frown
On me thus frowardly to rob me of my joy ?
What cruel envious hand hath taken thee away ;
And with thee, my content, my comfort and my stay ?
Thou only wast the ease of trouble and annoy :
When they did me assail, in thee my hopes did rest.
Alas, what now is left but grief that night and day
Afflicts this woeful life, and with continual rage
Torments ten thousand ways my miserable breast ?
O greedy envious heaven ! what needed thee to have
Enriched with such a jewel this unhappy age ;
To take it back again so soon ?   Alas, when shall
Mine eyes see ought that may content them, since thy grave
My only treasure hides, the joy of my poor heart ?
As here with thee on earth I lived, even so equal
Methinks it were, with thee in heaven I did abide :
And as our troubles all, we here on earth did part ;
So reason would that there, of thy most happy state
I had my share.   Alas, if thou my trusty guide
Were wont to be : how canst thou leave me thus alone
In darkness and astray ; weak, weary, desolate,
Plunged in a world of woe—refusing for to take

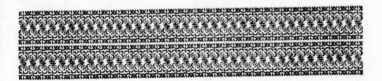

Me with thee, to the place of rest where thou art gone ?"
This said, she held her peace, for sorrow tied her tongue :
And instead of more words, seemed that her eyes a lake
Of tears had been, they flowed so plenteously therefrom :
And with her sobs and sighs th'air round about her rung.

If VENUS when she wailed her dear ADONIS slain,
Ought moved in thy fierce heart, compassion of her woe:
His noble sister's plaints, her sighs and tears emong ;
Would sure have made thee mild, and inly rue her pain.
AURORA half so fair, herself did never show;
When from old TITHON'S bed, she weeping did arise.
The blinded archer-boy, like lark in shower of rain,
Sat bathing of his wings, and glad the time did spend
Under those crystal drops which fell from her fair eyes ;
And at their brightest beams him proined in lovely wise.
Yet sorry for her grief, which he could not amend ;
The gentle boy 'gan wipe her eyes, and clear those lights :
Those lights through which his glory and his conquests shine.
The Graces tuckt her hair, which hung like threads of gold
Along her ivory breast, the treasure of delights.
All things with her to weep, it seemèd did incline ;
The trees, the hills, the dales, the caves, the stones so cold.
The air did help them mourn, with dark clouds, rain and
    mist ;
Forbearing many a day to clear itself again :
Which made them eftsoons fear the days of PYRRHA should
Of creatures spoil the earth, their fatal threads untwist.

For PHŒBUS' gladsome rays were wishèd for in vain,
And with her quivering light LATONA'S daughter fair;
And Charles' Wain eke refused to be the shipman's guide.
On NEPTUNE, war was made by ÆOLUS and his train.
Who letting loose the winds, tost and tormented th'air,
So that on every coast, men shipwreck did abide,
Or else were swallowed up in open sea with waves :
And such as came to shore were beaten with despair.
The Medway's silver streams that wont so still to slide,
Were troubled now and wroth; whose hidden hollow caves
Along his banks, with fog then shrouded from man's eye,
Aye "PHILIP" did resound, aye "PHILIP" they did cry.
His nymphs were seen no more, though custom still it
    craves,
With hair spread to the wind, themselves to bathe or sport;
Or with the hook or net, barefooted wantonly
The pleasant dainty fish to entangle or deceive.
The shepherds left their wonted places of resort,
Their bagpipes now were still, their lovely merry lays
Were quite forgot; and now their flocks, men might perceive
To wander and to stray, all carelessly neglect :
And in the stead of mirth and pleasure, nights and days
Nought else was to be heard, but woes, complaints and
    moan.
  But thou, O blessèd soul! dost haply not respect
These tears we shed, though full of loving pure affect;
Having affixt thine eyes on that most glorious throne,

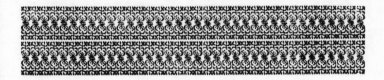

Where full of majesty, the high Creator reigns.
In whose bright shining face thy joys are all complete,
Whose love kindles thy sprite, where happy always one,
Thou liv'st in bliss that earthly passion never stains ;
Where from the purest spring the sacred nectar sweet
Is thy continual drink : where thou dost gather now
Of well-employed life, th'estimable gains.
There VENUS on thee smiles, APOLLO gives thee place ;
And MARS in reverent wise doth to thy virtue bow,
And decks his fiery sphere, to do thee honour most.
In highest part whereof, thy valour for to grace,
A chair of gold he sets to thee, and there doth tell
Thy noble acts arew ; whereby even they that boast
Themselves of ancient fame, as PYRRHUS, HANNIBAL,
SCIPIO and CÆSAR, with the rest that did excel
In martial prowess ; high thy glory do admire.

 All hail ! therefore, O worthy PHILIP immortal !
The flower of SIDNEY's race, the honour of thy name.
Whose worthy praise to sing, my Muses not aspire.
But sorrowful and sad these tears to thee let fall :
Yet wish their verses might so far and wide thy fame
Extend, that ENVY's rage nor time might end the same.

A pastoral Eclogue upon the death of Sir Philip Sidney, Knight, &c.

Lycon. Colin.

Lycon. Colin! well fits thy sad cheer this sad
   stound,
   This woeful stound, wherein all things
   complain
This great mishap, this grievous loss of ours.
Hear'st thou the Orown? How with hollow sound
He slides away, and murmuring doth plain,
And seems to say unto the fading flowers
Along his banks, unto the barèd trees;
Phillisides is dead. Up, jolly swain!
Thou that with skill canst tune a doleful lay;
Help him to mourn! My heart with grief doth freeze;
Hoarse is my voice with crying, else a part
Sure would I bear, though rude: but as I may,
With sobs and sighs I second will thy song;
And so express the sorrows of my heart.

Colin. Ah Lycon! Lycon! what need skill to teach
A grievèd mind pour forth his plaints? How long
Hath the poor turtle gone to school, weenest thou,
To learn to mourn her lost make? No, no, each
Creature by nature can tell how to wail.
Seest not these flocks; how sad they wander now?
Seemeth their leader's bell, their bleating tunes
In doleful sound. Like him, not one doth fail,
With hanging head to show a heavy cheer.
What bird, I pray thee, hast thou seen that prunes
Himself of late? Did any cheerful note
Come to thine ears, or gladsome sight appear
Unto thine eyes, since that same fatal hour?
Hath not the air put on his mourning coat,
And testified his grief with flowing tears?
Sith then, it seemeth each thing to his power,
Doth us invite to make a sad consort:
Come let us join our mournful song with theirs!
Grief will indite, and sorrow will enforce
Thy voice; and Echo will our words report.

Lycon. Though my rude rhymes, ill with thy verses
That others far excel: yet will I force   [frame,
Myself to answer thee the best I can;
And honour my base words with his high name.
But if my plaints annoy thee where thou sit
In secret shade or cave; vouchsafe, O Pan!

To pardon me ; and hear this hard constraint
With patience, while I sing ; and pity it.
And eke ye rural Muses, that do dwell
In these wild woods : if ever piteous plaint
We did indite, or taught a woeful mind
With words of pure affect, his grief to tell ;
Instruct me now ! Now COLIN then go on ;
And I will follow thee, though far behind.

   Colin. PHILLISIDES is dead ! O harmful death !
O deadly harm ! Unhappy Albion !
When shalt thou see emong thy shepherds ail
Any so sage, so perfect ? Whom uneath
Envy could touch for virtuous life and skill ;
Courteous, valiant, and liberal.
Behold the sacred PALES ! where with hair
Untrusst, she sits in shade of yonder hill ;
And her fair face bent sadly down, doth send
A flood of tears to bathe the earth : and there
Doth call the heavens despiteful, envious ;
Cruel his fate, that made so short an end
Of that same life, well worthy to have been
Prolonged with many years, happy and famous.
The Nymphs and Oreades her round about
Do sit lamenting on the grassy green ;
And with shrill cries, beating their whitest breasts,
Accuse the direful dart that DEATH sent out

To give the fatal stroke.   The stars they blame ;
That deaf or careless seem at their request.
The pleasant shade of stately groves they shun.
They leave their crystal springs, where they wont frame
Sweet bowers of myrtle twigs and laurel fair ;
To sport themselves free from the scorching sun.
And now the hollow caves, where HORROR dark
Doth dwell, whence banished is the gladsome air
They seek ; and there in mourning spend their time
With wailful tunes ; whiles wolves do howl and bark,
And seem to bear a bourdon to their plaint.

   Lycon. PHILLISIDES is dead!   O doleful rhyme!
Why should my tongue express thee ?   Who is left
Now to uphold thy hopes, when they do faint ;
LYCON unfortunate ?   What spiteful fate ?
What luckless destiny hath thee bereft
Of thy chief comfort, of thy only stay ?
Where is become thy wonted happy state ?
Alas, wherein through many a hill and dale,
Through pleasant woods, and many an unknown way,
Along the banks of many silver streams,
Thou with him yodest ; and with him did scale
The craggy rocks of th'Alps and Appennine ?
Still with the Muses sporting, while those beams
Of virtue kindled in his noble breast ;
Which after did so gloriously forth shine ?

But, woe is me, they now yquenched are
All suddenly, and death hath them oppressed,
Lo, father NEPTUNE ! with sad countenance,
How he sits mourning on the strond now bare
Yonder ; where th'OCEAN with his rolling waves
The white feet washeth, wailing this mischance,
Of Dover cliffs.   His sacred skirt about
The sea gods all are set ; from their moist caves,
All for his comfort gathered there they be.
The Thamis rich, the Humber rough and stout,
The fruitful Severn, with the rest ; are come
To help their lord to mourn, and eke to see
The doleful sight, and sad pomp funeral
Of the dead corps passing through his kingdom ;
And all their heads with cypress garlands crowned :
With woeful shrieks salute him, great and small.
Eke wailful ECHO, forgetting her dear
NARCISSUS, their last accents doth resound.

Colin. PHILLISIDES is dead !   O luckless age !
O widow world !   O brooks and fountains clear !
O hills !   O dales !   O woods that oft have rung
With his sweet carolling, which could assuage
The fiercest wrath of tiger or of bear !
Ye sylvans, fawns and satyrs, that emong
These thickets oft have danced after his pipe !
Ye Nymphs and Naiads with golden hair

That oft have left your purest crystal springs
To hearken to his lays, that coulden wipe
Away all grief and sorrow from your hearts!
Alas! who now is left that like him sings?
When shall you hear again like harmony?
So sweet a sound, who to you now imparts?
Lo where engravèd by his hand yet lives
The name of STELLA in yonder bay tree.
Happy name! happy tree! Fair may you grow
And spread your sacred branch, which honour gives,
To famous emperors; and poets crown.
Unhappy flock! that wander scattered now.
What marvel if through grief, ye woxen lean,
Forsake your food, and hang your heads adown?
For such a shepherd never shall you guide;
Whose parting, hath of weal bereft you clean.

    Lycon. PHILLISIDES is dead! O happy sprite!
That now in heaven with blessèd souls dost bide.
Look down awhile from where thou sitt'st above,
And see how busy shepherds be to indite
Sad songs of grief, their sorrows to declare;
And grateful memory of their kind love.
Behold myself with COLIN gentle swain,
Whose learned Muse thou cherisht most whilere,
Where we thy name recording, seek to ease
The inward torment and tormenting pain

That thy departure to us both hath bred;
Ne can each other's sorrow yet appease.
Behold the fountains now left desolate,
And withered grass with cypress boughs bespread!
Behold these flowers which on thy grave we strew!
Which faded, show the givers' faded state;
(Though eke they show their fervent zeal and pure)
Whose only comfort on thy welfare grew.
Whose prayers importune shall the heavens for aye,
That to thy ashes, rest they may assure;
That learnedst shepherds honour may thy name
With yearly praises; and the nymphs alway,
Thy tomb may deck with fresh and sweetest flowers;
And that for ever may endure thy fame.

Colin. The sun, lo, hastened hath his face to steep
In western waves, and th'air with stormy showers,
Warns us to drive homewards our silly sheep.
LYCON! let's rise, and take of them good keep.

Virtute summa ; cætera fortuna.

L. B.

An Elegy, or Friend's Passion
for his ASTROPHIL.

Written upon the death of the Right Honourable Sir PHILIP SIDNEY, Knight, Lord Governor of Flushing.

S THEN, no wind at all there blew,
No swelling cloud accloyed the air,
The sky, like grass of watchet hue,
Reflected PHŒBUS' golden hair;
 The garnished tree no pendant stirred,
 No voice was heard of any bird.

There might you see the burly bear,
The lion king, the elephant.
The maiden unicorn was there,
So was ACTÆON's hornèd plant:
 And what of wild or tame are found,
 Were couched in order on the ground.

ALCIDES' speckled poplar tree ;
The palm that monarchs do obtain;
With love juice stained, the mulberry,
The fruit that dews the poet's brain ;
    And PHILLIS' filbert there away
    Compared with myrtle and the bay :

The tree that coffins doth adorn,
With stately height threat'ning the sky,
And for the bed of love forlorn,
The black and doleful ebony :
    All in a circle compassed were
    Like to an amphitheatre.

Upon the branches of those trees,
The air-winged people sat,
Distinguishèd in odd degrees ;
One sort is this, another that.
    Here PHILOMEL that knows full well
    What force and wit in love doth dwell.

The sky-bred eagle, royal bird,
Perched there upon an oak above ;
The turtle by him never stirred,
Example of immortal love.
    The swan that sings about to die ;
    Leaving MEANDER, stood thereby.

And that which was of wonder most,
The Phœnix left sweet Araby;
And on a cedar in this coast,
Built up her tomb of spicery.
 As I conjecture by the same,
 Prepared to take her dying flame.

In midst and centre of this plot,
I saw one grovelling on the grass;
A man or stone, I knew not what.
No stone; of man, the figure was.
 And yet I could not count him one,
 More than the image made of stone.

At length I might perceive him rear
His body on his elbows' end:
Earthly and pale with ghastly cheer,
Upon his knees he upward tend;
 Seeming like one in uncouth stound,
 To be ascending out the ground.

A grievous sigh forthwith he throws,
As might have torn the vital strings;
Then down his cheeks the tears so flows
As doth the stream of many springs.
 So thunder rends the cloud in twain,
 And makes a passage for the rain.

Incontinent with trembling sound,
He woefully 'gan to complain;
Such were the accents as might wound,
And tear a diamond rock in twain.
 After his throbs did somewhat stay,
 Thus heavily he 'gan to say.

" O sun ! " said he, seeing the sun,
" On wretched me, why dost thou shine ?
My star is fallen, my comfort done;
Out is the apple of my eyen.
 Shine upon those possess delight,
 And let me live in endless night ! "

" O grief! that liest upon my soul,
As heavy as a mount of lead;
The remnant of my life control,
Consort me quickly with the dead!
 Half of this heart, this sprite and will,
 Died in the breast of ASTROPHIL."

" And you compassionate of my woe,
Gentle birds, beasts, and shady trees !
I am assured ye long to know
What be the sorrows me aggrieves;
 Listen ye then to what ensu'th,
 And hear a tale of tears and ruth."

" You knew, who knew not ASTROPHIL ?
(That I should live to say I knew,
And have not in possession still !)
Things known, permit me to renew :
 Of him you know, his merit such,
 I cannot say, you hear too much."

" Within these woods of Arcady,
His chief delight and pleasure took :
And on the mountain Partheny,
Upon the crystal liquid brook,
 The Muses met him every day ;
 That taught him sing, to write, and say."

" When he descended down the mount,
His personage seemed most divine ;
A thousand graces one might count
Upon his lovely cheerful eyen :
 To hear him speak, and sweetly smile ;
 You were in Paradise the while."

" A sweet attractive kind of grace ;
A full assurance given by looks ;
Continual comfort in a face,
The lineaments of Gospel books.
 I trow that countenance cannot lie,
 Whose thoughts are legible in the eye."

" Was ever eye did see that face ;
Was never ear did hear that tongue ;
Was never mind did mind his grace ;
That ever thought the travail long :
 But eyes and ears and every thought,
 Were with his sweet perfections caught."

"O GOD ! that such a worthy man,
In whom so rare deserts did reign ;
Desired thus, must leave us then :
And we to wish for him in vain.
 O could the stars that bred that wit,
 In force no longer fixèd sit."

" Then being filled with learned dew,
The Muses willèd him to love :
That instrument can aptly show,
How finely our conceits will move.
 As BACCHUS opes dissembled hearts,
 So LOVE sets out our better parts."

" STELLA, a nymph within this wood,
Most rare, and rich of heavenly bliss ;
The highest in his fancy stood,
And she could well demerit this.
 'Tis likely, they acquainted soon :
 He was a sun, and she a moon."

" Our ASTROPHIL did STELLA love.
  O STELLA! vaunt of ASTROPHIL!
  Albeit thy graces gods may move ;
  Where wilt thou find an ASTROPHIL?
        The rose and lily have their prime ;
        And so hath beauty but a time,"

"Although thy beauty do exceed
  In common sight of every eye;
  Yet in his poesies when we read,
  It is apparent more thereby.
        He that hath love and judgment too,
        Sees more than any others do."

" Then ASTROPHIL hath honoured thee.
  For when thy body is extinct,
  Thy graces shall eternal be.
  And live by virtue of his ink.
        For by his verses he doth give
        To shortlived beauty aye to live."

" Above all others this is he,
  Which erst approvèd in his song
  That love and honour might agree,
  And that pure love will do no wrong.
        Sweet saints! it is no sin nor blame
        To love a man of virtuous name."

" Did never love so sweetly breathe
    In any mortal breast before ?
Did never Muse inspire beneath,
    A poet's brain with finer store ?
        He wrote of love with high conceit ;
        And beauty reared above her height."

" Then PALLAS afterward attired
    Our ASTROPHIL with her device,
Whom in his armour heaven admired,
    As of the nation of the skies :
        He sparkled in his arms afar,
        As he were dight with fiery stars."

" The blaze whereof, when MARS beheld
    (An envious eye doth see afar)
' Such majesty,' quoth he, ' is seld.
Such majesty, my mart may mar.
        Perhaps this may a suitor be
        To set MARS by his deity.' "

" In this surmise, he made with speed
    An iron can, wherein he put
The thunders that in clouds do breed ;
The flame and bolt together shut,
        With privy force burst out again ;
        And so our ASTROPHIL was slain."

His word, " was slain," straightway did move,
And Nature's inward life-strings twitch,
The sky immediately above,
Was dimmed with hideous clouds of pitch.
 The wrastling winds, from out the ground
 Filled all the air with rattling sound.

The bending trees expressed a groan,
And sighed the sorrow of his fall ;
The forest beasts made ruthful moan ;
The birds did tune their mourning call,
 And Philomel for Astrophil,
 Unto her notes, annexed a " phil."

The turtle dove with tones of ruth,
Showed feeling passion of his death ;
Methought she said " I tell thee truth,
Was never he that drew in breath,
 Unto his love more trusty found,
 Than he for whom our griefs abound."

The swan that was in presence here,
Began his funeral dirge to sing ;
" Good things," quoth he, " may scarce appear ;
But pass away with speedy wing.
 This mortal life as death is tried,
 And death gives life, and so he died."

The general sorrow that was made
Among the creatures of kind,
Fired the Phœnix where she laid,
Her ashes flying with the wind.
  So as I might with reason see
  That such a Phœnix ne'er should be.

Haply, the cinders driven about,
May breed an offspring near that kind;
But hardly a peer to that, I doubt:
It cannot sink into my mind
  That under branches e'er can be,
  Of worth and value as the tree.

The eagle marked with piercing sight
The mournful habit of the place;
And parted thence with mounting flight,
To signify to JOVE the case:
  What sorrow Nature doth sustain,
  For ASTROPHIL, by ENVY slain.

And while I followed with mine eye
The flight the eagle upward took;
All things did vanish by and by,
And disappearèd from my look.
  The trees, beasts, birds and grove were gone:
  So was the friend that made this moan.

This spectacle had firmly wrought
A deep compassion in my sprite;
My molten heart issued, methought,
In streams forth at mine eyes aright:
And here my pen is forced to shrink;
My tears discolour so mine ink.

An Epitaph upon the Right Honourable Sir PHILIP SIDNEY, Knight, Lord Governor of Flushing.

O PRAISE thy life or wail thy worthy death;
And want thy wit, thy wit pure, high, divine:
Is far beyond the power of mortal line,
Nor any one hath worth that draweth breath.

Yet rich in zeal, though poor in learning's lore;
And friendly care obscured in secret breast,
And love that envy in thy life supprest,
Thy dear life done, and death hath doubled more.

And I, that in thy time and living state,
Did only praise thy virtues in my thought;
As one that seld the rising sun hath sought:
With words and tears now wail thy timeless fate.

Drawn was thy race aright from princely line,
Nor less than such (by gifts that Nature gave,
The common mother that all creatures have)
Doth virtue show, and princely lineage shine.

A King gave thee thy name; a kingly mind
That GOD thee gave : who found it now too dear
For this base world ; and hath resumed it near,
To sit in skies, and 'sort with powers divine.

Kent, thy birthdays ; and Oxford held thy youth.
The heavens made haste, and stayed nor years nor time ;
The fruits of age grew ripe in thy first prime :
Thy will, thy words ; thy words, the seals of truth.

Great gifts and wisdom rare employed thee thence,
To treat from kings, with those more great than kings.
Such hope men had to lay the highest things
On thy wise youth, to be transported thence.

Whence to sharp wars, sweet Honour did thee call,
Thy country's love, religion, and thy friends :
Of worthy men, the marks, the lives and ends ;
And her defence, for whom we labour all.

These didst thou vanquish shame and tedious age,
Grief, sorrow, sickness and base fortune's might.
Thy rising day saw never woeful night,
But passed with praise from off this worldly stage.

Back to the camp, by thee that day was brought
First, thine own death ; and after, thy long fame ;
Tears to the soldiers ; the proud Castilians' shame ;
Virtue expressed ; and honour truly taught.

What hath he lost ? that such great grace hath won.
Young years, for endless years ; and hope unsure
Of fortune's gifts, for wealth that still shall 'dure.
O happy race ! with so great praises run.

England doth hold thy limbs, that bred the same ;
Flanders, thy valour ; where it last was tried.
The camp, thy sorrow ; where thy body died.
Thy friends, thy want ; the world, thy virtue's fame.

Nations, thy wit ; our minds lay up thy love.
Letters, thy learning ; thy loss, years long to come.
In worthy hearts, sorrow hath made thy tomb ;
Thy soul and sprite enrich the heavens above.

Thy liberal heart embalmed in grateful tears,
Young sighs, sweet sighs, sage sighs bewail thy fall.
ENVY, her sting; and SPITE, hath left her gall.
MALICE herself, a mourning garment wears.

That day their HANNIBAL died, our SCIPIO fell:
SCIPIO, CICERO, and PETRARCH of our time:
Whose virtues, wounded by my worthless rhyme,
Let angels speak; and heaven, thy praises tell.

Another of the same.

ILENCE augmenteth grief! writing increaseth rage!
Stald are my thoughts, which loved and lost the
    wonder of our age.
Yet quickened now with fire, though dead with frost
    ere now,
    Enraged I write, I know not what. Dead, quick,
    I know not how.

Hard-hearted minds relent, and RIGOUR's tears abound,
And ENVY strangely rues his end, in whom no fault she
    found;

KNOWLEDGE her light hath lost; VALOUR hath slain her
    Knight :
SIDNEY is dead! Dead is my friend! Dead is the world's
    delight.

PLACE pensive wails his fall, whose presence was her pride.
TIME crieth out "my ebb is come; his life was my springtide."
FAME mourns in that she lost the ground of her reports.
Each living wight laments his lack, and all in sundry sorts.

He was (woe worth that word!) to each well-thinking mind,
A spotless friend, a matchless man, whose virtue ever shined :
Declaring in his thoughts, his life, and that he writ ;
Highest conceits, longest foresights, and deepest works of
    wit.

He only like himself, was second unto none,
Whose death (though life) we rue, and wrong, and all in
    vain do moan.
Their loss, not him ; wail they, that fill the world with cries.
DEATH slew not him ; but he made death his ladder to the
    skies.

Now sink of sorrow I, who live, the more the wrong,
Who wishing death, whom death denies, whose thread is all
    too long;
Who tied to wretched life, who looks for no relief,
Must spend my ever-dying days in never-ending grief.

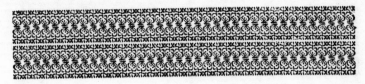

Heartsease and only I like parallels run on,
Whose equal length keep equal breadth, and never meet in
one:
Yet for not wronging him, my thoughts, my sorrows' cell,
Shall not run out; though leak they will, for liking him so
well.

Farewell to you! my hopes, my wonted waking dreams.
Farewell sometimes enjoyèd joy! Eclipsèd are thy beams.
Farewell self-pleasing thoughts! which quietness brings
forth.
And farewell friendship's sacred league! uniting minds of
worth.

And farewell, merry heart! the gift of guiltless minds;
And all sports! which for life's restore, variety assigns.
Let all that sweet is, void! In me no mirth may dwell.
PHILIP, the cause of all this woe, my life's content, farewell!

Now rhyme, the son of rage, which art no kin to skill;
And endless grief which deads my life, yet knows not how
to kill:
Go, seek that hapless tomb! which if ye hap to find;
Salute the stones that keep the limbs that held so good a
mind.

FINIS.

ALCILIA:

PHILOPARTHEN's

Loving Folly.

Non Deus (ut perhibent) amor est, sea
amaror, et error.

AT LONDON.

Printed by R. R. for William Mattes,
dwelling in Fleet street, at the sign of the
Hand and Plough.

1595.

[The only copy of the 1595 edition, at present known, is in the City Library, at Hamburg.

It was recovered, and reprinted in 1875 by Herr WILHELM WAGNER, Ph.D., in Vol. X. of the *Deutschen Shakespeare-Gesellschaft Jahrbuch* ; copies of this particular text being also separately printed.

A limited Subscription edition, of fifty-one copies, was printed by Rev. A. B. GROSART, LL.D., F.S.A., of Blackburn, in 1879 : with a fresh collation of the text by B. S. LEESON, Esq., of Hamburg.

The present modernized text is based on a comparison of the above two reprints of the 1595 edition with the text of the London edition of 1613 in which some headings (therein inserted between [ ], on *pp.* 256, 276, 278) first occur.]

A Letter written by a Gentleman to the Author, his friend.

FRIEND PHILOPARTHEN,

IN PERUSING your Loving Folly, and your Declining from it; I do behold Reason conquering Passion. The infirmity of loving argueth you are a man; the firmness thereof, discovereth a good wit and the best nature: and the falling from it, true virtue. Beauty was always of force to mislead the wisest; and men of greatest perfection have had no power to resist Love. The best are accompanied with vices, to exercise their virtues; whose glory shineth brightest in resisting motives of pleasure, and in subduing affections. And though I cannot altogether excuse your Loving Folly; yet I do the less blame you, in that you loved such a one as was more to be commended for her virtue, than beauty: albeit even for that too, she was so well accomplished with the gifts of Nature as in mine conceit (which, for good cause, I must submit as inferior to yours) there was nothing wanting, either in the one or the other, that might add more to her worth, except it were a more due and better regard of your love; which she requited not according to your deserts, nor answerable to herself in her other parts of perfection. Yet herein it appeareth you have made good use of Reason; that being heretofore lost in youthful vanity, have now, by timely discretion, found yourself!

X   10

Let me entreat you to suffer these your Passionate Sonnets to be published! which may, peradventure, make others, possessed with the like Humour of Loving, to follow your example, in leaving; and move other ALCILIAS (if there be any) to embrace deserving love, while they may!

Hereby, also, she shall know, and, it may be, inwardly repent the loss of your love, and see how much her perfections are blemished by ingratitude; which will make your happiness greater by adding to your reputation, than your contentment could have been in enjoying her love. At the least wise, the wiser sort, however in censuring them, they may dislike of your errors; yet they cannot but commend and allow of your reformation: and all others that shall with indifference read them, may reap thereby some benefit, or contentment.

Thus much I have written as a testimony of the good will I bear you! with whom I do suffer or rejoice according to the quality of your misfortune or good hap. And so I take my leave; resting, as always,

Yours most assured,

PHILARETES.

Author ipse φιλοπάρθενος ad libellum suum.

ARVE liber Domini vanos dicture labores,
 Insomnes noctes, sollicitosque dies,
Errores varios, languentis tædia vitæ,
 Mærores certos, gaudia certa minus,
Peruigiles curas, suspiria, vota, querelas,
 Et quæcunque pati dura coegit amor.
I precor intrepidus, duram comiterque salutans
 Hæc me ejus causa sustinuisse refer.
Te grato excipiet vultu rubicundula, nomen
 Cum titulo inscriptum viderit esse suum.
Forsitan et nostri miserebitur illa doloris,
 Dicet et, ah quantum deseruisse dolet :
Seque nimis sævam, crudelemque ipsa vocabit,
 Cui non est fidei debita cura meæ ;
Quod siquidem eveniet, Domino solaminis illud,
 Et tibi supremi muneris instar erit.
Si quis (ut est æquum) fatuos damnaverit ignes,
 Pigritiæ fructus ingeniique levis :
Tu Dominum cæcis tenebris errasse, sed ipsum
 Erroris tandem pænituisse sui,
Me quoque re vera nec tot, nec tanta tulisse,
 Sed ficta ad placitum multa fuisse refer.

Ab quanto satius (nisi mens mihi vana) fuisset
    Ista meo penitus delituisse sinu :
Quam levia in lucem prodire, aut luce carentis
    Insanam Domini prodere stultitiam.
Nil amor est aliud, quam mentis morbus et error
    Nil sapienter agit, nil bene, quisquis amat.
Sed non cuique datur sapere, aut melioribus uti,
    Forte erit alterius, qui meus error erat.
Cautior incedit, qui nunquam labitur, atqui
    Jam proprio evadam cautior ipse malo.
Si cui delicto gravior mea pœna videtur ;
    Illius in laudes officiosus eris.
Te si quis simili qui carpitur igne videbit,
    Ille suam sortem flebit, et ille meam.
ALCILIÆ obsequium supplex præstare memento,
    Non minima officii pars erit illa tui.
Te fortasse sua secura recondet in arca,
    Et Solis posthæc luminis orbus eris.
Nil referet, fateor me non prudenter amasse ;
    Ultima deceptæ sors erit illa spei.
Bis proprio PHŒBUS cursu lustraverat orbem,
    Conscius erroris, stultitiæque meæ,
A quo primus amor cœpit penetrare medullas,
    Et falsa accensos nutriit arte focos.
Desino jam nugas amplecti, seria posthæc
    (Ut Ratio monet) ac utiliora sequor.

Amoris Præludium.

[*Vel, Epistola ad Amicam.*]

TO THEE, ALCILIA! solace of my youth!
These rude and scattered rhymes I have addressed!
The certain Witness of my Love and Truth,
That truly cannot be in words expressed :
Which, if I shall perceive thou tak'st in gree,
I will, from henceforth, write of none but thee!

Here may you find the wounds yourself have made!
The many sorrows, I have long sustained!
Here may you see that LOVE must be obeyed!
How much I hoped, how little I have gained!
That as for you, the pains have been endured;
Even so by you, they may, at length, be cured!

I will not call for aid to any Muse
(It is for learned Poets so to do) :
Affection must, my want of Art excuse,
My works must have their patronage from You!
Whose sweet assistance, if obtain I might!
I should be able both to speak and write.

Meanwhile, vouchsafe to read this, as assigned
To no man's censure ; but to yours alone !
Pardon the faults, that you therein shall find ;
And think the writer's heart was not his own !
Experience of examples daily prove   *Nemini datur*
                                          amare simul
"That no man can be well advised, and love!" *et sapere.*

And though the work itself deserve it not
(Such is your Worth, with my great Wants compared !);
Yet may my love unfeignèd, without spot,
Challenge so much (if more cannot be spared !).
Then, lovely Virgin ! take this in good part !
The rest, unseen, is sealed up in the heart.

Judge not by this, the depth of my affection !
Which far exceeds the measure of my skill ;
But rather note herein your own perfection !
So shall appear my want of Art, not will :
Wherefore, this now, as part in lieu of greater,
I offer as an insufficient debtor !

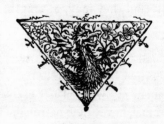

Sic incipit Stultorum Tragicomedia.

T was my chance, unhappy chance to me!
As, all alone, I wandered on my way;
Void of distrust, from doubt of dangers free,
To pass a grove where LOVE in ambush lay:
Who aiming at me with his feathered dart,
Conveyed it by mine eye unto my heart.

Where, retchless boy! he let the arrow stick,
When I, as one amazèd, senseless stood.
The hurt was great, yet seemèd but a prick!
The wound was deep, and yet appeared no blood!
But inwardly it bleeds.   Proof teacheth this.
When wounds do so, the danger greater is.

Pausing a while, and grievèd with my wound,
I looked about, expecting some relief:
Small hope of help, no ease of pain I found.
Like, all at once, to perish in my grief:
When hastily, I pluckèd forth the dart;
But left the head fast fixèd in my heart.

Fast fixèd in my heart, I left the head,
From whence I doubt it will not be removed.
Ah, what unlucky chance that way me led?
O LOVE! thy force thou might'st elsewhere have proved!
And shewed thy power, where thou art not obeyed!
"The conquest's small, where no resist is made."

But nought, alas, avails it to complain;
I rest resolved, with patience to endure.
The fire being once dispersed through every vein,
It is too late to hope for present cure.
Now PHILOPARTHEN must new follies prove,
And learn a little, what it is to love!

*These Sonnets following were written by the Author
(who giveth himself this feigned name of PHILOPARTHEN
as his accidental attribute), at divers times, and upon
divers occasions; and therefore in the form and
matter they differ, and sometimes are quite
contrary one to another: which ought not to
be misliked, considering the very nature
and quality of Love; which is
a Passion full of variety,
and contrariety
in itself.*

I.

UNHAPPY Eyes! that first my heart betrayed,
Had you not seen, my grief had not been such!
And yet, how may I, justly, you upbraid!
Since what I saw delighted me so much?
But hence, alas, proceedeth all my smart:
Unhappy Eyes! that first betrayed my
heart!

*Ut vidi, ut perii,
ut me malus
abstulit error.*

I I.

To seek adventures, as Fate hath assigned,
My slender Bark now floats upon the main;
Each troubled thought, an Oar; each sigh, a Wind,
Whose often puffs have rent my Sails in twain.
LOVE steers the Boat, which (for that sight, he lacks)
Is still in danger of ten thousand wracks.

I I I.

What sudden chance hath changed my wonted cheer,
Which makes me other than I seem to be?
My days of joy, that once were bright and clear,
Are turned to nights! my mirth, to misery!
Ah, well I ween that somewhat is amiss;
But, sooth to say, I know not what it is!

I V.

What, am I dead? Then could I feel no smart!
But still in me the sense of grief reviveth.
Am I alive? Ah, no! I have no heart;
For she that hath it, me of life depriveth.
O that she would restore my heart again;
Or give me hers, to countervail my pain!

V.

If it be Love, to waste long hours in grief;
If it be Love, to wish, and not obtain;
If it be Love, to pine without relief;
If it be Love, to hope and never gain;
Then may you think that he hath truly loved,
Who, for your sake! all this and more, hath proved!

V I.

If that, in ought, mine eyes have done amiss;
Let them receive deservèd punishment!
For so the perfect rule of Justice is,
Each for his own deeds, should be praised, or shent.
Then, doubtless, is it both 'gainst Law and Sense,
My Heart should suffer for mine Eyes' offence.

V I I.

I am not sick, and yet I am not sound;
I eat and sleep, and yet, methinks, I thrive not.
I sport and laugh, and yet my griefs abound;
I am not dead, and yet, methinks, I live not.
"What uncouth cause hath these strange passions bred,
To make at once, sick, sound, alive, and dead?"

V I I I.

Something I want; but what, I cannot say.
O, now I know! It is myself I want!
My Love, with her, hath ta'en my heart away;
Yea, heart and all, and left me very scant.
"Such power hath Love, and nought but Love alone,
To make divided creatures live in one."

I X.

PHILOPAR- "Come, gentle Death! and strike me with thy
THEN.   dart!
        Life is but loathsome to a man opprest."

DEATH.   " How can I kill thee! when thou hast no heart?
        That which thou hadst, is in another's breast!"

PHILOPAR- "Then, must I live, and languish still in
THEN.   pain?"

DEATH.   " Yea, till thy Love restore thy heart again!"

X.

Were Love a Fire, my tears might quench it lightly;
Or were it Water, my hot heart might dry it.
If Air, then might it pass away more slightly;
Or were it Earth, the world might soon descry it.
If Fire nor Water, Air nor Earth it be;
What then is it, that thus tormenteth me?

X I.

To paint her outward shape and gifts of mind,
It doth exceed my wit and cunning far.
She hath no fault, but that she is unkind.
All other parts in her so complete are,
That who, to view them throughly would devise,
Must have his body nothing else but eyes.

X I I.

Fair is my Love! whose parts are so well framed,
By Nature's special order and direction;
That She herself is more than half ashamed,
In having made a work of such perfection.
And well may Nature blush at such a feature;
Seeing herself excelled in her creature.

X I I I.

Her body is straight, slender, and upright;
Her visage comely, and her looks demure
Mixt with a cheerful grace that yields delight;
Her eyes, like stars, bright, shining, clear and pure:
Which I describing, LOVE bids stay my pen,
And says, "It's not a work for mortal men!"

X I V.

The ancient poets write of Graces three,
Which meeting all together in one creature,
In all points, perfect make the Frame to be;
For inward virtues, and for outward feature
But smile, ALCILIA! and the world shall see
That in thine eyes, a hundred Graces be!

X V.

As LOVE had drawn his bow, ready to shoot,
Aiming at me, with resolute intent;
Straight, bow and shaft he cast down at his foot,
And said, " Why, needless, should one shaft be spent?
I'll spare it then, and now it shall suffice
Instead of shafts, to use ALCILIA's eyes."

X V I.

Blush not, my Love! for fear lest PHŒBUS spy!
Which if he do, then, doubtless, he will say,
" Thou seek'st to dim his clearness with thine eye!"
That clearness, which, from East, brings gladsome day:
But most of all, lest JOVE should see, I dread;
And take thee up to heaven like GANYMEDE.

X V I I.

PHILOPARTHEN. " What is the cause ALCILIA is displeased?"
LOVE.   " Because she wants that which should
                    most content her."   [eased!"
PHILOPARTHEN. "O did I know it, soon should she be
LOVE.   " Perhaps, thou dost! and that doth most
                    torment her."
PHILOPARTHEN. " Yet, let her ask! what she desires to have."
LOVE.   " Guess, by thyself!   For maidens must not
                    crave!"

X V I I I.

My Love, by chance, her tender finger pricked;
As, in the dark, I strivèd for a kiss:
Whose blood, I seeing, offered to have licked,
But half in anger, she refusèd this.
O that she knew the difference of the smart
'Twixt her pricked finger, and my piercèd heart!

XIX.

PHILOPAR- "I pray thee, tell! What makes my heart to
THEN.   tremble,
         When, on a sudden, I, ALCILIA spy?"

LOVE.   "Because thy heart cannot thy joy dissemble!
         Thy life and death are both lodged in her eye."

PHILOPAR- "Dost thou not her, with self-same passion
THEN.   strike?"

LOVE.   "O, no! Her heart and thine are not alike."

XX.

Such are thy parts of body and of mind;
That if I should not love thee as I do,
I should too much degenerate from Kind,
And think the world would blame my weakness too.
For he, whom such perfections cannot move,
Is either senseless, or not born to love.

XXI.

ALCILIA's eyes have set my heart on fire,
The pleasing object that my pain doth feed:
Yet still to see those eyes I do desire,
As if my help should from my hurt proceed.
Happy were I, might there in her be found
A will to heal, as there was power to wound.

XXII.

Unwise was he, that painted LOVE a boy;
Who, for his strength, a giant should have been.
It's strange a child should work so great annoy;
Yet howsoever strange, too truly seen.
"But what is he? that dares at LOVE repine;
Whose works are wonders, and himself divine!"

XXIII.

My fair ALCILIA! gladly would I know it,
If ever Loving Passion pierced thy heart?
O, no! For, then, thy kindness soon would show it!
And of my pains, thyself wouldst bear some part.
Full little knoweth he that hath not proved,
What hell it is to love, and not be loved.

XXIV.

LOVE ! Art thou blind ? Nay, thou canst see too well !
And they are blind that so report of thee !
That thou dost see, myself by proof can tell ;
(A hapless proof thereof is made by me) ;
For sure I am, hadst thou not had thy sight,
Thou never couldst have hit my heart so right.

XXV.

Long have I languished, and endured much smart
Since hapless I, the Cruel Fair did love ;
And lodged her in the centre of my heart.
Who, there abiding, Reason should her move.
Though of my pains she no compassion take ;
Yet to respect me, for her own sweet sake.

XXVI.

In midst of winter season, as the snow,
Whose milk white mantle overspreads the ground ;
In part, the colour of my love is so.
Yet their effects, I have contrary found :
For when the sun appears, snow melts anon ;
But I melt always when my sun is gone.

XXVII.

The sweet content, at first, I seemed to prove
(While yet Desire unfledged, could scarcely fly),
Did make me think there was no life to Love ;
Till all too late, Time taught the contrary.
For, like a fly, I sported with the flame ;
Till, like a fool, I perished in the same.

XXVIII.

After dark night, the cheerful day appeareth ;
After an ebb, the river flows again ;
After a storm, the cloudy heaven cleareth :
All labours have their end, or ease of pain.
Each creature hath relief and rest, save I,
Who only dying, live ; and living, die !

XXIX.

Sometimes I seek for company to sport,
Whereby I might my pensive thoughts beguile;
Sometimes, again, I hide me from resort,
And muse alone : but yet, alas, the while
In changing place, I cannot change my mind;
For wheresoe'er I fly, myself I find.

XXX.

Fain would I speak, but straight my heart doth tremble,
And checks my tongue that should my griefs reveal :
And so I strive my Passions to dissemble,
Which all the art I have, cannot conceal.
Thus standing mute, my heart with longing starveth !
" It grieves a man to ask, what he deserveth." *Meritum petere grave*

XXXI.

Since you desire of me the cause to know,
For which these divers Passions I have proved ;
Look in your glass! which will not fail to show
The shadowed portrait of my best beloved.
If that suffice not, look into my heart!
Where it's engraven by a new found art.

XXXII.

The painful ploughman hath his heart's delight;
Who, though his daily toil his body tireth,
Yet merrily comes whistling home at night,
And sweetly takes the ease his pain requireth :
But neither days nor nights can yield me rest ;
Born to be wretched, and to live opprest !

XXXIII.

O well were it, if Nature would devise
That men with men together might engender,
As grafts of trees, one from another rise ;
Then nought, of due, to women should we render !
But, vain conceit ! that Nature should do this ;
Since, well we know, herself a woman is !

XXXIV.

Upon the altar where LOVE'S fires burnèd,
My Sighs and Tears for sacrifice I offered ;
When LOVE, in rage, from me his countenance turnèd,
And did reject what I so humbly proffered.
If he, my heart expect, alas, it's gone !
" How can a man give that, is not his own ? "

XXXV.

ALCILIA said, " She did not know my mind,
Because my words did not declare my love ! "
Thus, where I merit most, least help I find ;
And her unkindness all too late I prove.
Grant, LOVE ! that She, of whom thou art neglected,
May one day love, and little be respected !

XXXVI.

The Cynic * being asked, " When he should love ? " *DIOGENES.*
Made answer, " When he nothing had to do ;
For Love was Sloth ! " But he did never prove
By his experience, what belonged thereto.   *Amor est*
For had he tasted but so much as I,   *otiosorum*
He would have soon reformed his heresy.   *negotium.*

XXXVII.

O judge me not, sweet Love, by outward show
Though sometimes strange I seem, and to neglect thee !
Yet didst thou, but my inward Passions know,
Thou shouldst perceive how highly I respect thee !
" When looks are fixed, the heart ofttimes doth tremble ! '
" Little loves he, that cannot much dissemble ! "

XXXVIII.

Parting from thee ! even from myself I part.
Thou art the star, by which my life is guided !
I have the body, but thou hast the heart !
The better part is from itself divided.
Thus do I live, and this I do sustain,
Till gracious Fortune make us meet again !

X X X I X.

Open the sluices of my feeble eyes,
And let my tears have passage from their fountain !
Fill all the earth, with plaints ! the air, with cries !
Which may pierce rocks, and reach the highest mountain
That so, LOVE's wrath, by these extremes appeased ;
My griefs may cease, and my poor heart be eased.

X L.

" After long sickness, health brings more delight."
" Seas seem more calm, by storms once overblown."
" The day more cheerful, by the passed night."
" Each thing is, by his contrary best known."
" Continual ease is pain : Change sometimes meeter."
" Discords in music make music sweeter."

X L I.

Fear to offend forbids my tongue to speak,
And signs and sighs must tell my inward woe :
But (ay the while) my heart with grief doth break,
And she, by signs, my sorrow will not know.
" The stillest streams we see in deepest fords ;
And Love is greatest, when it wanteth words."

X L I I.

" No pain so great but may be eased by Art.'
" Though much we suffer, yet despair we should not."
" In midst of griefs, Hope always hath some part ;
And Time may heal, what Art and Reason could not.'
O what is then this Passion I endure,
Which neither Reason, Art, nor Time can cure ?

X L I I I.

Pale Jealousy ! Fiend of the eternal Night !
Misshapen creature, born before thy time !
The Imp of Horror ! Foe to sweet Delight !
Making each error seem an heinous crime.
Ah, too great pity ! (were there remedy),
That ever Love should keep Thee company !

XLIV.

The days are now come to their shortest date ; *Solstit: brumal.*
And must, in time, by course, increase again. *This Sonnet was devised upon the shortest day of the year.*
But only I continue at one state,
Void of all hope of help, or ease of pain ;
For days of joy must still be short with me,
And nights of sorrow must prolongèd be.

XLV.

Sleep now, my Muse ! and henceforth take thy rest !
Which all too long thyself in vain hath wasted.
Let it suffice I still must live opprest ;
And of my pains, the fruit must ne'er be tasted.
Then sleep, my Muse ! " Fate cannot be withstood."
" It's better sleep ; than wake, and do no good."

XLVI.

Why should I love, since She doth prove ungrateful :
Since, for reward, I reap nought but disdain.
Love thus to be requited, it is hateful !
And Reason would, I should not love in vain.
Yet all in vain, when all is out of season,
For " Love hath no society with Reason."

XLVII.

Heart's Ease and I have been at odds, too long !
I follow fast, but still he flies from me !
I sue for grace, and yet sustain the wrong ;
So gladly would I reconcilèd be.
LOVE ! make us one ! So shalt thou work a wonder ;
Uniting them, that were so far asunder.

XLVIII.

" Uncouth, unkist," our ancient Poet * said. * *CHAUCER.*
And he that hides his wants, when he hath need,
May, after, have his want of wit bewrayed ;
And fail of his desire, when others speed.
Then boldly speak ! " The worst is at first entering ! "
" Much good success men miss, for lack of venturing ! "

XLIX.

Declare the griefs wherewith thou art opprest,
And let the world be witness of thy woes!
Let not thy thoughts lie buried in thy breast;
But let thy tongue, thy discontents disclose!
For " who conceals his pain when he is grieved,
May well be pitied, but no way relieved."

L.

Wretched is he that loving, sets his heart
On her, whose love, from pure affection swerveth;
Who doth permit each one to have a part
Of that, which none but he alone deserveth.
Give all, or none!   For once, of this be sure!   *Ne amor ne*
" Lordship and Love no partners may endure."   *signoria vuole*
                                                 compagnia.

L I.

Who spends the weary day in pensive thought,
And night in dreams of horror and affright;
Whose wealth is want; whose hope is come to nought;
Himself, the mark for Love's and Fortune's spite:
Let him appear, if any such there be!
His case and mine more fitly will agree.

L I I.

Fair tree, but fruitless! sometimes full of sap!
Which now yields nought at all, that may delight me!
Some cruel frost, or some untimely hap
Hath made thee barren, only to despite me!
Such trees, in vain, with hope do feed Desire;
And serve for fuel to increase Love's fire.

L I I I.

In company (whiles sad and mute I sit,
My thoughts elsewhere, than there I seem to be)
Possessed with some deep melancholy fit;
One of my friends observes the same in me,
And says in jest, which I in earnest prove,
" He looks like one, that had lost his First Love!"

LIV.

'Twixt Hope and Fear, in doubtful balance peazed,
My fate, my fortune, and my love depends.
Sometimes my Hope is raised, when LOVE is pleased;
Which Fear weighs down, when ought his will offends.
The heavens are sometimes clear, and sometimes lower;
And " he that loves, must taste both sweet and sour ! "

LV.

Retire, my wandering Thoughts ! unto your rest !
Do not, henceforth, consume yourselves in vain !
No mortal man, in all points, can be blest ;
What now is mine, may be another's pain.
The watery clouds are clear, when storms are past ;
And " things, in their extremes, long cannot last."

LVI.

The fire of Love is first bred in the Eye,
And thence conveys his heat unto the Heart,
Where it lies hid, till time his force descry.   *Visus.*
The Tongue thereto adds fuel for his part ;   *Sermo.*
   Tactus.
The touch of Lips, which doth succeed the same,
Kindles the rest, and so it proves a flame.

LVII.

The tender Sprigs that sprouted in the field,
And promised hope of fruit to him that planted ;
Instead of fruit, doth nought but blossoms yield,
Though care, and pain to prune them never wanted :
Even so, my hopes do nought but blossoms prove,
And yield no fruits to recompense my love.

LVIII.

Though little sign of love in show appear ;
Yet think, True Love, of colours hath no need !
It's not the glorious garments, which men wear,
That makes them other than they are indeed :
" In meanest show, the most affection dwells ;
And richest pearls are found in simplest shells."

LIX.

Let not thy tongue, thy inward thoughts disclose!
Or tell the sorrows that thy heart endures!
Let no man's ears be witness of thy woes!
Since pity, neither help nor ease procures: *MARTIAL.*
And "only he is, truly, said to moan, *Ille dolet*
Whose griefs none knoweth but himself alone." *vere, qui sine teste dolet.*

LX.

A thousand times; I curse these idle rhymes,
Which do their Maker's follies vain set forth;
Yet bless I them again, as many times,
For that in them, I blaze ALCILIA's worth. *Alteri*
Meanwhile, I fare, as doth the torch by night, *inserviens meipsum*
Which wastes itself in giving others light. *conficio.*

LXI.

Enough of this! For all is nought regarded!
And She, not once, with my complaints is moved.
Die, hapless love! since thou art not rewarded;
Yet ere thou die, to witness that I loved!
Report my truth! and tell the Fair unkind,
That "She hath lost, what none but She shall find!"

LXII.

Lovers, lament! You that have truly loved!
For PHILOPARTHEN, now, hath lost his love:
The greatest loss that ever lover proved.
O let his hard hap some compassion move!
Who had not rued the loss of her so much;
But that he knows the world yields no more such.

LXIII.

Upon the ocean of conceited error,
My weary spirits, many storms have past;
Which now in harbour, free from wonted terror,
Joy the possession of their rest at last.
And, henceforth, safely may they lie at road!
And never rove for "Had I wist!" abroad!

L O V E's Accusation at the Judgement Seat of R E A S O N; wherein the Author's whole success in his love is covertly deciphered.

[Compare this, with GASCOIGNE's poem, *Vol. I. p.* 63.]

N REASON's Court, myself being Plaintiff
    there,
    LOVE was, by process, summoned to appear.
    That so the wrongs, which he had done to me,
    Might be made known; and all the world
        might see :
And seeing, rue what to my cost I proved ;
While faithful, but unfortunate I loved.

After I had obtainèd audience ;
I thus began to give in evidence.

[*The Author's Evidence against* LOVE.]

" Most sacred Queen ! and Sovereign of man's heart !
Which of the mind dost rule the better part !
First bred in heaven, and from thence, hither sent
To guide men's actions by thy regiment !
Vouchsafe a while to hear the sad complaint
Of him that LOVE hath long kept in restraint ;

And, as to you it properly belongs,
Grant justice of my undeservèd wrongs!

It's now two years, as I remember well,
Since first this wretch, (sent from the nether hell,
To plague the world with new-found cruelties),
Under the shadow of two crystal Eyes,
Betrayed my Sense; and, as I slumbering lay,
Feloniously conveyed my heart away;
Which most unjustly he detained from me,
And exercisèd thereon strange tyranny.

Sometime his manner was, in sport and game,
With briars and thorns, to raze and prick the same;
Sometime with nettles of Desire to sting it;
Sometime with pincons* of Despair to wring it; [*_pincers._]
Sometime again, he would anoint the sore,
And heal the place that he had hurt before:
But hurtful helps! and ministered in vain!
Which servèd only to renew my pain.
For, after that, more wounds he added still;
Which piercèd deep, but had no power to kill.
Unhappy medicine! which, instead of cure,
Gives strength to make the patient more endure!

But that which was most strange of all the rest
(Myself being thus 'twixt life and death distrest),
Ofttimes, when as my pain exceeded measure,
He would persuade me that the same was pleasure;
My solemn sadness, but contentment meet;
My travail, rest; and all my sour, sweet;
My wounds, but gentle strokes: whereat he smiled,
And by these slights, my careless youth beguiled.

Thus did I fare, as one that living died,
(For greater pains, I think, hath no man tried)

Disquiet thoughts, like furies in my breast
Nourished the poison that my spirits possesst.
Now Grief, then Joy; now War, then Peace unstable,
Nought sure I had, but to be miserable.
    I cannot utter all, I must confess.
Men may conceive more than they can express !
But (to be short), which cannot be excused,
With vain illusions, LOVE, my hope abused ;
Persuading me I stood upon firm ground
When, unawares, myself on sands I found.
This is the point which most I do enforce !
That Love, without all pity or remorse,
Did suffer me to languish still in grief
Void of contentment, succour, or relief :
And when I looked my pains should be rewarded,
I did perceive, that they were nought regarded.
    For why ?   Alas, these hapless eyes did see
ALCILIA loved another more than me !
So in the end, when I expected most ;
My hope, my love, and fortune thus were crost."

    Proceeding further, REASON bad me stay
For the Defendant had some thing to say.
Then to the Judge, for justice, loud I cried !
And so I pausèd : and LOVE thus replied.

[*Love's Reply to the Author.*]

    " Since REASON ought to lend indifferent ears
Unto both parties, and judge as truth appears ;
Most gracious Lady ! give me leave to speak,
And answer his Complaint, that seeks to wreak
His spite and malice on me, without cause ;

In charging me to have transgressed thy laws!
Of all his follies, he imputes the blame
To me, poor LOVE! that nought deserves the same.
Himself it is, that hath abusèd me!
As by mine answer, shall well proved be.

    Fond youth! thou knowest what I for thee effected!
Though, now, I find it little be respected.
I purged thy wit, which was before but gross.
The metal pure, I severed from the dross,
And did inspire thee with my sweetest fire
That kindled in thee Courage and Desire:
Not like unto those servile Passions
Which cumber men's imaginations
With Avarice, Ambition, and Vainglory;
Desire of things fleeting and transitory.
No base conceit, but such as Powers above
Have known and felt, I mean, th' Instinct of Love;
Which making men, all earthly things despise,
Transports them to a heavenly paradise.

    Where thou complain'st of sorrows in thy heart,
Who lives on earth but therein hath his part?
Are these thy fruits?   Are these thy best rewards
For all the pleasing glances, sly regards,
The sweet stol'n kisses, amorous conceits,
So many smiles, so many fair intreats,
Such kindness as ALCILIA did bestow
All for my sake! as well thyself dost know?
That LOVE should thus be used, it is hateful!
But 'all is lost, that's done for one ungrateful.'

    Where he allegeth that he was abusèd
In that he truly loving, was refusèd:
That's most untrue! and plainly may be tried.

Who never asked, could never be denied!
But he affected rather single life,
Than yoke of marriage, matching with a wife.
And most men, now, make love to none but heires[ses]
Poor love! GOD wot! that poverty empairs.
Worldly respects, LOVE little doth regard.
'Who loves, hath only love for his reward!'

He merits a lover's name, indeed!
That casts no doubts, which vain suspicion
   breed:

The description of a foolhardy Lover.

But desperately at hazard, throws the dice,
Neglecting due regard of friends' advice;
That wrestles with his fortune and his fate,
Which had ordained to better his estate;
That hath no care of wealth, no fear of lack,
But ventures forward, though he see his wrack;
That with Hope's wings, like ICARUS doth fly,
Though for his rashness, he like fortune try;
That, to his fame, the world of him may tell
How, while he soared aloft, adown he fell.
And so True Love awarded him his doom
In scaling heaven, to have made the sea his tomb;
That making shipwreck of his dearest fame,
Betrays himself to poverty and shame;
That hath no sense of sorrow, or repent,
No dread of perils far or imminent;
But doth prefer before all pomp or pelf,
The sweet of love as dearer than himself.
Who, were his passage stopped by sword and fire,
Would make way through, to compass his Desire.
For which he would (though heaven and earth forbad it)
Hazard to lose a kingdom, if he had it.

These be the things wherein I glory most,
Whereof, this my Accuser cannot boast :
Who was indifferent to his loss or gain ;
And better pleased to fail, than to obtain.
All qualified affections, LOVE doth hate !
And likes him best that's most intemperate.
But hence, proceeds his malice and despite ;
While he himself bars of his own delight.
For when as he, ALCILIA first affected,
(Like one in show, that love little respected)
He masqued, disguised, and entertained his thought
With hope of that, which he in secret sought ;
And still forbare to utter his desire,
Till his delay receive her worthy hire.
And well we know, what maids themselves would have,
Men must sue for, and by petition crave.
But he regarding more his Wealth, than Will ;
Hath little care his Fancy to fulfil.
Yet when he saw ALCILIA loved another ;
The secret fire, which in his breast did smother,
Began to smoke, and soon had proved a flame :
If Temperance had not allayed the same.
Which, afterward, so quenched he did not find
But that some sparks remainèd still behind.
Thus, when time served, he did refuse to crave it ;
And yet envied another man should have it !
     As though, fair maids should wait, at young men's
       pleasure,
Whilst they, 'twixt sport and earnest, love at leisure.
Nay, at the first ! when it is kindly proffered !
Maids must accept ; least twice, it be not offered !
Else though their beauty seem their good t'importune,

Yet may they lose the better of their fortune.

   Thus, as this Fondling coldly went about it;
So in the end, he clearly went without it.
For while he, doubtful, seemed to make a stay,
A Mongrel stole the maiden's heart away;
For which, though he lamented much in shew,
Yet was he, inward, glad it fell out so.

   Now, REASON! you may plainly judge by this,
Not I, but he, the false dissembler is:
Who, while fond hope his lukewarm love did feed,
Made sign of more than he sustained indeed:
And filled his rhymes with fables and with lies,
Which, without Passion, he did oft devise;
So to delude the ignorance of such
That pitied him, thinking he loved too much.
And with conceit, rather to shew his Wit,
Than manifest his faithful Love by it.

   Much more than this, could I lay to his charge;
But time would fail to open all at large.
Let this suffice to prove his bad intent,
And prove that LOVE is clear and innocent."

   Thus, at the length, though late, he made an end,
And both of us did earnestly, attend
The final judgement, REASON should award:
When thus she 'gan to speak. "With due regard,
The matter hath been heard, on either side.
For judgement, you must longer time abide!
The cause is weighty, and of great import."
And so she, smiling, did adjourn the Court.

   Little availed it, then, to argue more;
So I returned in worse case than before.

Love Deciphered.

Love and I are now divided,
  Conceit, by Error, was misguided.
  ALCILIA hath my love despised!
  "No man loves, that is advised."
"Time at length, hath Truth detected."
Love hath missed what he expected.
Yet missing that, which long he sought;
I have found that, I little thought.
"Errors, in time, may be redrest,"
"The shortest follies are the best."

Love and Youth are now asunder;
Reason's glory, Nature's wonder.
My thoughts, long bound, are now enlarged;
My Folly's penance is discharged:
Thus Time hath altered my estate.
"Repentance never comes too late."
Ah, well I find that Love is nought
But folly, and an idle thought.
The difference is 'twixt Love and me,
That he is blind, and I can see.

Love is honey mixed with gall!
A thraldom free, a freedom thrall!
A bitter sweet, a pleasant sour!
Got in a year, lost in an hour!
A peaceful war, a warlike peace!
Whose wealth brings want; whose want, increase!
Full long pursuit, and little gain!
Uncertain pleasure, certain pain!
Regard of neither right nor wrong!
For short delights, repentance long!

Love is the sickness of the thought!
Conceit of pleasure, dearly bought!
A restless Passion of the mind!
A labyrinth of errors blind!
A sugared poison! fair deceit!
A bait for fools! a furious heat!
A chilling cold! a wondrous passion
Exceeding man's imagination!
Which none can tell in whole, or part,
But only he that feels the smart.

Love is sorrow mixt with gladness!
Fear, with hope! and hope, with madness!
Long did I love, but all in vain;
I loving, was not loved again:
For which my heart sustained much woe.
It fits not maids to use men so!
Just deserts are not regarded,
Never love so ill rewarded!
But "all is lost that is not sought!"
"Oft wit proves best, that's dearest bought!"

Women were made for men's relief;
To comfort, not to cause their grief.
Where most I merit, least I find:
No marvel! since that love is blind.
Had She been kind, as She was fair,
My case had been more strange and rare.
But women love not by desert!
Reason in them hath weakest part!
Then, henceforth, let them love that list,
I will beware of "Had I wist!"

These faults had better been concealed,
Than to my shame abroad revealed.
Yet though my youth did thus miscarry,
My harms may make others more wary.
Love is but a youthful fit,
And şome men say " It's sign of wit ! "
But he that loves as I have done ;
To pass the day, and see no sun :
Must change his note, and sing *Erravi !*
Or else may chance to cry *Peccavi !*

The longest day must have his night,
Reason triumphs in Love's despite.
I follow now Discretion's lore ;
" Henceforth to like ; but love no more ! "
Then gently pardon what is past !
For LOVE draws onwards to his last.
" He walks," they say, " with wary eye ;
Whose footsteps never tread awry ! "
My Muse a better work intends :
And here my Loving Folly ends.

After long storms and tempests past,
I see the haven at the last ;
Where I must rest my weary bark,
And there unlade my care and cark.
My pains and travails long endured,
And all my wounds must there be cured.
Joys, out of date, shall be renewed ;
To think of perils past eschewed.
When I shall sit full blithe and jolly,
And talk of lovers and their folly.

Then LOVE and FOLLY, both adieu!
Long have I been misled by you.
FOLLY may new adventures try!
But REASON says that "LOVE must die!"
Yea, die indeed, although grieve him;
For my cold heart cannot relieve him!
Yet for her sake, whom once I loved,
(Though all in vain, as time hath proved)
I'll take the pain, if She consent!
To write his Will and Testament.

LOVE's last Will and Testament.

Y SPIRIT, I bequeath unto the air!
　　My Body shall unto the earth repair!
　　My Burning Brand, unto the Prince of Hell;
　　T"increase men's pains that there in darkness
　　　　dwell!
For well I ween, above nor under ground,
A greater pain than that, may not be found.
　　My sweet Conceits of Pleasure and Delight,
To EREBUS! and to Eternal Night!
　　My Sighs, my Tears, my Passions, and Laments,
Distrust, Despair; all these my hourly rents,
With other plagues that lovers' minds enthral:
Unto OBLIVION, I bequeath them all!
　　My broken Bow, and Shafts, I give to REASON!
　　My Cruelties, my Slights, and forgèd Treason,
To Womankind! and to their seed, for aye!
To wreak their spite, and work poor men's decay.
Reserving only for ALCILIA's part,
Small kindness, and less care of lovers' smart.

For She is from the vulgar sort excepted;
And had She, PHILOPARTHEN's love respected,
Requiting it with like affection,
She might have had the praise of all perfection.

   This done; if I have any Faith and Troth;
To PHILOPARTHEN, I assign them both!
For unto him, of right, they do belong
Who loving truly, suffered too much wrong.

   TIME shall be sole Executor of my will;
Who may these things, in order due fulfil,
   To warrant this my Testament for good;
I have subscribed it, with my dying blood."

And so he died, that all this bale had bred.
And yet my heart misdoubts he is not dead:
For, sure, I fear, should I ALCILIA spy;
She might, eftsoons, revive him with her eye!
Such power divine remaineth in her sight;
To make him live again, in Death's despite.

The Sonnets following were written by the Author,
after he began to decline from his Passionate
Affection; and in them, he seemeth to
please himself with describing the
Vanity of Love, the Frailty
of Beauty, and the
sour fruits of
Repentance.

I.

Ow have I spun the web of my own woes,
And laboured long to purchase my own loss.
Too late I see, I was beguiled with shows.
And that which once seemed gold, now
    proves but dross.
Thus am I, both of help and hope bereaved.
" He never tried that never was deceived.

II.

Chi non si
fida, non viene
ingannato.

Once did I love, but more than once repent ;
When vintage came, my grapes were sour, or rotten.
Long time in grief and pensive thoughts I spent ;
And all for that, which Time hath made forgotten.
O strange effects of time ! which, once being lost,
Make men secure of that they lovèd most.

III.

Thus have I long in th'air of Error hovered,
And run my ship upon Repentance's shelf.
Truth hath the veil of Ignorance uncovered,
And made me see ; and seeing, know myself.
Of former follies, now, I must repent,
And count this work, part of my time ill spent.

I V .

What thing is LOVE?   " A tyrant of the Mind ! "
" Begot by heat of Youth ; brought forth by Sloth ;
   Nursed with vain Thoughts, and changing as the wind ! "
" A deep Dissembler, void of faith and troth ! "
" Fraught with fond errors, doubts, despite, disdain,
   And all the plagues that earth and hell contain ! "

V .

Like to a man that wanders all the day
Through ways unknown, to seek a thing of worth,
And, at the night, sees he hath gone astray;
As near his end, as when he first set forth :
Such is my case, whose hope untimely crost,
After long errors, proves my labour lost.

V I .

Failed of that hap, whereto my hope aspired,
Deprived of that which might have been mine own :
Another, now, must have what I desired ;
And things too late, by their events are known.
Thus do we wish for that cannot be got ;
And when it may, then we regard it not.

V I I .

Ingrateful LOVE ! since thou hast played thy part !
(Enthralling him, whom Time hath since made free)
It rests with me, to use both Wit and Art,
That of my wrongs I may revengèd be :
And in those eyes, where first thou took'st thy fire !
Thyself shalt perish, through my cold desire.

V I I I .

" Grieve not thyself, for that cannot be had !
And things, once cureless, let them cureless rest ! "
" Blame not thy fortune, though thou deem it bad !
What's past and gone will never be redrest."
" The only help, for that cannot be gained,
Is to forget it might have been obtained."

I X .

How happy, once, did I myself esteem!
While Love with Hope, my fond Desire did cherish:
My state as blissful as a King's did seem,
Had I been sure my joys should never perish.
" The thoughts of men are fed with expectation."
" Pleasures themselves are but imagination."

X .

Why should we hope for that which is to come,
Where the event is doubtful, and unknown?
Such fond presumptions soon receive their doom,
When things expected we count as our own ;
Whose issue, ofttimes, in the end proves nought
But hope! a shadow, and an idle thought.

X I .

In vain do we complain our life is short,
(Which well disposed, great matters might effect)
While we ourselves, in toys and idle sport,
Consume the better part without respect.
And careless (as though time should never end it)
'Twixt sleep, and waking, prodigally spend it.

X I I .

Youthful Desire is like the summer season
That lasts not long ; for winter must succeed :
And so our Passions must give place to Reason ;
And riper years, more ripe effects must breed.
Of all the seed, Youth sowed in vain desires,
I reapèd nought, but thistles, thorns, and briars.

X I I I .

"To err and do amiss, is given to men by Kind."
" Who walks so sure, but sometimes treads awry ? "
But to continue still in errors blind,
A bad and bestial nature doth descry.
" Who proves not ; fails not ; and brings nought *Chi non fa,*
to end : *non falla ; chi falla, l'amenda.*
Who proves and fails, may, afterward, amend."

X I V.

There was but One, and doubtless She the best!
Whom I did more than all the world esteem :
She having failed, I disavow the rest ;
For, now, I find " things are not as they seem."
" Default of that, wherein our will is crost,
Ofttimes, unto our good availeth most."

X V.

I fare like him who, now his land-hope spent,
By unknown seas, sails to the Indian shore ;
Returning thence no richer than he went,
Yet cannot much his fortune blame therefore.
Since " Whoso ventures forth upon the Main,
Makes a good mart, if he return again."

*Chi va, e
ritorna,
fa buon
viaggio.*

X V I.

Lovers' Conceits are like a flatt'ring Glass,
That makes the lookers fairer than they are ;
Who, pleased in their deceit, contented pass.
Such once was mine, who thought there was none fair,
None witty, modest, virtuous but She ;
Yet now I find the Glass abusèd me.

X V I I.

Adieu, fond Love ! the Mother of all Error !
Replete with hope and fear, with joy and pain.
False fire of Fancy ! full of care and terror.
Shadow of pleasures fleeting, short, and vain !
Die, loathèd Love ! Receive thy latest doom !
" Night be thy grave ! and Oblivion be thy tomb !"

X V I I I.

Who would be rapt up into the third heaven
To see a world of strange imaginations ?
Who, careless, would leave all at six and seven,
To wander in a labyrinth of Passions ?
Who would, at once, all kinds of folly prove ;
When he hath nought to do, then let him love !

*Nihil agendo
male agere
discimus.*

X I X.

What thing is Beauty?　" Nature's dearest Minion ! "
" The Snare of Youth ! like the inconstant moon
Waxing and waning ! "　" Error of Opinion ! "
" A Morning's Flower, that withereth ere noon ! "
" A swelling Fruit ! no sooner ripe, than rotten ! "
" Which sickness makes forlorn, and time forgotten ! "

X X.

The Spring of Youth, which now is in his prime ;
Winter of Age, with hoary frosts shall nip !
Beauty shall then be made the prey of Time !
And sour Remorse, deceitful Pleasures whip !
Then, henceforth, let Discretion rule Desire !
And Reason quench the flame of CUPID's fire !

X X I.

O what a life was that sometime I led !
When Love with Passions did my peace encumber ;
While, like a man neither alive nor dead,
I was rapt from myself, as one in slumber :
Whose idle senses, charmed with fond illusion,
Did nourish that which bred their own confusion.

X X I I.

The child, for ever after, dreads the fire ;
That once therewith by chance his finger burned.
Water of Time distilled doth cool Desire.
" And far he ran," they say, " that never turned."
After long storms, I see the port at last.
Farewell, Folly ! For now my love is past !

X X I I I.

Base servile thoughts of men, too much dejected,
That seek, and crouch, and kneel for women's grace !
Of whom, your pain and service is neglected ;
Yourselves, despised ; rivals, before your face !
The more you sue, the less you shall obtain !
The less you win, the more shall be your gain !

X X I V.

In looking back unto my follies past;
While I the present, with times past compare,
And think how many hours I then did waste
Painting on clouds, and building in the air:
I sigh within myself, and say in sadness,
"This thing which fools call Love, is nought but Madness!"

X X V.

"The things we have, we most of all neglect;
And that we have not, greedily we crave.
The things we may have, little we respect;
And still we covet, that we cannot have.
Yet, howsoe'er, in our conceit, we prize them;
No sooner gotten, but we straight despise them."

X X V I.

Who seats his love upon a woman's will,
And thinks thereon to build a happy state;
Shall be deceived, when least he thinks of ill,
And rue his folly when it is too late.
He ploughs on sand, and sows upon the wind,
That hopes for constant love in Womankind.

X X V I I.

I will no longer spend my time in toys!
Seeing Love is Error, Folly, and Offence;
An idle fit for fond and reckless boys,
Or else for men deprived of common sense.
'Twixt Lunacy and Love, these odds appear;
Th' one makes fools, monthly; th' other, all the year.

X X V I I I.

While season served to sow, my plough stood still;
My graffs unset, when other's trees did bloom.
I spent the Spring in sloth, and slept my fill;
But never thought of Winter's cold to come;
Till Spring was past, the Summer well nigh gone;
When I awaked, and saw my harvest none.

XXIX.

Now LOVE sits all alone, in black attire;
His broken bow, and arrows lying by him;
His fire extinct, that whilom fed Desire;
Himself the scorn of lovers that pass by him:
Who, this day, freely may disport and play;
For it is PHILOPARTHEN'S Holiday.

XXX.

Nay, think not LOVE! with all thy cunning slight,
To catch me once again! Thou com'st too late!
Stern Industry puts Idleness to flight:
And Time hath changèd both my name and state.
Then seek elsewhere for mates, that may befriend *Otia si tollas*
  thee!   *periere*
                Cupidinis
For I am busy, and cannot attend thee!   *arcus.*

XXXI.

Loose Idleness! the Nurse of fond Desire!
Root of all ills that do our youth betide;
That, whilom, didst, through love, my wrack conspire:
I banish thee! and rather wish t'abide
All austere hardness, and continual pain;
Than to revoke thee! or to love again!

XXXII.

The time will come when, looking in a glass,
Thy rivelled face, with sorrow thou shalt see!
And sighing, say, "It is not as it was!
These cheeks were wont more fresh and fair to be!
But now, what once made me so much admired
Is least regarded, and of none desired!"

XXXIII.

Though thou be fair, think Beauty but a blast!
A morning's dew! a shadow quickly gone!
A painted flower, whose colour will not last!
Time steals away, when least we think thereon.
Most precious time! too wastefully expended; *Temporis solius*
Of which alone, the sparing is commended.   *honesta est*
                  avaritia.

XXXIV.

How vain is Youth that, crossed in his Desire,
Doth fret and fume, and inwardly repine ;
As though 'gainst heaven itself, he would conspire ;
And with his fraility, 'gainst his fate combine,
Who of itself continues constant still ;
And doth us good, ofttimes against our will.

XXXV.

In prime of Youth, when years and Wit were ripe,
Unhappy Will, to ruin led the way.
Wit danced about, when Folly 'gan to pipe ;
And Will and he together went astray.
Nought then but Pleasure, was the good they sought !
Which now Repentance proves too dearly bought.

XXXVI.

He that in matters of delight and pleasure,
Can bridle his outrageous affection ;
And temper it in some indifferent measure,
Doth prove himself a man of good direction. *Est virtus*
In conquering Will, true courage most is shown ; *placitis*
And sweet temptations makes men's virtues known. *abstinuisse bonis.*

XXXVII.

Each natural thing, by course of Kind, we see,
In his perfection long continueth not.
Fruits once full ripe, will then fall from the tree ;
Or in due time not gathered, soon will rot. *Invidia*
It is decreed, by doom of Powers Divine, *fatorum series*
Things at their height, must thence again decline. *summisque negatum stare diu.*

XXXVIII.

Thy large smooth forehead, wrinkled shall appear !
Vermillion hue, to pale and wan shall turn !
Time shall deface what Youth has held most dear !
Yea, these clear Eyes (which once my heart did burn)
Shall, in their hollow circles, lodge the night ;
And yield more cause of terror, than delight !

XXXIX.

Lo here, the Record of my follies past,
The fruits of Wit unstaid, and hours misspent!
Full wise is he that perils can forecast,
And so, by others' harms, his own prevent.
All Worldly Pleasure that delights the Sense,   *Quanto piace*
Is but a short Sleep, and Time's vain expense!   *al mondo, e breue sogno.*

XL.

The sun hath twice his annual course performed,
Since first unhappy I, began to love;
Whose errors now, by Reason's rule reformed,
Conceits of Love but smoke and shadows prove.
Who, of his folly, seeks more praise to win;
Where I have made an end, let him begin!

J. C.

FINIS.

DAIPHANTUS,

OR

The Passions of Love.

Comical to read,

But Tragical to act:

As full of Wit, as Experience.

By A n. S c. Gentleman.

Fœlix quem faciunt aliena pericula cautum.

Whereunto is added,

The Passionate Man's Pilgrimage.

LONDON:

Printed by T. C. for William Cotton: and are
to be sold at his shop, near Ludgate. 1604.

The Argument.

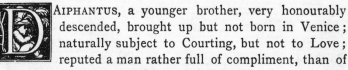

AIPHANTUS, a younger brother, very honourably descended, brought up but not born in Venice; naturally subject to Courting, but not to Love; reputed a man rather full of compliment, than of true courtesy; more desirous to be thought honest, than so to be wordish beyond discretion; promising more to all, than friendship could challenge; mutable in all his actions, but his affections aiming indeed to gain opinion rather than goodwill; challenging love from greatness, not from merit; studious to abuse his own wit, by the common sale of his infirmities; lastly, under the colour of his natural affection (which indeed was very pleasant and delightful) coveted to disgrace every other to his own discontent: a scourge to Beauty, a traitor to Women, and an infidel to Love.

This He, this creature, at length, falls in love with two at one instant; yea, two of his nearest allies: and so indifferently [*equally*] yet outrageously, as what was commendable in the one, was admirable in the other. By which means, as not despised, not regarded! if not deceived, not pitied! They esteemed him as he was in deed, not words. He protested, they jested! He swore he loved in sadness; they in sooth believed, but seemed to give no credence to him: thinking him so humorous as no resolution could be long good ; and holding this his attestation to them of affection in that kind, [no] more than his contesting against it before time.

Thus overcome of that he seemed to conquer, he became a slave to his own fortunes. Laden with much misery, utter mischief seized upon him. He fell in love with another, a wedded Lady. Then with a fourth, named VITULLIA. And so far was he imparadised in her beauty (She not re-comforting him) that he fell from Love to Passion, so to Distraction, then to Admiration [*wonderment*] and Con-templation, lastly to Madness. Thus did he *act* the Tragical scenes, who only penned the Comical : became, if not as brutish as ACTÆON, as furious as ORLANDO. Of whose Humours and Passions, I had rather you should read them, than I act them !

In the end, by one, or rather by all, he was recovered. A Voice did mad him ; and a Song did recure him ! Four in one sent him out of this world ; and one with four redeemed him to the world. To whose unusual strains in Music, and emphatical emphasis in Love ; I will leave you to turn over a new leaf !

This only I will end with :

> Who, of Love should better write,
> Than he that Love learns to indite ?

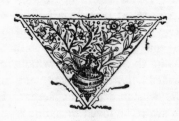

To the mighty, learned, and ancient Poten-
tate, QUISQUIS, Emperor of ✠, King of
Great and Little A., Prince of B. C. and
D., &c.; ALIQUIS wisheth the much
increase of true subjects, free from
Passion, spleen, and melancholy;
and endued with virtue,
wisdom, and mag-
nanimity.

Or to the Reader.

AN EPISTLE to the Reader! Why! that must have
his Forehead or first entrance like a Courtier, fair-
spoken and full of expectation; his Middle or centre
like your citizen's warehouse, beautified with enticing
vanities, though the true riches consist of bald commodi-
ties; his Rendezvous or conclusion like the lawyer's case, able
to pocket up any matter; but let good words be your best evidence!
In the General or foundation, he must be like Paul's Church, resolved to let every Knight and Gull travel upon him: yet his Par-
ticulars or lineaments may be Royal as the Exchange, with ascending
steps, promising new but costly devices and fashions. It must have
Teeth like a Satyr, Eyes like a critic; and yet may your Tongue
speak false Latin, like your panders and bawds of poetry. Your
Genius and Species should march in battle array with our politi-
cians: yet your Genius ought to live with an honest soul indeed.

It should be like the never-too-well-read Arcadia, where the
Prose and Verse, Matter and Words, are like his [SIDNEY'S]
Mistress's eyes! one still excelling another, and without corrival! or to come home to the vulgar's element, like friendly
SHAKE-SPEARE'S Tragedies, where the Comedian rides, when
the Tragedian stands on tiptoe. Faith, it should please all, like
Prince HAMLET! But, in sadness, then it were to be feared,
he would run mad. In sooth, I will not be moonsick, to please!
nor out of my wits, though I displease all! What? Poet! are
you in Passion, or out of Love? This is as strange as true!

*Well, well ! if I seem mystical or tyrannical ; whether I be
a fool or a Lord's-Ingle ; all's one ! If you be angry, you are not
well advised ! I will tell you, it is an Indian humour I have
snuffed up from Divine Tobacco ! and it is most gentlemanlike,
to puff it out at any place or person !*

I'll no Epistle *! It were worse than one of* HERCULES'
*labours ! but will conclude honesty is a man's best virtue. And
but for the Lord Mayor and the two Sheriffs, the Inns of Court,
and many Gallants elsewhere, this last year might have been burned !
As for* MOMUS (*carp and bark who will !*), *if the* noble Ass *bray
not, I am as good a Knight Poet, as* Ætatis suæ, *Master* An.
Dom.'*s son-in-law.*

*Let your critic look to the rowels of his spurs, the pad of his
saddle, and the jerk of his wand ! then let him ride me and my
rhymes down, as hotly as he would. I care not ! We shall meet
and be friends again, with the breaking of a spear or two ! and
who would do less, for a fair Lady ?*

There I leave you, where you shall ever find me !

Passionate DAIPHANTUS, *your loving subject,*
Gives you to understand, he is a Man in Print, *and it is enough
he hath undergone a* Pressing, *though for your sakes and for
Ladies : protesting for this poor infant of his brain, as it was the
price of his virginity, born into the world with tears : so (but for a
many his dear friends that took much pains for it) it had died,
and never been laughed at ! and that if Truth have wrote less than
Fiction ; yet it is better to err in Knowledge than in Judgement !
Also, if he have caught up half a line of any other's, it was out of
his memory, not of any ignorance !*

*Why he dedicates it to All, and not to any Particular, as his
Mistress or so? His answer is, He is better born, than to creep into
women's favours, and ask their leave afterwards.*

*Also he desireth you to help to correct such errors of the Printer,
which (because the Author is dead, or was out of the City) hath been
committed. And it was his folly, or the Stationer's, you had not
an* Epistle *to the purpose.*

Thus like a lover, wooes he for your favour ;
Which, if you grant, then Omnia vincit Amor.

DAIPHANTUS.

Proem

 Sing the old World in an infant story!
I sing the new World in an ancient ditty!
I sing this World; yes, this World's shame
   and glory!
I sing a Medley of rigour and of pity!
 I sing the Court's, City's, and the Country's fashions!
 Yet sing I but of Love and her strange Passions!

I sing that anthem lovers sigh in sadness!
I sing sweet times of joys in wo[e]-ven verses!
I sing those lines, I once did act in madness!
I sing and weep! (tears follow birth and hearses!)
 I sing a *Dirge*! a Fury did indite it!
 I sing Myself! whilst I myself do write it.

2 A   10

I invocate, to grace my Artless labour,
The faithful goddess, men call MEMORY
(True Poet's treasure, and their Wit's best favour) ;
To deck my Muse with truest poesy !
    Though Love write well, yet Passion blinds th'affection.
    Man ne'er rules right, that's in the least subjection.

Sweet Memory ! Soul's life, new life increasing !
The Eye of Justice ! Tongue of Eloquence !
The Lock of Learning ! Fountain never ceasing !
The Cabinet of Secrets ! Caske[t] of Sense !
    Which governest Nature, teacheth Man his awe !
    That art all Conscience, and yet rul'st by Law !

Bless thou, this Love Song-Air of my best wishes !
(Thou art the Parent nourisheth Desire !)
Blow, gentle winds ! safe land me at my blisses !
Love still mounts high, though lovers not aspire.
    My Poem 's Truth ! Fond poets feign at pleasure !
    A loving subject is a Prince's treasure.

THE PASSIONS OF LOVE.

N VENICE fair, the city most admired ;
Their lived a Gallant, who DAIPHANTUS hight,
Right nobly born, well lettered, loved, desired
Of every Courtier in their most delight :
   So full of pleasance, that he seemed to be
   A man begot in VENUS' infancy.

His face was fair, full comely was his feature ;
Lipped like the cherry, with a wanton's eye :
A MARS in anger, yet a VENUS' creature ;
Made part of CYNTHIA, most of MERCURY :
   A pitied soul, so made of Love and Hate,
   Though still beloved, in love unfortunate.

Thus made by Nature, Fortune did conspire
To balance him, with weight of CUPID's wings ;
Passant in Love, yet oft in great Desire ;
Sudden in Love, not staid in anything.
   He courted all, not loved : and much did strive
   To die for Love, yet never meant to wive !

As Nature made him fair, so likewise witty;
(She not content) his thoughts thus very fickle.
Fortune that gained him, placed him in this city,
To wheel his head, which she had made most tickle.
    Fortune made him beloved, and so distraught him!
    His reins let forth, he fell; and CUPID caught him.

Not far from Venice, in an Abbey fair,
Well walled about, two worthy Ladies dwelt:
Who virgins were, so sweet and debonair,
The ground they trod on, of their odour smelt.
    Two virgin Sisters, matchless in a phere,
    Had livèd virgins well nigh eighteen year.

EURIALÆ, the elder sister's named;
The other was URANIA the wise.
Nature for making them was surely blamed:
VENUS herself, by them all did despise!
    Such beauties with such virtue! so combined,
    That all exceeds, yet nought excels their mind.

EURIALÆ so shows as doth the sun,
When mounted on the continent of heaven:
Yet oft she's clouded; but when her glory's come,
Two suns appear! to make her glory even.
    Her smiles send brightness when the sun's not bright!
    Her looks give beauty, when the sun lends light!

Modest and humble, of nature mild and sweet;
Unmatchèd beauty with her virtue meeting:
Proud that her lowly 'beisance doth re-greet
With her chaste silence.   Virtue ever keeping.
    This is the sun, that sets before it rise!
    This is a star! no less are both her eyes!

Her beauty peerless ! peerless is her mind !
Her body matchless ! matchless are her thoughts !
Herself but one ! but one like her, we find !
Her wealth 's her virtue ! Such virtue is not bought !
 This is a heaven on earth, makes her divine !
 This is the sun, obscures where it doth shine !

URANIA next. O that I had that Art
Could write her worth ! her worth no eye may see !
Or that her tongue (O heaven !) were now my heart,
What silver lines in showers should drop from me !
 My heart she keeps ! how can I then indite ?
 No heart-less creature can Love Passions write !

As a black veil upon the wings of morn,
Brings forth a day as clear as VENUS' face ;
Or a fair jewel, by an Ethiope worn,
Enricheth much the eye, which it doth grace :
 Such is her beauty, if it well be told !
 Placed in a jetty chariot set with gold.

Her hair, Night's canopy in mourning weeds
Is still enthroned, when locked within is seen
A Deity, drawn by a pair of steeds
Like VENUS' eyes ! And if the like have been,
 Her eyes two radiant stars, but yet divine !
 Her face day's sun (heaven all !) if once they shine !

Upon the left side of this heavenly feature,
In curious work, Nature hath set a seal,
Wherein is writ, *This is a matchless creature !*
Where Wit and Beauty strives for the appeal :
 The Judges choosed are Love and Fancy. They rise,
 And looking on her, with her, left their eyes !

Her Wit and Beauty were at many frays,
" Whether the deep impressions did cause ? "
" Nature ! " said Beauty ; Art, her Wit did praise :
Love thought her Face ; her tongue had Truth's applause.
    Whilst they contend, Which was the better part ?
    I lent an eye ; She robbed me of my heart !

Sisters these two are, like the Day and Night :
Their glories, by their virtues they do merit,
One as the Day to see the other's might ;
The other's Night to shadow a high spirit.
    If all were Day, how could a lover rest ?
    Or if all Night, lovers were too much blest !

Both fair ; as eke their bodies tall and slender :
Both wise, yet silence shews their modesty :
Both grave, although they both are young and tender :
Both humble hearted, not in policy.
    So fair, wise, grave, and humble are esteemed ;
    Yet what men see, the worst of them is deemed !

Nature that made them fair, doth love perfection.
What Youth counts wisdom, Age doth bring to trial.
Grave years in Youth, in Age needs no direction.
A humble heart deserves, finds, no denial.
    Fairs ring their knells, and yet Fame never dies !
    True judgement 's from the heart, not from the eyes !

These two, two sisters, cousins to this lover ;
He often courts, as was his wonted fashion.
Who swears all 's fair, yet hath no heart to prove her,
Seems still in Love or in a lover's Passion,
    Now learns this lesson ! and love-scoffers find it !
    CUPID hits rightest, when Lovers do least mind it !

Although his guise were fashioned to his mind,
And wording Love, as compliment he used ;
Seemed still to jest at Love and lovers' kind,
Never obtained, but where he was refused :
  Yet now, his words with wit so are rewarded ;
  He loves ! loves two ! loves all ! of none regarded.

Now he that laughed to hear true lovers sigh,
Can bite his lips, until his heart doth bleed !
Who jibed at all, loves all ! each day 's his night !
Who scorned, now weeps and howls ! writes his own meed !
  He that would bandy Love, is now the ball !
  Who feared no hazard, himself hath ta'en the fall !

Beauty and Virtue, who did praise the fashion ;
Who, Love and Fancy thought a comedy :
Now is turned Poet ! and writes Love in Passion !
His verses fit the bleeding Tragedy !
  In willow weeds, right well he acts his part !
  His Scenes are tears, whose embryon was his heart !

He loves, where Love to all doth prove disaster !
His eyes no sooner see, but he 's straight blind !
His kindred, friends, or foes, he follows faster
Than his own good !   He 's now but too too kind !
  He that spent all, would fain find out Love's treasure !
  Extremities are, for extremes the measure.

Thus thinks he, of the words he spent in vain ;
And wishes now, his tongue had eloquence !
He 's dumb ! all motion that a world could gain,
A centre now without circumference !
  CUPID, with words who fought ! would teach him Art,
  Hath lost his tongue ; and with it, left his heart !

He swears he loves! (the heat doth prove the fire!)
He weeps his Love, his tears shew his Affection.
He writes his Love, his lines plead his Desire.
He sings his Love, the ditty mourns the action.
    He sings, writes, weeps, and swears that he's in sadness!
    It is believed, *Not cured, Love turns to madness!*

Love once dissembled, oaths are a grace most slender!
Tears oft are heard, Ambassadors for Beauty!
Words writ in gold, an iron heart may render!
A Passion Song shews much more hope than duty!
    Oaths spoke in tears; words, song; prove no true ditty:
    A feignèd Love must find a feignèd Pity!

Thus is the good DAIPHANTUS like the fly,
Who playing with the candle feels the flame.
The smiles of scorn are lovers' misery:
That soul's most vex't, is grievèd with his name.
    Though kind DAIPHANTUS do most love protest;
    Yet is his cross, still to be thought in jest!

Poor tortured lover! Like a perjured soul,
Swears till he's hoarse, yet never is believed!
(Who's once a villain, still is counted foul!)
O woful pity! when with wind relieved,
    Learns this by wrote, *Though Love unconstant be,*
    They must prove constant, will her comforts see!

Now to the humble heart of his dread Saint,
EURIALÆ, he kneels; but 's not regarded!
Then to URANIA sighs, till he grows faint:
Such is her Wit, in silence he's rewarded!
    His humble voice, EURIALÆ accuseth!
    His sighing Passion, URANIA refuseth!

Then lifts he up his eyes, but Heaven frowneth!
Bows down his head, Earth is a mass of sorrow!
Runs to the seas; the sea, it storms and howleth!
Hies to the woods, the birds sad tunes do borrow!
 Heaven, Earth, sea, woods, and all things do conspire
 He burn in Love, yet freeze in his Desire!

The Ladies jest! command him to feign still!
Tell him, how, one day, he may be in love!
That lover's reason hath not Love's free will!
Smile in disdain, to think of that he proves!
 (O me, DAIPHANTUS! how art thou advised?
 When he's less pitied, then he is despised!)

They hold this but his humour! seem so wise!
And many lovers' stories forth do bring!
Court him with shadows, whilst he catcheth flies,
Biting his fingers till the blood forth spring!
 Then do they much commend his careless Passion!
 Call him " a lover of our Courtiers' fashion! "

All this they do in modesty; yet free
From thinking him so honest, as in truth:
Much less so kind, as to love two or three,
Him near allied; and he himself a youth!
 Till with the sweat, which from his sufferings rise,
 His face is pearled, like the lights his eyes.

Then with his look down-cast, and trembling hand,
A High Dutch colour, and a tongue like ice,
Apart with this EURIALÆ to stand
Endeavours he. This was his last device,
 Yet in so humble strains, this Gallant courts her;
 The wind being high, his breath it never hurts her!

Speechless thus stands he, till She feared him dead,
And rubs his temples, calls and cries for aid.
Water is fetched and spunged into his head :
Who then starts up ; from dreaming, as he said,
   And craving absence of all, but this Saint,
   He 'gan to court her, but with a heart right faint.

" Bright Star of PHŒBUS ! Goddess of my thought !
Behold thy vassal, humbled on his knee !
Behold for thee, what gods and Art hath wrought,
A man adoring ! of Love, the lowest degree.
   I love ! I honour thee ! " No more ; there stayed
   As if foresworn; even so, was he afraid !

EURIALÆ now spake, yet seemed in wonder,
Her lips when parting, heaven did ope his treasure,
" O do not, do not love !   I will not sunder
A heart in two !   Love hath nor height nor measure !
   Live still a virgin !   Then I'll be thy lover ! "
   Heaven here did close.   No tongue could after move her.

As if in heaven, he was ravished so.
O love ! O voice ! O face ! which is the glory?
O day! O night! O Age ! O worlds of joy !
Of every part, true love might write a story.
   Convert my sighs, O to some angel's tongue.
   To die for Love is life !   Death is best young !

She gone, URANIA came.   He, on the flower,
But sight of her revived his noble fire :
And as if MARS did thunder, words did shower!
(Love speaks in heat, when 'tis in most Desire)
   She made him mad, whose sight had him revived;
   Now speaks he plainly !   Storms past, the air is glide.

"Why was I made, to bear such woe and grief?
Why was I born, but in Love to be nourished?
Why then for Love (Love, of all virtues chief),
And I not pitied, though I be not cherished?
    What! did my eyes offend in virtue seeing?
    O no! True Virtue is the lover's being!

"Beauty and Virtue are the twins of life;
Love is the mother which them forth doth bring.
Wit with discretion ends the lover's strife.
Patience with silence is a glorious thing.
    Love crowns a man, Love gives to all due merit;
    Men without love are bodies without spirit.

"Love to a mortal is both life and treasure.
Love changed to Wedlock doubleth in her glory.
Love is the gem, whose worth is without measure.
Fame dies, if not entombed within Love's story.
    Man that lives, lives not, if he wants Content.
    Man that dies, dies not, if with Love's consent."

Thus spake DAIPHANTUS, and thus spake he well;
Which wise URANIA well did understand:
So well she like it, as it did excel.
Now graced she him with her white slender hand,
    With words most sweet, a colour fresh and fair,
    In heavenly speech, she 'gan his woes declare.

"My good DAIPHANTUS! Love, it is no toy!
CUPID, though blind, yet strikes the heart at last.
His force, you feel! whose power must breed your joy;
This is the meed for scoffs, you on him cast!
    You love, who scorned! your love, with scorn is quite!
    You love, yet want! your love, with want is spite!

" Love plays the wanton, where she means to kill.
Love rides the fool, and spurs without direction.
Love weeps like you, yet laughs at your good will.
Love is, of all things, but the true confection.
    Love is of everything ; yet itself's but one thing.
    Love is anything, yet indeed is nothing.

" We virgins know this, though not the force of Love.
For we two sisters live as in a cell :
Nor do we scorn it, though we it not approve ;
By prayer we hope, her charms for to repell !
    And thus adieu ! But you, in Progress go,
    To find fit place to warble forth your woe.

" Who first seeks mercy, is the last for grief,"
Thus did She part ; whose image stayed behind.
He in a trance stands mute, finds no relief
(For She was absent, whose tongue pleased his mind),
    But like a heartless and a hurtless creature,
    In admiration of so sweet a feature.

At length looked up, his shadow only seeing,
Sighs to himself and weeps, yet silent stands ;
Kneels, riseth, walks, all this without True Being,
Sure he was there, though fettered in Love's bands.
    His lips departed, parted were his blisses :
    Yet for pure love, each lip the other kisses.

Revived by this, or else Imagination,
Recalls things past, the time to come laments ;
Records his love, but with an acclamation !
Repents himself and all these accidents.
    Now with the wings of Love, he 'gins to raise,
    His Love to gain, this woman he doth praise.

" Women than Men are purer creatures far !
The Soul of souls ! the blessed Gift of Nature !
To men, a heaven ! to men, the brightest star !
The pearl that 's matchless ! high, without all stature !
 So full of goodness, that Bounty waiteth still
 Upon their trencher ! feeds them with free will !

" Where seek we Virtue, learn true Art or Glory;
Where find we Joy that lasteth, still is spending,
But in sweet Women ? of man's life, the Story !
Alpha, they are ! Omega is their ending !
 Their virtues shine with such a sun of brightness !
 Yet he 's unwise, that looks in them for lightness ! "

(O let my pen relate mine own decay !
There are, which are not, or which should not be,
Some shaped like Saints, whose steps are not the way.
O let my Verse not name their infamy !
 These hurt not all, but even the wandering eye,
 Which fondly gapes for his own misery.

These do not harm the honest or the just,
The faithful lover, or the virtuous dame;
But those whose souls be only given to lust,
Care more for pleasure, than for worthy fame.
 But peace, my Muse ! For now, methinks I hear
 An angel's voice come warbling in my ear !)

Not distant far, within a garden fair,
The sweet ARTESIA sang unto her lute,
Her voice charmed CUPID, and perfumed the air,
Made beasts stand still, and birds for to be mute.
 Her voice and beauty proved so sad a ditty;
 Who saw, was blind ! who heard, soon sued for pity !

This Lady was no virgin like the rest,
Yet near allied.   By Florence city dwelling
(Nature and Art; within her both were blest;
Music in her, and Love had his excelling).
    To visit her fair cousins oft she came;
    Perhaps more jocund, but no whit to blame.

Fortune had crossed her with a churlish Mate,
Who STRYMON hight.   A Palmer was his sire,
Full nobly born and of a wealthy state;
His son a child not born to his Desire.
    Thus was she crossed, which causèd her thereby,
    DAIPHANTUS' grief to mourn, by sympathy.

DAIPHANTUS hearing such a swan-tuned voice,
Was ravished, as with angels' melody;
Though in this labyrinth blest, could not rejoice,
Nor yet could see what brought this harmony.
    At length, this goddess ceased; began draw near,
    Who, when he saw; he saw not, 'twas her sphere!

Away then crept he on his hands and knees,
To hide himself: thought VENUS came to plague him!
Which she espying, like the sun she stands;
As with her beams, she thought for to assuage him.
    But like the sun, which gazed on blinds the eye,
    So he by her! and so resolved to die.

At this, in wonder softly did she pace it;
Yet suddenly was stayed.   His verses seized her,
Which he late writ, forgot.   Thus was he graced.
She read them over, and the writing pleased her.
    For CUPID framed two mottoes in her heart:
    The one as DIAN's, the other, for his dart.

She read and pitied ; reading, Pity taught.
She loved and hated ; hate to Love did turn.
She smiled and wept ; her weeping Smiling brought.
She hoped and feared ; her Hopes in fear did mourn.
　　She read, loved, smiled, and hoped ; but 'twas in vain :
　　Her tears, still dread ; and pity, hate did gain.

She could have loved him, such true verses making ;
She might have loved him, and yet love beguiling.
She would have kissed him, but feared his awaking ;
She might have kissed him, and sleep sweetly smiling.
　　She thus afeared, did fear what she most wished.
　　He thus in hope, still hoped for that he missed.

He looked ! They two, long each on other gazed !
Sweet silence pleaded what each other thought.
Thus Love and Fancy both alike amazed,
As if their tongues and hearts had been distraught.
　　ARTESIA's voice thus courted him at length.
　　The more she spake, the greater was his strength !

" Good gentle Sir ! your fortunes I bemoan,
And wish my state so happy as to ease you !
But She that grieved you, She it is alone,
Whose breath can cure, and whose kind words appease you !
　　Were I that She, heaven should my star extinguish,
　　If you but loved me, ere I would relinquish.

" Yet, noble Sir ! I can no love protest,
For I am wedded (O word full fraught with woe !)
But in such manner as good love is blest,
In honest kindness, I'll not prove your foe !
　　Mine own experience doth my counsel prove,
　　I know to pity, yet not care to love !

" A sister, yet Nature hath given me,
A virgin true, right fair, and sweetly kind.
I for her good, Fortune hath driven me
To be a comfort.   Your heart shall be her mind.
    My woes yet tell me, she is best a maid ! "
    And here she stopped her tears, her words thus stayed.

DAIPHANTUS then, in number without measure,
Began her praises, which no pen can end.
" O Saint ! O sun of heaven, and earth the treasure !
Who lives, if not thy honour to defend ?
    Ah me ! what mortal can be in love so strange,
    That wedding Virtue will a wand'ring range ?

" She, like the morning, is still fresh and fair.
The Elements, of her, they all do borrow ;
The Earth, the Fire, the Waters, and the Air ;
Their strength, heat, moisture, liveliness.   No sorrow
    Can Virtue change ! Beauty hath but one place.
    The heart 's still perfect ; though empaled the face.

" O eyes ! no eyes, but stars still clearly shining !
O face ! no face but shape of angels' fashion !
O lips ! no lips, but bliss by kiss refining !
O heart ! no heart, but of true love right Passion !
    O eyes, face, lips, and heart, if not too cruel ;
    To see, feel, taste, and love earth's rarest jewel."

This said, he paused, new praises now devising,
Kneels to APOLLO for his skill and Art :
When came the Ladies ! At which, he arising,
'Twixt lip and lip, he had nor lips nor heart.
    His eyes, their eyes so sweetly did incumber :
    Although awaked, yet in a golden slumber.

Most like a lion raised from slumbering ease,
He cast his looks, fall grimly them among.
At length, he firmly knit what might appease
His brow; looked stedfastly and long
   At one, till all their eyes with his eyes met alike
   On fair VITULLIA, who his heart did strike.

VITULLIA fair, yet brown; as mixed together
As Art and Nature strove which was the purest.
So sweet her smilings were, a grace to either!
That heaven's glory in that face seemed truest.
   VENUS, excepted when the god her wooed,
   Was ne'er so fair! so tempting, yet so good!

Wonder not, mortals, though the Poets feign!
The Muses' graces were in this She's favour:
Nor wonder, though She strove his tongue to gain!
For I lose mine, in thinking of his labour.
   " Well may he love," I write, " and all Wits praise her,
   She 's so all humble, Learning cannot raise her ! "

DAIPHANTUS oft sighed: " Oh ! " oft said " Fair ! "
Then looks and sighs, and then cries wonderful ;
Thus did he long, and truly 'twas not rare :
The object was ! which made his mind so dull.
   Pray pardon him ! for better to cry " Oh ! "
   Than feel that Passion which caused him sigh so.

Now, all were silent, not alone this Lover,
Till came ISMENIO, brother to this Saint,
Whose haste made sweat, his tongue he could not prove her,
For this against him, that his heart was faint :
   Thus all amazed, none knowing any cause,
   ISMENIO breathless, here had time to pause.

At length, ISMENIO, who had wit and skill,
Questioned the reason of this strong effect :
At last related, haste outwent his will,
He told them, "He was sent, them to direct,
  Where hunting sports, their eyes should better please!"
  Who first went forth, DAIPHANTUS most did ease.

They gone, DAIPHANTUS to his standish highs!
Thinks, in his writs VITULLIA's beauties were :
But what he wrote, his Muse not justifies,
Bids him take time! "Love badly writes in fear!
  Her worthy praise, if he would truly write,
  Her kisses' nectar must the same indite."

" Art, and sweet Nature! Let your influence drop
From me like rain! Yes, yes, in golden showers!
(Whose end is Virtue, let him never stop!)
But fall on her, like dew on sprinkling flowers!
  That both together meeting, may beget
  An ORPHEUS! two gems in a soil richly set!"

Thus ravished, then distracted, as was deemed,
Not taught to write of Love in this extreme ;
In love, in fear; yea, trembling (as it seemed),
If praising her, he should not keep the mean!
  Thus vexed, he wept! His tears intreated pity,
  But Love unconstant, tunes a woful ditty.

Now kneels to VENUS. Faithfulness protested
To this, none else! This was his only Saint!
Vowed e'er his service, or to be arrested
To VENUS' censure! Thus he left to faint.
  His love brought Wit, and Wit engendered Spirit ;
  True Love and Wit thus learned him to indite.

" As the mild lamb runs forth from shepherd's fold,
By ravenous wolves is caught and made a prey :
So is my Sense, by which Love taketh hold,
Tormented more than any tongue can say.
   The difference is, they tortured so, do die !
   I feed the torment breeds my misery.

" Consumed by her I live, such is her glory !
Despised of her I love, I more adore her !
I'll ne'er write ought, but of her virtue's story !
Beauty unblasted is the eye's rich storer,
   If I should die, O who would ring love's knell ? "
   Faint not, DAIPHANTUS ! Wise men love not so well !

" Like heaven's artist, the astronomer,
Gazing on stars, oft to the earth doth fall :
So I, DAIPHANTUS, now Lover's Harbinger,
Am quite condemned to Love's funeral !
   Who falls by women, by them oft doth rise ;
   Ladies have lips to kiss, as well as eyes ! "

But tush, thou fool ! thou lov'st all thou seest.
Who once thou lovest, thou should'st change her never !
Constant in love, DAIPHANTUS, see thou beest !
If thou hope comfort, Love but once, and ever !
   " Fortune ! O be so good to let me find
   A lady living, of this constant mind ! "

" O, I would wear her in my heart's heart-gore !
And place her on the continent of stars !
Think heaven and earth, like her had not one more !
Would fight for her till all my face were scars !
   But if that women be such fickle Shees ;
   Men may be like them in infirmities ! "

O no, DAIPHANTUS! Women are not so
'Tis but their shadows, pictures merely painted!
Then turn poor lover! "O heaven! not to my woe!
Then to VITULLIA!" With that word, he fainted.
 Yet she that wounds, did heal. Like her, no heaven.
 Odds in a man, a woman can make even!

"O my VITULLIA! Let me write that down!
O sweet VITULLIA! Nature made thee sweet!
O kind VITULLIA! Truth hath the surest ground!
I'll weep or laugh, so that our hearts may meet!"
 Love is not always merry, nor still weeping:
 A drop of each, Love's joys are sweets in sleeping.

"Her name, in golden letters, on my breast I'll 'grave!
Around my temples, in a garland wear!
My Art shall be, her favour for to have!
My Learning still her honour high to rear!
 My lips shall close but to her sacred name!
 My tongue be silent but to spread her fame!

"In woods, groves, hills, VITULLIA's name shall ring!
In meadows, orchards, gardens, sweetest and fair!
I'll learn the birds her name alone to sing!
All quires shall chant it in a heavenly air!
 The Day shall be her Usher! Night, her Page!
 Heaven, her Palace! and this Earth, her Stage!

"Virgin's pure chasteness, in her eyes shall be!
Women, true love, from her true mind shall learn!
Widows, their mourning in her face shall see!
Children, their duty in her speech discern!
 And all of them in love with each, but I:
 Who fear her love, will make me fear to die!

" My Orisons are still to please this creature !
My Valour sleeps but when She is defended !
My Wits still jaded but when I praise her feature !
My Life is hers ; in her begun and ended !
  O happy day wherein I wear not willow !
  Thrice blessed night, wherein her breast's my pillow !

" I'll serve her, as the Mistress of all Pleasure !
I'll love her, as the Goddess of my soul !
I'll keep her, as the Jewel of all treasure !
I'll live with her, yet out of LOVE's control !
  That all may know, I will not from her part,
  I'll double lock her in my lips and heart !

If e'er I sigh, it shall be for her pity !
If e'er I mourn, her funeral draws near !
If e'er I sing, her virtue is the ditty !
If e'er I smile, her beauty is the sphere !
  All that I do, is that I may admire her !
  All that I wish, is that I still desire her ! "

But peace, DAIPHANTUS ! Music is only sweet,
When without discord. A consort makes a heaven.
The ear is ravished when true voices meet.
Odds, but in music, never makes things even.
    In voices' difference breeds a pleasant ditty,
    In Love, a difference brings a scornful pity.

Whose was the tongue, EURIALÆ defended ?
Whose was the wit, URANIA did praise ?
Whose were the lips, ARTESIA's voice commended ?
Whose was the heart loved all ? all crowned with bays ?
  " Sure 'twas myself ! What did I ? O I tremble !
  Yet I'll not weep ! Wise men may love dissemble.

"Fie, no! Fond Love hath ever his reward!
A sea of tears! a world of sighs and groans!
Ah me! VITULLIA will have no regard
To ease my grief, and cure me of my moans;
 If once her ear should hearken to that voice,
 Relates my fortunes in Love's fickle choice.

But now, I will, their worth with hers declare,
That Truth by Error may have her true being;
Things good are lessened by the thing that 's rare.
Beauty increaseth by a blackness seeing.
 Whoso is fair and chaste, they, sure, are best!
 Such is VITULLIA! such are all the rest!

"But she is fair, and chaste, and wise." What then,
So are they all, without a difference!
"She 's fair, chaste, wise, and kind, yes, to all men."
The rest are so! Number makes Excellence.
 "She 's fair, chaste, wise, kind, rich, yet humble."
 They three, her equal! Virtue can never stumble.

"VITULLIA is the sun; they stars of night!"
Yet night is the bosom wherein the sun doth rest.
"The moon herself borrows of the sun's light,"
All by the stars take counsel to be blest.
 The day 's the sun, yet Cupid can it blind;
 The stars at night, Sleep cures the troubled mind.

"She is a rose, the fairer, so the sweeter!
She is a lute, whose belly tunes the music!
She is my prose, yet makes me speak all metre!
She is my life, yet sickens me with physic!
 She is a virgin, that makes her a jewel!
 She will not love me, therein She is cruel!

" Eurialæ is like Sleep when one is weary
Urania is like a golden Slumber.
Artesia's voice, like Dreams that make men merry.
Vitullia, like a Bed, all these encumber.
   1. Sleep, 2. Slumber, 3. Dreams upon a 4. Bed are best ;
   First, Second, Third, but in the Fourth is blest.

" O but Vitullia, what ? She 's wondrous pretty !
O I, and what ? so is She very fair !
O yes, and what ? She 's like herself most witty !
And yet, what is She ? She is all but air !
   What can earth be, but earth ? So we are all !
   Peace, then, my Muse ! Opinion oft doth fall !

" Eurialæ, I honour for humility !
Urania, I reverence for her wit !
Artesia, I adore for true agility !
Three Graces for the goddesses most fit.
   Each of these gifts are blessèd in their faces,
   O, what's Vitullia, who hath all these Graces ? "

She is but a Lady ! So are all the rest.
As pure, as sweet, as modest, yea as loyal ;
Yes, She 's the Shadow (shadows are the least !),
Which tells the Hour of Virtue by her dial.
   By her, men see there is on earth a heaven !
   By them, men know her virtues are matched even !

In praising all, much time he vainly spent,
Yet thought none worthy but Vitullia ;
Then called to mind, he could not well repent
The love he bare the wise Urania.
   Eurialæ, Artesia, all, such beauties had,
   Which as they pleased him, made him well nigh mad.

EURIALÆ, her beauty, his eyesight harmed!
URANIA, her wit, his tongue incensed!
ARTESIA, her voice, his ears had charmed!
Thus poor DAIPHANTUS was, with love tormented.
    VITULLIA's beauty, as he did impart,
    The others' virtues vanquishèd his heart.

At length, he grew as in an ecstasy
'Twixt Love and Love, Whose beauty was the truer?
His thoughts thus diverse, as in a lunacy,
He starts and stares, to see Whose was the purer?
    Oft treads a maze, runs, suddenly then stays,
    Thus with himself, himself makes many frays.

Now with his fingers, like a barber snaps!
Plays with the fire-pan, as it were a lute!
Unties his shoe-strings! Then his lips, he laps!
Whistles awhile, and thinks it is a flute!
    At length, a glass presents it to his sight,
    Where well he acts fond Love in Passions right.

His chin he strokes! swears " beardless men kiss best!"
His lips anoints, says " Ladies use such fashions!"
Spits on his napkin, terms that "the bathing jest."
Then on the dust, describes the Courtiers' Passion.
    Then humble calls, " Though they do still aspire;
    Ladies then fall, when Lords rise by desire."

Then straddling goes, says, " Frenchmen fear no bears!"
Vows "he will travel to the Siege of Brest!"
Swears, " Captains, they do all against the hair!"
Protests " Tobacco is a smoke-dried jest!"
    Takes up his pen for a tobacco pipe,
    Thus all besmeared, each lip, the other wipe.

His breath, he thinks the smoke! his tongue, a coal!
Then runs for bottle-ale to quench his thirst;
Runs to his ink-pot, drinks! then stops the hole!
And thus grows madder than he was at first.
 TASSO he finds, by that of HAMLET thinks
 Terms him a madman, then of his inkhorn drinks!

Calls players "fools! The Fool, he judgeth wiseth,
Will learn them action out of Chaucer's *Pander*,
Proves of their poets bawds, even in the highest,
Then drinks a health! and swears it is no slander."
 Puts off his clothes! his shirt he only wears!
 Much like mad HAMLET, thus, as Passion tears!

" Who calls me forth, from my distracted thought?
O Cerberus! if thou? I prithee speak!
Revenge, if thou? I was thy rival ought!
In purple gores, I'll make the ghosts to reek!
 VITULLIA! O VITULLIA, be thou still!
 I'll have revenge, or harrow up my will!

" I'll fallow up the wrinkles of the earth!
Go down to hell, and knock at PLUTO's gate!
I'll turn the hills to valleys! make a dearth
Of virtuous honour to eternal Fate!
 I'll beat the winds, and make the tides keep back!
 Reign in the sea, that lovers have no wrack!

" Yes, tell the Earth, ' It is a murderer!
Hath slain VITULLIA!' O VITULLIA's dead!
I'll count blind CUPID for a conjurer,
And with wild horses will I rend his head!
 I, with a pickaxe, will pluck out his brains!
 Laugh at this boy! ease lovers of much pains!

" O then, I'll fly! I'll swim! yet stay, and then
I'll ride the moon, and make the clouds my horse!
Make me a ladder of the heads of men,
Climb up to heaven! Yes, my tongue will force
   To gods and angels! O, I'll never end,
   Till for VITULLIA, all my cries I spend!

" Then I, like a Spirit of pure Innocence,
I'll be all white! and yet behold I'll cry
' Revenge!' O lovers! this my sufference;
Or else for love, for love, a soul must die!
   EURIALÆ! URANIA! ARTESIA! so!—"
   Heart rent in sunder, with these words of woe.

" But soft, here comes! Who comes? and not calls out
Of rape and murder, love and villainy?
Stay, wretched man! Who runs? doth never doubt
It is thy soul! thy Saint! thy deity!
   Then call the birds to ring a mourning Knell,
   For mad DAIPHANTUS, who doth love so well!

" O sing a song, parted in parcels three,
I'll bear the burden still of all your grief;
Who is all Woe, can tune his misery
To discontents; but not to his relief.
   O kiss her! kiss her! And yet do not do so!
   They bring some joy, but with short joys, long woe!

Upon his knees, " O goddesses behold
A caitiff wretch bemoaning his mishap!
If ever pity were hired without gold,
Lament DAIPHANTUS, once in Fortune's lap!
   Lament DAIPHANTUS, whose good deeds now slumber!
   Lament a lover, whose woe no tongue can number!

" My woes—" There did he stay, fell to the ground,
Rightly divided into blood and tears,
As if those words had given a mortal wound,
So lay he foaming, with the weight of cares.
   Who this had seen, and seeing had not wept,
   Their hearts were, sure, from crosses ever kept!

The Ladies all, who late from hunting came,
Untimely came to view this Map of Sorrow.
Surely all wept! and sooth it was no shame,
For, from his grief, the world might truly borrow:
   As he lay speechless grovelling, all undressed;
   So they stood weeping, Silence was their best.

ISMENIO with these Ladies bare a part,
And much bemoaned him, though he knew not why;
But kind compassion struck him to the heart,
To see him mad.   Much better see one die!
   Thus walks ISMENIO, and yet oft did pause,
   At length, a writing made him know the cause.

He read, till words, like thunder, pierced his heart;
He sighed, till Sorrow seemed itself to mourn;
He wept till tears like ysacles [*icicles*] did part,
He pitied so, that pity, hate did scorn.
   He read to sigh, and weep for pity's sake;
   The less he read, the less his heart did quake.

At length resolved, he up the writing takes
And to the Ladies travails as with child;
The birth was Love, such love as discord makes,
The midwife Patience; thus in words full mild,
   He writ with tears that which with blood was writ;
   The more he read, the more they pitied it.

They look upon DAIPHANTUS, he not seeing :
And wondered at him, but his sense was parted.
They loved him much, though little was his being,
And sought to cure him, though he was faint-hearted,
　　ISMENIO thus, with speed resolves to ease him ;
　　By a sweet song, his sister should appease him !

ISMENIO was resolved he would be eased,
And was resolved of no means but by Music,
Which is so heavenly that it hath released
The danger oft, not to be cured by physic.
　　Her tongue and hand thus married together,
　　Could not but please him, who so loved either.

But first before his madness were allayed,
They offered incense at DIANA's shrine,
And much besought her, now to be apaid ;
Which was soon granted to these saints divine :
　　Yet so, that mad DAIPHANTUS must agree
　　Never to love, but live in chastity.

Thus they adjured him, by the gods on high,
Never henceforth to shoot with CUPID's quiver !
Nor love to feign : for there 's no remedy,
If once relapsed, then was he mad for ever !
　　Tortured DAIPHANTUS, now a sign did make ;
　　And kind ISMENIO this did undertake.

Then 'gan ARTESIA to play upon her lute,
Whose voice sang sweetly, now a mourning ditty ;
LOVE her admired, though he that loved were mute,
CUPID himself feared he should sue for pity.
　　O wondrous virtue ! Words spoken are but wind ;
　　But sung to Prick Song, they are joys divine !

I heard her sing, but still methought I dreamed.
I heard her play, but I methought did sleep.
The Day and Night, till now, were never weaned.
VENUS and DIAN ravished, both did weep.
   They which each hated, now agreed to say
   This was the goddess both of night and day.

My heart and ears, so ravished with the voice
I still forgot, what still I heard her sing :
The tune, surely, of Sonnets, this was all the choice.
Poets do keep it as a charming thing.
   What think you of the joys that DAIPHANTUS had,
   When for such music, I would still be mad !

The birds came chirping to the windows round,
And so stood still, as if they ravished were ;
Beasts forth the forest came, brought with the sound ;
The lion laid him down as if in fear.
   The fishes in fresh rivers swam to shore ;
   Yea, had not Nature stayed them, had done more.

This was a sight, whose eyes had never seen ;
This was a voice, such music ne'er was heard ;
This Paradise was it, where who had been,
Might well have thought of hell, and not afeard.
   Sure, hell itself was heaven, in this sphere,
   Madmen, wild beasts, and all here tamèd were.

Like as a king, his chair of state ascendeth,
Being newly made a god upon the earth,
In state amounts, till step by step he endeth,
Thinks it to heaven a true-ascending birth.
   So hies DAIPHANTUS, on his legs and feet,
   As if DAIPHANTUS now some god should meet.

He looks upon himself, not without wonder.
He wonders at himself, what he might be.
He laughs unto himself: thinks he 's aslumber.
He weeps unto himself, himself to see.
 And sure to hear and see what he had done
 Might make him swear but now the world begun.

Fully revived, at last ARTESIA ceased,
When birds and beasts so hideous noise did make,
That almost all turned fury, fear was the least;
Yea, such a fear as forced them cry and quake;
 Till that DAIPHANTUS, more of reason had
 Than they which moaned him, lately being mad.

He with more joy than words could well declare,
And with more words than his new tongue could tell,
Did strive to speak (such was his love and care
Thus to be thankful); but yet knew not well
 Whether his tongue (not tuned unto his heart),
 Or modest silence, would best act his part?

But speak he will! Then give attentive ear
To hear him tell a woful lover's story!
His hands and eyes to heaven up did he rear,
Grief taught him speech, though he to speak were sorry.
 But whatsoever be a Lover's Passion,
 DAIPHANTUS speaks his, in a mourning fashion.

As o'er the mountains walks the wandering soul,
Seeking for rest in his unresting spirit,
So good DAIPHANTUS, thinking to enrol
Himself in grace, by telling of Love's merit
 Was so distracted, how he should commend it,
 Where he began, he wishèd still to end it.

" EURIALÆ, my eyes are hers in right !
URANIA, my tongue is as her due !
ARTESIA, my ears to her I 'dite !
My heart to each ! and yet my heart to you,
   To you, VITULLIA ! to you, and all the rest,
    Who once me cursed, now to make me blest !

" 1 Beauty and 2 Wit, did 1 wound and 2 pierce my heart,
3 Music and 4 Favour, 3 gained and 4 kept it sure :
Love led by Fancy to the 4 last I part,
Love led by Reason to the 1 first is truer.
   1 Beauty and 2 Wit first conquered, made me yield,
   3 Music and 4 Favour rescued got the field.

"To 2 Wit and 1 Beauty, my first love I give !
3 Music and 4 Favours, my second love have gained !
All made me mad, and all did me relieve,
Though one recured me, when I was sustained.
   Thus, troth to say, to All I love did owe ;
   Therefore to All my love I ever vow ! "

Thus to the first 1 and 2, his right hand he did tender :
His left hand to the 3 and 4 ; last most lovingly 4.
His tongue kind thanks, first to the last did render,
The whiles his looks were bent indifferently.
   Thus he salutes All : and to increase his blisses,
   From lip to lip, each Lady now he kisses.

ISMENIO in humble wise salutes he,
With gracious language he returns his heart,
His words so sweetly to his tongue now suits he,
As what he speaks shew Learning with good Art.
   ISMENIO pleased DAIPHANTUS, DAIPHANTUS All ;
   When love gains love for love, this Love we call !

URANIA now bethought what was protested
By young ISMENIO at DIANA's shrine,
Conjured DAIPHANTUS that, no more he jested
With Love or Fancy! for they were Divine:
   And if he did, that there they all would pray
   He still might live in love, both night and day!

This grieved him much (but folly 'twere to grieve!)
His now obedience shewed his own free will.
He swore " he would not love, in shew, achieve!
But live a virgin, chaste and spotless still.
   Which said, such music suddenly delighted,
   As all were ravished, and yet all affrighted.

Here parted all, not without joy and sadness.
Some wept, some smiled ; a world it was to hear them!
Both springs here met. Woe here was clothed with gladness.
Heaven was their comfort. It alone did cheer them.
   DAIPHANTUS from these springs, some fruit did gather.
   Experience is an infant, though an ancient father!

"Sweet Lady! know the Soul looks through our eyesights!
Content lives not in shews or beauty seeing!
Peace, not from number, nor strength in high spirits!
Joy dies with Virtue, yet lives in Virtue's being!
   Beauty is masked, where Virtue is not hidden!
   Man still desires that fruit, he 's most forbidden!

" Jewels, for virtue, not for beauty prized!
What 's seldom seen breeds wonder, we admire it!
King's lines are rare, and therefore well advised.
Wise men, not often talk, Fools still desire it.
   Women are books! Kept close, they hold much treasure ;
   Unclasped, sweet ills! Most woe lies hid in pleasure.

" Who studies Arts alike, can he prove Doctor ?
Who surfeits, hardly lives ! drunkards recover !
Whose will 's his law, that conscience needs no Proctor !
When men turn beasts, look there for brutish lovers !
   Those eyes are pore-blind, look equally on any
   Though 't be a virtue to hinder one by many.

" Who gains by travel, lose Lordships for their Manors,
Must TARQUIN ravish some ?   Hell on that glory !
Whose life 's in healths, death soonest gains those banners !
Lust still is punished, though Treason write the story !
   A rolling eye, a globe, new worlds discover !
   Who still wheels round is but a damnèd lover.

" Doth Faith and Troth lie bathing ?   Is Lust, pleasure ?
Can commons be as sweet as land enclosed ?
Then virgin sin may well be counted pleasure !
Where such lords rule, who lives not ill-disposed !
   True Love 's a Phœnix, but One until it dies :
   Lust is a Cockatrice in all, but in her eyes."

Here did he end more blessed than his wishes.
(Fame 's at the high, when Love indites the Story)
The private life brings with it heavenly blisses.
Sweet Contemplation much increaseth glory.
   I'll leave him to the learning of Love's spell !
   " Better part friends, that follow fiends to hell ! "

ISMENIO, with VITULLIA went together,
Perhaps both wounded with blind CUPID's dart ;
Yet durst they not relate their love to either,
Love if once pitied, pierceth to the heart :
   But, sure, VITULLIA is so fair a mark,
   CUPID would court her, though but by the dark.

ARTESIA, she must go, the more She 's grieved,
To churlish STRYMON, her adopted Mate ;
CUPID, though blind, yet pitied and relieved
This modest Lady with some happy fate.
    For what but Virtue, which doth all good nourish,
    Could brook her fortunes, much less love and cherish.

EURIALÆ, with good URANIA stayed,
Where Virtue dwells, they only had their being ;
Beauty and Wit still fear, are not dismayed,
For where they dwell, Love ever will be prying.
    These two were one.   All good, each could impart.
    One was their fortune, and one was their heart.

Beauty and Virtue were true friends to either.
Heaven is the sphere where all men seek for glory.
Earth is the grave where sinners join together.
Hell keeps the book, enrols each lustful story.
    Live as we will, Death makes, of all conclusion :
    Die then to live ! or life is thy confusion.

Beauty and Wit in these, fed on Affection.
Labour and Industry were their twins of life.
Love and True Bounty were in their subjection,
Their bodies, with their spirits, had no strife.
    Such were these two, as grace did them defend :
    Such are these two, as with these two I end.

FINIS.

Non Amori sed Virtuti.

The Passionate Man's Pilgrimage.

Supposed to be written by one at the point of death.

IVE me my Scalop Shell of quiet,
My Staff of faith to walk upon,
My Scrip of joy, immortal diet !
My Bottle of salvation,
My Gown of glory, hope's true gage,
And thus I'll take my Pilgrimage !

Blood must be my body's balmer,
No other balm will there be given !
Whilst my Soul, like a white Palmer,
Travels to the land of heaven,
Over the silver mountains,
Where spring the nectar fountains :
And there I'll kiss
The bowl of bliss,
And drink my eternal fill
On every milken hill !
My Soul will be a dry before ;
But, after it, will ne'er thirst more !

And by the happy blissful way,
More peaceful pilgrims I shall see
That have shook off their gowns of clay,
And go apparelled fresh like me.
I'll bring them first
To slake their thirst,
And then to taste those nectar suckets
At the clear wells
Where sweetness dwells,
Drawn up by Saints in crystal buckets.

And when our bottles and all we,
Are filled with immortality,
Then the holy paths we'll travel,
Strewed with rubies thick as gravel,
Ceilings of diamonds, sapphire floors,
High walls of coral, and pearl bowers.

From thence, to Heaven's bribeless Hall,
Where no corrupted voices brawl.
No conscience molten into gold;
Nor forged accusers bought and sold.
No cause deferred, nor vain spent journey;
For there, CHRIST is the King's Attorney,
Who pleads for all without degrees;
And he hath angels, but no fees!
When the grand twelve million Jury,
Of our sins and sinful fury, .
'Gainst our souls, black verdicts give:
CHRIST pleads his death, and then we live!
Be thou, my speaker, taintless Pleader!
Unblotted Lawyer! true Proceeder!
Thou movest salvation, even for alms!
Not with a bribèd lawyer's palms.

And this is my eternal Plea,
To Him that made heaven, earth, and sea;
Seeing my flesh must die so soon,
And want a head to dine next noon;
Just at the stroke, when my veins start and spread,
Set on my Soul, an everlasting head!
Then am I ready, like a Palmer fit
To tread those blest paths, which before I writ.

FINIS.

Michael Drayton.

Odes.

[1606, and 1619.]

To the Reader.

ODES I have called these, the first of my few Poems ;
which how happy soever they prove, yet Criti-
cism itself cannot say, That the name is wrong-
fully usurped.   For (not to begin with Definitions,
against the Rule of Oratory ; nor *ab ovo*, against
the Prescript of Poetry in a poetical argument : but somewhat only to season thy palate with a slight description) an Ode is known to have been properly a Song
moduled to the ancient harp : and neither too short-
breathed, as hastening to the end ; nor composed of [the]
longest verses, as unfit for the sudden turns and lofty tricks
with which APOLLO used to menage it.

They are, as the Learned say, divers :
Some transcendently lofty ; and far more high than the
Epic, commonly called the Heroic, Poem—witness those of the
inimitable PINDARUS consecrated to the glory and renown

of such as returned in triumph from [the Games at] Olympus, Elis, Isthmus, or the like.

Others, among the Greeks, are amorous, soft, and made for chambers ; as others for theatres : as were ANACREON's, the very delicacies of the Grecian ERATO ; which Muse seemed to have been the Minion of that Teian old man, which composed them.

Of a mixed kind were HORACE's. And [we] may truly therefore call these mixed ; whatsoever else are mine : little partaking of the high dialect of the first

> Though we be *all* to seek
> Of PINDAR, that great Greek,

nor altogether of ANACREON ; the Arguments being amorous, moral, or what else the Muse pleaseth.

To write much in this kind neither know I how it will relish : nor, in so doing, can I but injuriously presuppose ignorance or sloth in thee ; or draw censure upon myself for sinning against the decorum of a Preface, by reading a Lecture, where it is enough to sum the points. New they are, and the work of Playing Hours : but what other commendation is theirs, and whether inherent in the subject, must be thine to judge.

But to act the Go-Between of my Poems and thy applause, is neither my modesty nor confidence : that, oftener than once, have acknowledged thee, kind ; and do not doubt hereafter to do somewhat in which I shall not fear thee, just. And would, at this time, also gladly let thee understand what I think, above the rest, of the last Ode of the number ; or, if thou wilt, Ballad in my book. For both the great Master of Italian rymes PETRARCH, and our CHAUCER, and others of the Upper House of the Muses, have thought their Canzons honoured in the title of a *Ballad*: which for that I labour to meet truly therein with the old English garb, I hope as ably to justify as the learned COLIN CLOUT his *Roundelay*.

Thus requesting thee, in thy better judgment, to correct such faults as have escaped in the printing ; I bid thee farewell.

⌊M. DRAYTON.]

O D E S.
[1606.]

ODE I.

To Himself, and the Harp.

AND why not I, as he
That 's greatest, if as free,
  (In sundry strains that strive,
Since there so many be),
  Th' old Lyric kind revive?

I will, yea; and I may:
Who shall oppose my way?
  For what is he alone,
That of himself can say,
  He 's Heir of Helicon.

APOLLO and the Nine
Forbid no man their shrine,
  That cometh with hands pure;
Else, they be so divine,
  They will not him endure.

For they be such coy things;
That they care not for Kings,
  And dare let them know it:
Nor may he touch their Springs
  That is not born a Poet.

The Phocean it did prove,
Whom when foul lust did move
  Those Maids, unchaste to make;
Fell as with them he strove,
  His neck and justly brake.

PYRENÆUS,
King of Phocis
attempting to
ravish the
Muses.

That instrument ne'er heard,
Struck by the skilful Bard,
  It strongly to awake ;
But it th' infernals scared,
  And made Olympus quake.

1 Samuel xvi.

As those prophetic strings,
Whose sounds with fiery wings
  Drave fiends from their abode ;
Touched by the best of Kings,
  That sang the holy Ode.

ORPHEUS the
Thracian Poet.
*Caput, Hebre,
lyramque
excipis, &c.*
OVID.
Metam. xi.

So his, which women slew :
And it int' Hebrus threw ;
  Such sounds yet forth it sent,
The banks to weep that drew,
  As down the stream it went.

MERCURY,
inventor of the
harp, as HORACE.
Ode 10, Lib. I.,
*curvæque lyræ
parentem.*

That by the tortoise shell,
To MAYA's son it fell,
  The most thereof not doubt :
But sure some Power did dwell
  In him who found it out.

The wildest of the field,
And air, with rivers t' yield,
  Which moved ; that sturdy glebes,
And mossy oaks could wield,

Thebes feigned
to have been
raised by music.

  To raise the piles of Thebes.

And diversely though strung,
So anciently We sung
  To it ; that now scarce known,
If first it did belong
  To Greece, or if our own.

The ancient
British Priests,
so called of their
abode in woods.

The Druids embrued
With gore, on altars rude
  With sacrifices crowned,
In hollow woods bedewed,
  Adored the trembling sound.

Though we be *all* to seek
Of PINDAR, that great Greek,
  To finger it aright;
The soul with power to strike:
  His hand retained such might.

PINDAR, Prince
of the Greek
Lyrics, of whom
HORACE,
*PINDARUM
quisquis studet,*
&c. Ode 2, Lib.
IV.

Or him that Rome did grace,
Whose Airs we all embrace:
  That scarcely found his peer;
Nor giveth PHŒBUS place,
  For strokes divinely clear.

HORACE, first of
the Romans in
that kind.

The Irish I admire,
And still cleave to that Lyre
  As our Music's mother:
And think, till I expire,
  APOLLO's such another.

The Irish Harp.

As Britons that so long
Have held this antique Song;
  And let all our carpers
Forbear their fame to wrong:
  Th'are right skilful harpers.

SOOWTHERN, I long thee spare;
Yet wish thee well to fare,
  Who me pleasedst greatly:
As first, therefore more rare,
  Handling thy harp neatly.

SOOWTHERN, an
English Lyric.
[His
PANDORA
was published in
1584.]

To those that with despite
Shall term these Numbers slight;
  Tell them, Their judgment's blind!
Much erring from the right.
  It is a noble kind.

Nor is 't the Verse doth make,
That giveth, or doth take:
  'Tis possible to climb,
To kindle, or to slake;
  Although in SKELTON's rhyme.

An old English
Rhymer.

ODE 2.

To the New Year.

ICH statue double faced!
With marble temples graced,
    To raise thy godhead higher;
In flames where, altars shining,
Before thy Priests divining,
    Do od'rous fumes expire.

Great JANUS, I thy pleasure,
With all the Thespian treasure,
    Do seriously pursue:
To th' passed year returning,
As though the Old adjourning;
    Yet bringing in the New.

Thy ancient Vigils yearly,
I have observèd clearly;
    Thy Feasts yet smoking be!
Since all thy store abroad is;
Give something to my goddess,
    As hath been used by thee!

Give her th' Eoan Brightness!
Winged with that subtle lightness
    That doth transpierce the air;
The Roses of the Morning!
The rising heaven adorning,
    To mesh with flames of hair;

Those ceaseless Sounds, above all,
Made by those orbs that move all;
    And ever swelling there:
Wrapped up in Numbers flowing,
Them actually bestowing
    For jewels at her ear.

O rapture great and holy,
Do thou transport me wholly
  So well her form to vary!
That I aloft may bear her
Where as I will insphere her
  In regions high and starry.

And in my choice Composures,
The soft and easy Closures
  So amorously shall meet,
That every lively Ceasure
Shall tread a perfect measure,
  Set on so equal feet.

That spray to fame so fert'le,
The lover-crowning myrtle,
  In wreaths of mixèd boughs;
Within whose shades are dwelling
Those beauties most excelling,
  Enthroned upon her brows.

Those parallels so even,
Drawn on the face of heaven,
  That curious Art supposes;
Direct those gems, whose clearness
Far off amaze by nearness,
  Each globe such fire encloses.

Her bosom full of blisses,
By Nature made for kisses;
  So pure and wondrous clear:
Where as a thousand Graces
Behold their lovely faces,
  As they are bathing there.

O thou self-little Blindness!
The kindness of unkindness,
  Yet one of those Divine:
Thy Brands to me were lever,
Thy Fascia, and thy Quiver,
  And thou this Quill of mine.

This heart so freshly bleeding,
Upon its own self feeding;
   Whose wounds still dropping be:
O Love, thyself confounding,
Her coldness so abounding,
   And yet such heat in me.

Yet, if I be inspirèd,
I'll leave thee so admirèd
   To all that shall succeed;
That were they more than many,
'Mongst all there is not any
   That Time so oft shall read.

Nor adamant ingravèd,
That hath been choicely savèd,
   IDEA's name outwears:
So large a dower as this is;
The greatest often misses,
   The diadem that bears.

ODE 3.

[*To Cupid.*]

 AIDENS, why spare ye?
   Or whether not dare ye
      Correct the blind Shooter?"
   " Because wanton VENUS,
   So oft that doth pain us,
      Is her son's tutor.

" Now in the Spring,
He proveth his wing;
   The field is his Bower:

And as the small bee,
About flyeth he,
  From flower to flower.

" And wantonly roves
Abroad in the groves,
  And in the air hovers ;
Which when it him deweth,
His feathers he meweth
  In sighs of true Lovers.

" And since doomed by Fate
(That well knew his hate)
  That he should be blind ;
For very despite,
Our eyes be his White :
  So wayward his kind !

" If his shafts losing
(Ill his mark choosing)
  Or his bow broken ;
The moan VENUS maketh,
And care that she taketh,
  Cannot be spoken.

" To VULCAN commending
Her love ; and straight sending
  Her doves and her sparrows,
With kisses, unto him :
And all but to woo him
  To make her son arrows.

" Telling what he hath done ;
Saith she, ' Right mine own son !'
  In her arms she him closes.
Sweets on him fans,
Laid in down of her swans ;
  His sheets, leaves of roses.

" And feeds him with kisses ;
Which oft when he misses,
   He ever is froward.
The mother's o'erjoying
Makes, by much coying,
   The child so untoward."

Yet in a fine net,
That a spider set,
   The Maidens had caught him.
Had she not been near him,
And chancèd to hear him ;
   More good they had taught him !

To my worthy friend Master JOHN SAVAGE
of the Inner Temple.

ODE 4.

PON this sinful earth,
   If Man can happy be,
And higher than his birth,
   Friend, take him thus of me :

Whom promise not deceives,
   That he the breach should rue ;
Nor constant reason leaves
   Opinion to pursue.

To raise his mean estate,
   That soothes no Wanton s sin :
Doth that preferment hate,
   That virtue doth not win.

Nor bravery doth admire:
  Nor doth more love profess
To that he doth desire,
  Than that he doth possess.

Loose humour nor to please,
  That neither spares nor spends;
But by discretion weighs
  What is to needful ends.

To him deserving not,
  Not yielding: nor doth hold
What is not his: doing what
  He ought, not what he could.

Whom the base tyrants' will
  So much could never awe
As him, for good or ill,
  From honesty to draw.

Whose constancy doth rise
  'Bove undeservèd spite;
Whose valuers to despise
  That most doth him delight.

That early leave doth take
  Of th' World, though to his pain,
For Virtue's only sake;
  And not till need constrain.

No man can be so free,
  Though in imperial seat;
Nor eminent: as he
  That deemeth nothing great.

ODE 5.

[*An Amouret Anacreontic.*]

 Ost good! most fair!
Or thing as rare!
To call you's lost;
For all the cost
Words can bestow
So poorly show
Upon your praise,
That all the ways
Sense hath, come short.
Whereby Report
Falls them under:
That when Wonder
More hath seized;
Yet not pleased
That it, in kind,
Nothing can find,
You to express.
Nevertheless
As by globes small
This mighty A L L
Is shewed, though far
From life; each star
A World being:
So we seeing
You, like as that,
Only trust what
Art doth us teach.
And when I reach
At Moral Things,
And that my strings
Gravely should strike;
Straight some mislike
Blotteth mine Ode;
As, with the Load,
The Steel we touch:
Forced ne'er so much;

Yet still removes
To that it loves,
Till there it stays.
So to your praise
I turn ever:
And though never
From you moving;
Happy so loving.

ODE 6.

[Love's Conquest.]

ER 'T granted me to choose,
How I would end my days,
    Since I this life must lose;
It should be in your praise:
For there are no Bays
    Can be set above You.

S' impossibly I love You;
And for You sit so high
    (Whence none may remove You)
In my clear Poesy,
That I oft deny
    You so ample merit.

The freedom of my spirit
Maintaining, still, my cause;
    Your sex not to inherit,
Urging the Salic Laws:
But your virtue draws
    From me every due.

Thus still You me pursue,
That nowhere I can dwell;
    By fear made just to You,

2 D

10

　　　Who naturally rebel;
　　　Of You that excel
　　　　That should I still endite.

　　　Yet will You want some rite.
　　That lost in your high praise,
　　　I wander to and fro;
　　As seeing sundry ways:
　　Yet which the right not know
　　　To get out of this Maze.

ODE 7.

[An Ode written in the Peak.]

HIS while we are abroad,
　　　Shall we not touch our Lyre?
　　Shall we not sing an Ode?
　　　Shall that holy fire,
　　In us that strongly glowed,
　　　In this cold air expire?

Long since the Summer laid
　　Her lusty bravery down;
The Autumn half is weighed,
　　And BOREAS 'gins to frown:
Since now I did behold
　　Great BRUTE's first builded town.

Though in the utmost Peak,
　　A while we do remain;
Amongst the mountains bleak,
　　Exposed to sleet and rain:
No sport our hours shall break,
　　To exercise our vein.

What though bright PHŒBUS' beams
  Refresh the southern ground;
And though the princely Thames
  With beauteous Nymphs abound;
And by old Camber's streams
  Be many wonders found:

Yet many rivers clear
  Here glide in silver swathes;
And what of all most dear,
  Buxton's delicious baths,
Strong ale, and noble cheer,
  T'assuage breem Winter's scathes.

Those grim and horrid caves,
  Whose looks affright the day;
Wherein nice Nature saves
  What she would not bewray:
Our better leisure craves,
  And doth invite our Lay.

In places far, or near,
  Or famous, or obscure;
Where wholesome is the air,
  Or where the most impure;
All times, and everywhere,
  The Muse is still in ure.

ODE 8.

ING we the Rose!
  Than which no flower there grows
    Is sweeter;
  And aptly her compare
With what in that is rare:
  A parallel none meeter.

Or made posies,
Of this that encloses
　　Such blisses :
That naturally flusheth,
　　As she blusheth
When she is robbed of kisses.

　　Or if strewed,
When with the mor　ing dewed ;
　　Or stilling ;
Or how to sense exposed :
All which in her enclosed,
Each place with sweetness filling.

　　That most renowned
By Nature richly crowned
　　With yellow ;
Of that delicious lair :
And as pure her hair,
Unto the same the fellow.

　　Fearing of harm ;
Nature that flower doth arm
　　From danger :
The touch gives her offence,
But with reverence
Unto herself, a stranger.

　　The red, or white,
Or mixed, the sense delight,
　　Beholding,
In her complexion :
All which perfection,
Such harmony infolding,

　　That divided,
Ere it was decided
　　Which most pure,
Began the grievous War
Of YORK and LANCASTER,
That did many years endure.

Conflicts as great
As were in all that heat,
    I sustain :
By her, as many hearts
As men on either parts,
That with her eyes hath slain.

The Primrose flower,
The first of FLORA's bower
    Is placed :
So is She first, as best :
Though excellent the rest ;
All gracing, by none graced.

ODE 9.

[A Skeltoniad.]

HE Muse should be sprightly ;
Yet not handling lightly
Things grave : as much loath
Things that be slight, to cloathe
Curiously.   To retain
The Comeliness in mean
Is true Knowledge and Wit.
Nor me forced rage doth fit,
That I thereto should lack
Tobacco, or need Sack ;
Which to the colder brain
Is the true Hippocrene.
Nor did I ever care
For Great Fools, nor them spare.
Virtue, though neglected,
Is not so dejected
As vilely to descend
To low baseness, their end :
Neither each rhyming slave

Deserves the name to have
Of Poet.   So, the rabble
Of Fools, for the table,
That have their jests by heart,
As an Actor his part,
Might assume them chairs
Amongst the Muses' heirs.
Parnassus is not clomb
By every such Mome :
Up whose steep side who swerves,
It behoves t' have strong nerves.
My resolution such
How *well*, and not how *much*,
To write.   Thus do I fare
Like some few good, that care
(The evil sort among)
How *well* to live, and not how *long*.

ODE 10.

[*His Defence against the idle Critic.*]

HE Ryme nor mars, nor makes ;
    Nor addeth it, nor takes,
        From that which we propose :
Things imaginary
Do so strangely vary
    That quickly we them lose.

And what 's quickly begot,
As soon again is not ;
    This do I truly know.
Yea, and what 's born with pain ;
That, Sense doth long'st retain,
    Gone with a greater flow.

Yet this Critic so stern,
(But whom, none must discern
　　Nor perfectly have seeing)
Strangely lays about him,
As nothing without him
　　Were worthy of being,

That I myself betray
To that most public way;
　　Where the World's old bawd
Custom, that doth humour,
And by idle rumour,
　　Her dotages applaud.

That whilst she still prefers
Those that be wholly hers,
　　Madness and Ignorance;
I creep behind the Time,
From spertling with their crime;
　　And glad too with my chance.

O wretched World the while,
When the evil most vile
　　Beareth the fairest face;
And inconstant lightness,
With a scornful slightness,
　　The best things doth disgrace!

Whilst this strange knowing beast,
Man; of himself the least,
　　His envy declaring,
Makes Virtue to descend,
Her title to defend
　　Against him; much preparing.

Yet these me not delude,
Nor from my place extrude,
　　By their resolvèd hate;
Their vileness that do know:
Which to myself I show,
　　To keep above my fate.

ODE II.

To the Virginian Voyage.

OU brave heroic minds,
　Worthy your country's name,
　　That Honour still pursue ;
　　Go and subdue !
Whilst loitering hinds
　　Lurk here at home with shame.

Britans, you stay too long ;
Quickly aboard bestow you !
　And with a merry gale
　Swell your stretched sail !
With vows as strong
As the winds that blow you.

Your course securely steer,
West-and-by-South forth keep !
　Rocks, Lee-shores, nor Shoals,
　When EOLUS scowls,
You need not fear !
So absolute the deep.

And cheerfully at sea,
Success you still entice,
　To get the pearl and gold ;
　And ours to hold,
Virginia,
Earth's only Paradise.

Where Nature hath in store
Fowl, venison, and fish :
　And the fruitful soïl ;
　Without your toil,
Three harvests more,
All greater than your wish.

And the ambitious vine
Crowns, with his purple mass,
  The cedar reaching high
  To kiss the sky.
The cypress, pine,
And useful sassafras.

To whose, the Golden Age
Still Nature's laws doth give :
  No other cares that tend,
  But them to defend
From winter's age,
That long there doth not live.

When as the luscious smell
Of that delicious land,
  Above the seas that flows,
  The clear wind throws,
Your hearts to swell,
Approaching the dear strand.

In kenning of the shore
(Thanks to GOD first given !)
  O you, the happiest men,
  Be frolic then !
Let cannons roar !
Frightening the wide heaven.

And in regions far,
Such heroes bring ye forth
  As those from whom We came !
  And plant our name
Under that Star
Not known unto our North !

And as there plenty grows
Of laurel everywhere,
  APOLLO's sacred tree ;
  You it may see
A Poet's brows
To crown, that may sing there.

Thy *Voyages* attend,
Industrious HAKLUYT !
  Whose reading shall inflame
  Men to seek fame ;
And much commend
To after Times thy wit.

ODE 12.

To the Cambro-Britans and their Harp, his
Ballad of Agincourt.

[Besides this Ballad : MICHAEL DRAYTON published, in 1627, a much
longer Poem upon this celebrated Battle.]

FAIR stood the wind for France,
  When we our sails advance ;
  Nor now to prove our chance
    Longer will tarry.
  But putting to the main ;
At Caux, the mouth of Seine,
With all his martial train
    Landed King HARRY.

And taking many a fort
Furnished in warlike sort,
Marcheth towards Agincourt
    In happy hour ;
Skirmishing, day by day,
With those that stopped his way,
Where the French General lay
    With all his Power.

Which, in his height of pride,
King HENRY to deride ;
His ransom to provide,
    To the King sending.

Which he neglects the while,
As from a nation vile ;
Yet, with an angry smile,
    Their fall portending.

And turning to his men,
Quoth our brave HENRY then :
" Though they to one be ten
    Be not amazèd !
Yet have we well begun :
Battles so bravely won
Have ever to the sun
    By Fame been raised ! "

" And for myself," quoth he,
" This my full rest shall be :
England ne'er mourn for me,
    Nor more esteem me !
Victor I will remain,
Or on this earth lie slain :
Never shall She sustain
    Loss to redeem me !

" Poitiers and Cressy tell,
When most their pride did swell,
Under our swords they fell.
    No less our skill is,
Than when our Grandsire great,
Claiming the regal seat,
By many a warlike feat
    Lopped the French lillies."

The Duke of YORK so dread
The eager Vanward led ;
With the Main, HENRY sped
    Amongst his henchmen :
EXETER had the Rear,
A braver man not there !
O Lord, how hot they were
    On the false Frenchmen !

They now to fight are gone;
Armour on armour shone;
Drum now to drum did groan:
    To hear, was wonder.
That, with cries they make,
The very earth did shake;
Trumpet, to trumpet spake;
    Thunder, to thunder.

Well it thine age became,
O noble ERPINGHAM!
Which didst the signal aim
    To our hid forces:
When, from a meadow by,
Like a storm suddenly,
The English Archery
    Stuck the French horses.

With Spanish yew so strong;
Arrows a cloth-yard long,
That like to serpents stung,
    Piercing the weather.
None from his fellow starts;
But, playing manly parts,
And like true English hearts,
    Stuck close together.

When down their bows they threw;
And forth their bilbowes [*swords*] drew
And on the French they flew:
    Not one was tardy.
Arms were from the shoulders sent
Scalps to the teeth were rent,
Down the French peasants went:
    Our men were hardy.

This while our noble King,
His broad sword brandishing,
Down the French host did ding
    As to o'erwhelm it.

And many a deep wound lent;
His arms with blood besprent,
And many a cruel dent
    Bruisèd his helmet.

GLOUCESTER that Duke so good,
Next of the royal blood,
For famous England stood
    With his brave brother.
CLARENCE, in steel so bright,
Though but a Maiden Knight;
Yet in that furious fight,
    Scarce such another!

WARWICK, in blood did wade;
OXFORD, the foe invade,
And cruel slaughter made,
    Still as they ran up.
SUFFOLK his axe did ply;
BEAUMONT and WILLOUGHBY
Bare them right doughtily:
    FERRERS, and FANHOPE.

Upon Saint CRISPIN'S Day,
Fought was this noble Fray;
Which Fame did not delay
    To England to carry.
O when shall English men
With such acts fill a pen?
Or England breed again
    Such a King HARRY?

F I N I S.

To the worthy Knight, and my noble friend,
Sir HENRY GOODERE, a Gentleman of
His Majesty's Privy Chamber.

HESE Lyric pieces, short, and few,
Most worthy Sir, I send to you;
  To read them be not weary!
They may become JOHN HEWES his lyre,
Which oft, at Polesworth,* by the fire,
Hath made us gravely merry.

Believe it, he must have the trick
Of Ryming, with Invention quick,
  That should do Lyrics well:
But how I have done in this kind,
Though in myself I cannot find,
  Your judgment best can tell.

Th' old British Bards (upon their harps
For falling Flats, and rising Sharps,
  That curiously were strung)
To stir their Youth to warlike rage,
Or their wild fury to assuage,
  In these loose Numbers sung.

No more I, for fools' censure pass,
Than for the braying of an ass;
  Nor once mine ear will lend them:
If you but please to take in gree
These *Odes*, sufficient 'tis to me:
  Your liking can commend them.

Yours,

MICHAEL DRAYTON.

* In Warwickshire.

WITH OTHER LYRIC POESIES.

To his Valentine.

USE, bid the Morn awake!
  Sad Winter now declines,
Each bird doth choose a Make;
  This day 's Saint VALENTINE'S.
For that good Bishop's sake
Get up, and let us see
What Beauty it shall be
  That Fortune us assigns!

But, lo, in happy hour,
  The place wherein she lies;
In yonder climbing Tower,
  Gilt by the glitt'ring Rise.
O, JOVE, that in a shower
(As once that Thunderer did,
When he in drops lay hid)
  That I could her surprise!

Her canopy I'll draw,
  With spangled plumes bedight:
No mortal ever saw
  So ravishing a sight;
That it the Gods might awe,
And pow'rfully transpierce
The globy Universe,
  Outshooting every light.

My lips I'll softly lay
  Upon her heavenly cheek,
Dyed like the dawning day,
  As polished ivory sleek;
And in her ear I'll say:
" O thou bright Morning Star!
'Tis I, that come so far,
  My Valentine to seek.

" Each little bird, this tide,
  Doth choose her lovèd pheere;

Which constantly abide
  In wedlock all the year,
As Nature is their guide ;
  So may we Two be true
This year, nor change for new ;
  As turtles coupled were.

" The sparrow, swan, the dove,
    Though VENUS' birds they be ;
Yet are they not for love,
    So absolute as we !
For reason us doth move ;
But they by billing woo.
Then try what we can do !
    To whom each sense is free.

" Which we have more than they,
    By livelier organs swayed ;
Our Appetite each way
    More by our Sense obeyed.
Our Passions to display,
This season us doth fit ;
Then let us follow it,
    As Nature us doth lead !

" One kiss in two let 's breathe !
    Confounded with the touch,
But half words let us speak !
    Our lips employed so much,
Until we both grow weak :
With sweetness of thy breath,
O smother me to death !
    Long let our joys be such !

" Let 's laugh at them that choose
    Their Valentines by lot ;
To wear their names that use,
    Whom idly they have got."
Saint VALENTINE, befriend !
We thus this Morn may spend :
    Else, Muse, awake her not !

The Heart.

IF thus we needs must go;
What shall our one Heart do,
This One made of our Two?

Madam, two Hearts we brake;
And from them both did take
The best, one Heart to make.

Half this is of your Heart,
Mine in the other part;
Joined by an equal Art.

Were it cemented, or sewn;
By shreds or pieces known,
We might each find our own.

But 'tis dissolved and fixed;
And with such cunning mixed,
No diff'rence that betwixt.

But how shall we agree,
By whom it kept shall be:
Whether by you or me?

It cannot two breasts fill;
One must be heart-less still,
Until the other will.

It came to me to-day:
When I willed it to say,
With Whether would it stay?

It told me, " In your breast,
Where it might hope to rest:
For if it were my guest,

" For certainty, it knew
That I would still anew
Be sending it to you!"

2 E   IO

Never, I think, had two
Such work, so much, to do:
A Unity to woo!

Yours was so cold and chaste:
Whilst mine with zeal did waste;
Like Fire with Water placed.

How did my Heart intreat!
How pant! How did it beat,
Till it could give yours heat!

Till to that temper brought,
Through our perfection wrought,
That blessing either's thought.

In such a height it lies
From this base World's dull eyes;
That Heaven it not envies.

All that this Earth can show,
Our Heart shall not once know!
For it's too vile and low.

The Sacrifice to APOLLO.

RIESTS of APOLLO, sacred be the room
For this learned meeting! Let no barbarous groom,
How brave soe'er he be,
Attempt to enter!
But of the Muses free,
None here may venture!
This for the Delphian Prophets is prepared:
The profane Vulgar are from hence debarred!

And since the Feast so happily begins;
Call up those fair Nine, with their violins!
    They are begot by JOVE.
    Then let us place them
    Where no clown in may shove,
    That may disgrace them:
But let them near to young APOLLO sit;
So shall his foot-pace overflow with wit.

Where be the Graces? Where be those fair Three?
In any hand, they may not absent be!
    They to the Gods are dear:
    And they can humbly
    Teach us, ourselves to bear,
    And do things comely.
They, and the Muses, rise both from one stem:
They grace the Muses; and the Muses, them.

Bring forth your flagons, filled with sparkling wine
(Whereon swollen BACCHUS, crownèd with a vine,
    Is graven); and fill out!
    It well bestowing
    To every man about,
    In goblets flowing!
Let not a man drink, but in draughts profound!
To our god PHŒBUS, let the Health go round!

Let your Jests fly at large; yet therewithal
See they be Salt, but yet not mixed with Gall!
    Not tending to disgrace:
    But fairly given,
    Becoming well the place,
    Modest and even,
That they, with tickling pleasure, may provoke
Laughter in him on whom the Jest is broke.

Or if the deeds of Heroes ye rehearse:
Let them be sung in so well-ordered Verse,
    That each word have its weight,
    Yet run with pleasure!

Holding one stately height
In so brave measure
That they may make the stiffest storm seem weak ;
And damp JOVE's thunder, when it loud'st doth speak.

And if ye list to exercise your vein,
Or in the Sock, or in the Buskined strain ;
Let Art and Nature go
One with the other !
Yet so, that Art may show
Nature her mother :
The thick-brained audience lively to awake,
Till with shrill claps the Theatre do shake.

Sing Hymns to BACCHUS then, with hands upreared !
Offer to JOVE, who most is to be feared !
From him the Muse we have.
From him proceedeth
More than we dare to crave.
'Tis he that feedeth
Them, whom the World would starve. Then let the lyre
Sound ! whilst his altars endless flames expire.

To his Rival.

HER loved I most,
By thee that 's lost,
Though she were won with leisure ;
She was my gain :
But to my pain,
Thou spoilest me of my treasure.

The ship full fraught
With gold, far sought,
Though ne'er so wisely helmèd,
May suffer wrack
In sailing back,
By tempest overwhelmèd.

But She, good Sir!
Did not prefer
You, for that I was ranging:
But for that She
Found faith in me,
And She loved to be changing.

Therefore boast not
Your happy lot;
Be silent now you have her!
The time I knew
She slighted you,
When I was in her favour.

None stands so fast
But may be cast
By Fortune, and disgracèd:
Once did I wear
Her garter there,
Where you her glove have placèd.

I had the vow
That thou hast now,
And glances to discover
Her love to me;
And She to thee,
Reads but old lessons over.

She hath no smile
That can beguile;
But, as my thought, I know it:
Yea to a hair,
Both when, and where,
And how, she will bestow it.

What now is thine
Was only mine,
And first to me was given;
Thou laugh'st at me!
I laugh at thee!
And thus we two are even.

2 E 2

But I'll not mourn,
But stay my turn ;
The wind may come about, Sir !
And once again
May bring me in ;
And help to bear you out, Sir !

The Crier.

OOD folk, for gold or hire,
But help me to a Crier !
For my poor Heart is run astray
After two Eyes, that passed this way.

Oh yes ! O yes ! O yes !
If there be any man,
In town or country, can
Bring me my Heart again ;
I'll please him for his pain.

And by these marks, I will you show
That only I this Heart do owe [*own*] :
It is a wounded Heart,
Wherein yet sticks the dart.
Every piece sore hurt throughout it :
Faith and Troth writ round about it.
It was a tame Heart, and a dear ;
And never used to roam :
But having got this haunt, I fear
'Twill hardly stay at home.

For God's sake, walking by the way,
If you my Heart do see ;
Either impound it for a Stray,
Or send it back to me !

To his coy Love.

A Canzonet.

PRAY thee leave!   Love me no more!
   Call home the heart you gave me!
I but in vain that Saint adore
   That can, but will not, save me.
These poor half kisses kill me quite!
   Was ever man thus servèd?
Amidst an ocean of delight,
   For pleasure to be starvèd.

Show me no more those snowy breasts
   With azure riverets branchèd!
Where whilst mine Eye with plenty feeds,
   Yet is my thirst not staunchèd.
O TANTALUS, thy pains ne'er tell!
   By me thou art prevented:
'Tis *nothing* to be plagued in Hell;
   But, *thus*, in Heaven, tormented!

Clip me no more in those dear arms;
   Nor thy "Life's Comfort" call me!
O these are but too powerful charms;
   And do but more enthrall me.
But see how patient I am grown,
   In all this coil about thee!
Come, nice Thing, let thy heart alone!
   I cannot live without thee!

A Hymn to his Lady's Birth-place.

OVENTRY, that dost adorn
   The country [*County*] wherein I was born:
Yet therein lies not thy praise;
Why I should crown thy Towers with bays?
'Tis not thy Wall, me to thee weds;   Coventry
Thy Ports; nor thy proud Pyramids;   finely walled.

The shoulder-bone of a Boar of mighty bigness.

Nor thy trophies of the Boar :
But that She which I adore,
(Which scarce Goodness's self can pair)
First there breathing, blest thy air.

IDEA ; in which name I hide
Her, in my heart deified.
For what good, Man's mind can see ;
Only her ideas be :
She, in whom the Virtues came
In Woman's shape, and took her name.
She so far past imitation
As (but Nature our creation
Could not alter) she had aimed
More than Woman to have framed.
She whose truly written story,
To thy poor name shall add more glory,
Than if it should have been thy chance
T' have bred our Kings that conquered France.

Two famous Pilgrimages : one in Norfolk, the other in Kent.

Had she been born the former Age,
That house had been a Pilgrimage ;
And reputed more Divine
Than Walsingham, or BECKET's Shrine.

GODIVA, Duke LEOFRIC's wife, who obtained the freedom of the city of her husband, by riding through it naked.

That Princess, to whom thou dost owe
Thy Freedom (whose clear blushing snow
The envious sun saw ; when as she
Naked rode to make thee free),
Was but her type : as to foretell
Thou shouldst bring forth One should excel
Her bounty ; by whom thou shouldst have
More Honour, than she Freedom gave.

Queen ELIZABETH.

And that great Queen, which but of late
Ruled this land in peace and State,
Had not been ; but Heaven had sworn
A Maid should reign when She was born.

Of thy streets, which thou hold'st best,
And most frequent of the rest ;

Happy *Mich Park!* Every year,
On the Fourth of August there,
Let thy Maids, from FLORA's bowers,
With their choice and daintiest flowers
Deck thee up! and from their store,
With brave garlands crown that door!

A noted street in Coventry.
His Mistress's birthday.

The old man passing by that way,
To his son, in time, shall say :
" There was that Lady born : which
Long to after Ages shall be sung."
Who, unawares being passed by,
Back to that house shall cast his eye ;
Speaking my verses as he goes,
And with a sigh shut every Close.

Dear City! travelling by thee,
When thy rising Spires I see,
Destined her Place of Birth ;
Yet methinks the very earth
Hallowed is, so far as I
Can thee possibly descry.
Then thou, dwelling in this place,
(Hearing some rude hind disgrace
Thy city, with some scurvy thing
Which some Jester forth did bring)
Speak these Lines, where thou dost come,
And strike the slave for ever dumb.

Edinburgh : T. and A. CONSTABLE, Printers to His Majesty